Saudi Arabia's Economy: Oil and the Search for Economic Development

CONTEMPORARY STUDIES IN ECONOMIC AND FINANCIAL ANALYSIS, VOLUME 67

Editors: Robert J. Thornton and J. Richard Aronson
Lehigh University

CONTEMPORARY STUDIES IN ECONOMIC AND FINANCIAL ANALYSIS

An International Series of Monographs

Series Editors: **Robert J. Thornton** and **J. Richard Aronson**
Lehigh University

Volume 1. **DYNAMICS OF FORECASTING FINANCIAL CYCLES: Theory, Technique and Implementation**
Lacy H. Hunt, II. *Fidelcor Inc. and the Fidelity Bank*

Volume 2. **COMPOSITE RESERVE ASSETS IN THE INTERNATIONAL MONETARY SYSTEM**
Jacob S. Dreyer, *Office of Monetary Research, U.S. Treasury.*

Volume 3. **APPLICATION OF CLASSIFICATION TECHNIQUES IN BUSINESS, BANKING AND FINANCE**
Edward I. Altman, *Graduate School of Business Administration, New York University.*
Robert B. Avery, Graduate School of Industrial Administration, Carnegie-Mellon University.
Robert A. Eisenheis, Federal Deposit Insurance Corporatio, and Joseph F. Sinkey, Jr., *College of Business Administration, University of Georgia*

Volume 4. **PROBLEM AND FAILED INSTITUTIONS IN THE COMMERCIAL BANKING INDUSTRY**
Joseph F. Sinkey, Jr., *College of Business Administration, University of Georgia*

Volume 5. **A NEW LOOK AT PORTFOLIO MANAGEMENT**
David M. Ahlers, *Graduate School of Business and Public Administration, Cornell University.*

Volume 6. **MULTINATIONAL ELECTRONIC COMPANIES AND NATIONAL ECONOMIC POLICIES**
Edmond Sciberras, *Science Policy Research Unit. University of Sussex*

Volume 7. **VENEZUELAN ECONOMIC DEVELOPMENT: A Politico-Economic Analysis**
Loring Allen, *University of Missouri, St. Louis*

Volume 8. **ENVIRONMENT, PLANNING AND THE MULTINATIONAL CORPORATION**
Thomas N. Gladwin, *New York University*

Volume 9. **FOREIGN DIRECT INVESTMENT, INDUSTRIALIZATION AND SOCIAL CHANGE**
Stephen J. Kobrin, *Sloan School of Management, Massachusetts Institute of Technology*

Volume 10. **IMPLICATIONS OF REGULATION ON BANK EXPANSION: A Simulation Analysis**
George S. Oldfield, Jr., *Graduate School of Business and Public Administration, Cornell University*

Volume 11. **IMPORT SUBSTITUTION, TRADE AND DEVELOPMENT**
Jaleel Ahmad, *Concordia University, Sir George Williams Campus*

Volume 12. **CORPORATE GROWTH AND COMMON STOCK RISK**
David R. Fewings, *McGill University*

Volume 13. **CAPITAL MARKET EQUILIBRIUM AND CORPORATE FINANCIAL DECISIONS**
Richard C. Stapleton, *Manchester Business and New York University,* and M.G. Subrahmanyam, *Indian Institute of Management and New York University*

Volume 14. **IMPENDING CHANGES FOR SECURITIES MARKETS: What Role for the Exchanges?**
Ernest Bloch and Robert A. Schwartz, *Graduate School of Business Administration, New York University*

Volume 15. **INDUSTRIAL INNOVATION AND INTERNATIONAL TRADING PERFORMANCE**
William B. Walker, *Science Policy Research Unit, University of Sussex*

Volume 16. **FINANCIAL POLICY, INFLATION AND ECONOMIC DEVELOPMENT: The Mexican Experience**
John K. Thompson, *Mellon Bank, N.A.*

Volume 17. **CORPORATE LIQUIDITY MANAGEMENT**
Michel Levasseur, *Centre d'Enseignement Superieur des Affaires, Jouy-en-Josas, France*

Volume 18. **STABILIZATION OF INTERNATIONAL COMMODITY MARKETS**
Paul Hallwood, *University of Aberdeen*

Volume 19. **PROBLEMS IN EUROPEAN CORPORATE FINANCE: Text and Cases**
Michel Schlosser, *Centre d'Enseignement Supeieur des Affaires, Jouy-en-Josas, France*

Volume 20. **THE MULTINATIONAL ENTERPRISE: International Investment and Host-County Impacts**
Thomas G. Parry, *School of Economics, University of New South Wales*

Volume 21. **POLICY RESPONSES TO RESOURCES DEPLETION: The Case of Mercury**
Nigel Roxburgh, *Management Studies Division, The Economist Intelligence Unit, Ltd.*

Volume 22. **THE INTERNATIONAL MONEY MARKET: An Assessment of Forecasting Techniques and Market Efficiency**
Richard M. Levich, *Graduate School of Business Administration, New York University*

Volume 23. **TRANSNATIONAL CONGLOMERATES AND THE ECONOMICS OF DEPENDENT DEVELOPMENT: A Case Study of the International Electrical Oligopoly and Brazil's Electrical Industry**
Richard Newfarmer, *University of Notre Dame*

Volume 24. **THE POLITICAL ECONOMY OF ENVIRONMENTAL PROTECTION**
Horst Siebert, *University of Mannheim,* and Ariane Berthoin Antal, *International Institute for Environment and Society, Science Center, Berlin*

Volume 25. **BIDDING AND OIL LEASES**
James B. Ramsey, *New York University*

Volume 26. **THE ECONOMICS OF EXPLORATION FOR ENERGY RESOURCES**
James B. Ramsey, *New York University*

Volume 27. **TECHNOLOGY TRANSFER TO DEVELOPING COUNTRIES: The Case of the Fertilizer Industry**
Subrata Ghatak, *University of Leicester and University of Guelph*

Volume 28. **MULTINATIONALS: Bank and Corporation Relationships**
Oliver Pastre, *Universite Paris-Nord*

Volume 29. **THE PRIMARY MARKET FOR MUNICIPAL DEBT: Bidding Rules and Cost of Long-Term Borrowing**
G.O. Bierwag, *University of Oregon*

Volume 30. **EFFICIENCY IN THE MUNICIPAL BOND MARKET: The Use of Tax Exempt Financing for "Private" Purposes**
George G. Kaufman, *Loyola University of Chicago*

Volume 31. **FOREIGN INVESTMENT AND TECHNOLOGY TRANSFER: The Industry in Latin America**
Peter West, *Caracas, Venezuela*

Volume 32. **DIMENSIONS OF ENERGY ECONOMICS**
Noel D. Uri, *Catholic University of America*

Volume 33. **INDIGENIZATION AND ECONOMIC DEVELOPMENT: The Nigerian Experience**
Nicholas Balabkins, *Lehigh University*

Volume 34. **INTERNATIONAL FINANCIAL MANAGEMENT: Problems, Issues, and Experiences**
John S. Oh, *Portland State University*

Volume 35. **PURCHASING POWER PARITY AND EXCHANGE RATES: Theory, Evidence and Relevance**
Lawrence H. Officer, *Michigan State University*

Volume 36. **FINANCIAL REPORTING RULES AND CORPORATE DECISIONS: A Study of Public Policy**
Bertrand Horwitz, *State University of New York-Binghamion*and Richard Kolodny, *University of Maryland*

Volume 37. **CONSUMER EMANCIPATION AND ECONOMIC DEVELOPMENT**
Hans B. Thorelli, *Villa Serbelloni, Bellagio and Indiana University* and Gerald D. Sentell, NIDA, Bangkok and the University of Tennessee

Volume 38. **INSURING NUCLEAR POWER: Liability, Safety and Economic Efficiency**
William C. Wood, *Owen Graduate School of Management, Vanderbilt University*

Volume 39. **NEW DIMENSIONS IN PUBLIC UTILITY PRICING**
Noel D. Uri, *Catholic University of America*

Volume 40. **ECONOMIC DECISIONS UNDER INFLATION: The Impact of Accounting Measurement Error**
Stephen M. Cross, *College of the Holy Cross*

Volume 41. **INNOVATIONS IN BOND PORTFOLIO MANAGEMENT**
George Kaufman, *Loyola University of Chicago,* G.O. Bierwag, *University of Arizona,* and Alden Toews, *University of Oregon*

Volume 42. **SMALL BUSINESS FINANCE**
Paul M. Horvitz and R. Richardson Petit, *University of Houston*

Volume 43. **IMPORT DEPENDENCE AND ECONOMIC VULNERABILITY**
Steven E. Plaut, *Technion-Israel Institute of Technology*

Volume 44. **EVALUATION OF THE INTERNAL PROCESSES OF MANAGED FUNDS**
Rank J. Finn, *University of Queensland*

Volume 45. **PUBLIC PLANNING-PARADIGM AND PARADOX. THE QUESTIONABLE BASES FOR PUBLIC PLANNING AND REGULATION BY LOCAL GOVERNMENTS IN AMERICA**
Leonard C. Moffitt, *Honolulu, Hawaii*

To

NAS

Saudi Arabia's Economy: Oil and the Search for Economic Development

by **Hossein Askari**
Department of Business Administration
George Washington University

with the assistance of
Babak Dastmaltschi
McKinsey and Company
Washington, D.C.

JAI PRESS INC.

Greenwich, Connecticut *London, England*

Library of Congress Cataloging-in-Publication Data
Askari, Hossein.
Saudi Arabia's economy : oil and the search for economic development / by Hossein Askari with Babak Dastmaltschi.
p. cm. — (Contemporary studies in economic and financial analysis ; v. 67)
Includes bibliographical references.
ISBN 1-55938-002-0
1. Saudi Arabia—Economic policy. 2. Petroleum industry and trade—Government policy—Saudi Arabia. 3. Saudi Arabia—Economic conditions. I. Dastmaltschi, Babak. II. Title. III. Series.
HC415.33.A83 1990
338.9538—dc20 89-49104

55 Old Post Road, No. 2
Greenwich, Connecticut 06830

JAI PRESS LTD.
118 Penvontille Road
London N1 9JN
England

ISBN NUMBER: 1-55938-002-0

Library of Congress Catalog Number 89-49104

Manufactured in the United States of America

CONTENTS

List of Figures

List of Tables

Chapter I

Chapter II

Chapter III

Chapter IV

Chapter V

Chapter VI

Appendix V

About the Authors

Hossein Askari received his Ph.D. in Economics in 1970 from the Massachusetts Institute of Technology. He has been an advisor to the Executive Director at the International Monetary Fund and advisor to the Minister of Finance of Saudi Arabia. From 1984 to 1986, he was the Director of the Economics and Finance Department of the Consulting Center in Riyadh; in this capacity, he directed the development of energy planning models (international, domestic, and GCC) for the Ministry of Planning of Saudi Arabia. He is currently professor of International Finance and Director of the International Business Program at George Washington University. He has also taught at the School of Advanced International Studies (The Johns Hopkins University), the University of Texas at Austin, and Tufts University.

Babak Dastmaltschi was involved for three years in the efforts to design and develop the long-term Energy Plan for the Kingdom of Saudi Arabia. He has also done numerous feasibility studies for industrial projects in the GCC. He has previously worked for the Gulf Center Management Consultants on issues of privatization in Saudi Arabia and is currently with McKinsey and Company.

Acknowledgments

In any endeavor such as this, one is invariably indebted to many friends and colleagues. In our case, the assistance is rather long and we can only mention a few names and even then we will not be able to do justice to their invaluable help and support.

We owe our biggest debt to the many Saudis who have enhanced our understanding of the Kingdom. Any author would be sufficiently rewarded to have Robert Solow write the Foreword to his manuscript. We are, to say the least, honored. We are grateful to Martin Weitzman for his outstanding contribution on the technical basis of an oil economy. Vahid Nowshirvani, Anne Patterson, Hossein Farzin, John Cummings, Vittorio Corbo, Howard Reed, and Mohan Agarwal have given us many ideas and have made numerous helpful suggestions. Ben Burdetsky and Adel El-Ansary have given us moral support and have generously given us technical assistance from the Department of Business Administration at the George Washington University. We have benefitted from Rodrigo Guimaraes, Albert Xu, Maziar Minovi, Philip Chase, and Asad Yaqub for research assistance. Irena Eva, and especially Debra Ervais and Greta Hendrickson have tirelessly typed drafts; to them many thanks. Many thanks are also due to Maria Deegan for improving the quality of this study. But we remain responsible for any shortcomings.

NOTE

The reader is to note that Appendix II provides a table of corresponding Hijri and Gregorian years.

Foreword

I do not mean to exaggerate, but there is a sense in which a book like this is a theorist's dream come true. Fifteen years ago, the first OPEC price shock had major effects on the world economy and the minor effect of focusing a few academic minds—including mine—on the economics of exhaustible resources. It must, after all, make a difference to the growth of an economy, and to the nature of its policy programs, if it is dependent on some resources that cannot be renewed and will eventually be gone. My first technical article on this subject tried to figure out, in an abstractly theoretical way, what determines the largest sustainable flow of consumption achievable in such an economy. That is exactly the criterion discussed by Martin Weitzman in Appendix I and applied by Hossein Askari in this detailed study of Saudi Arabia, an exhaustible-resource-based economy if ever there was one.

This book is a lovely example of the relation between theoretical thinking and applied work in economics. In my view, the economic theorist's job is to pick out one or two key aspects of the problem at hand—an act of judgment, by the way—and then try to analyze how they work, what makes them so important, what they imply for a broader view of the problem, including questions about how things are and about what should be done. Then it is the applied economist's job—it could be the same person, of course—to look more closely at the real world with its complications, using theoretical insights as a guide, a sort of flashlight, not as a straitjacket. Here, too, a lot of judgment comes into play. You need to know your subject intimately well. Judgment is not the same as prejudice; a prejudice is its own justification, but a judgment needs to be well-argued, with facts and figures and maybes.

That is exactly what Dr. Askari is doing in his thoughtful and valuable book. The problem is posed by nature and history. The Saudi Arabian economy starts with one asset: a vast pool of oil. Its job is to manage the use and using-up of that asset in such a way as to provide the best available flow of consumption benefits over time. That stream of benefits may well have to go on after the pool of oil is more or less exhausted, or is at least much diminished in value. To put the problem that way suggests immediately what the important issues will be: how rapidly to draw down the oil, how much of the proceeds to consume now and how much to invest in other assets to make up for the dwindling pool of oil, and how to choose an appropriate portfolio of assets at home and abroad, including intangible assets like education and social institutions. Dr. Askari discusses all of these issues and more. One of *his* assets has to be his knowledge of the Saudi Arabian economy, and his sense of the feasible. He is an excellent guide.

Economists like to talk glibly and wishfully about "natural experiments." I would not go so far as to call Saudi Arabia an experiment. There is too much historical contingency. But it is certainly a special and different sort of history, well worth studying and learning from.

Robert M. Solow

Chapter I

Introduction

During the span of three development plans (1970-1985), the economy of the Kingdom of Saudi Arabia has undergone a dramatic transformation. Because of its large export earnings from oil, Saudi Arabia was able to implement an extensive development program. Social services, infrastructure, and basic industries were constructed and developed at a rapid speed. Hospitals and clinics, universities and schools, houses and apartments, highways and roads, airports and ports, refineries and petrochemical plants, agribusiness and farms, and cities, have literally risen from the desert. All of these have provided the average citizen with a high standard of social services.[1]

During most of its recent history, Saudi Arabia has experienced increasing oil revenues. Exports, largely oil, increased from US $2.1 billion in 1970, to a high of US $111.1 billion in 1981. This dramatic increase in export revenues fueled euphoric feelings that the Kingdom was not, and perhaps would not be, subject to normal revenue constraints. This resulted in a rapid implementation of projects with social considerations in mind, but sometimes with less attention given to economic criteria and efficiency. But, with the decline in oil revenues, beginning in 1982, increased economic realism has been injected into decision making.

Since the early 1970s, the Kingdom has espoused the importance of diversification from oil; oil, a depleting resource, would not last forever. Each successive development plan has recognized this simple fact. But after more than 15 years of development planning, Saudi Arabia is still heavily dependent on oil. Real oil-GDP, as a percentage of the total GDP, decreased from 55 percent in 1978, to less than 24 percent in 1985 largely due to a massive decrease in oil production; while oil exports, as a percentage of total exports, remained at about 98 percent during the same period. The importance of this fact has been driven home by the decline (after 1981) in oil revenues and by the resulting domestic economic downturn. The high expectations of the populace still have to be met and it is better that the government evaluate its successes and failures and implement the necessary changes while it has more viable options.

Thus, this is an opportune time to look back at what has been accomplished, to assess the impact of the results of this effort, and to evaluate the success of the government's policies in bringing about economic development and diversification. It is also time to look ahead and explore future options.

ECONOMIC GROWTH

The Saudi Arabian economy has experienced an extraordinary transformation and expansion over a period of a decade and a half (1970-1985). A review of some selected key economic indicators brings this growth into perspective. Real GDP, measured in billions of 1970 U.S. dollars, grew from 3.8 in 1970, to nearly 16 in 1982, a fourfold increase over a 12-year period (see Table I.1). During this time the share of non-oil GDP, which includes electricity, gas, and water services as well as manufacturing, transportation and agriculture, increased from less than 40 percent of the total GDP, to 54

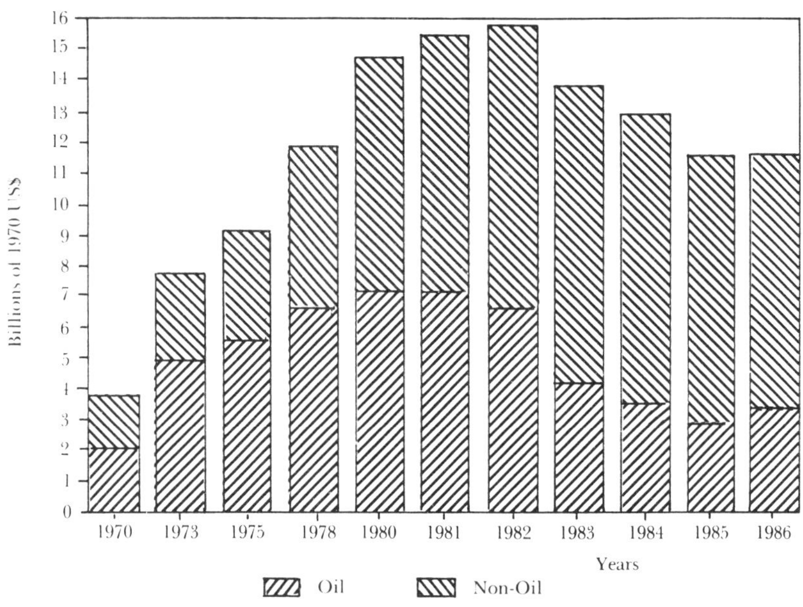

Figure I.1. Real Gross Domestic Product (Saudi Arabia)

Table I.1. Selected Key Economic Indicators[a]

		Non-Oil								
Year	*Oil GDP*	*Government (%)*	*Private (%)*	*Non-Oil GDP*	*Total GDP*	*Current Per Capita GDP (US$T)*[b]	*SAMA*[c] *Foreign Assets (US$B)*[d]	*Trade Balance (US$B)*	*Imports (US$B)*	*Exports (US$B)*
1970	2.1	28.5	71.5	1.7	3.8	0.6	0.9	1.3	0.8	2.1
1973	4.9	30.0	70.0	2.7	7.6	1.7	4.8	5.6	1.9	7.5
1975	5.4	34.4	65.6	3.6	9.0	5.5	38.7	21.3	6.0	27.3
1978	6.5	33.5	66.5	5.3	11.8	.80	60.0	17.0	20.0	37.0
1980	7.1	32.5	66.6	7.6	14.7	12.4	87.4	72.5	28.2	100.7
1981	7.1	32.5	67.5	8.3	15.4	15.6	128.8	81.2	29.9	111.1
1982	6.5	30.0	70.0	9.2	15.7	14.9	141.0	38.6	34.4	73.1
1983	4.1	28.5	71.5	9.7	13.8	11.1	132.6	12.5	33.2	45.7
1984	3.4	28.1	71.9	9.4	12.8	9.4	117.9	8.8	28.6	37.4
1985	2.7	26.7	73.3	8.8	11.5	8.1	109.2	6.9	20.4	27.3
1986[e]	3.2	29.8	70.2	8.3	11.5	8.0	88.5	3.4	16.6	20.0

Notes: a. Figures are in billions of 1970 U.S. Dollars unless otherwise indicated.
b. Figures are in thousands of U.S. Dollars.
c. Saudi Arabian Monetary Agency includes all official foreign assets (including funds managed by the SAMA).
d. Figures are in billions of U.S. Dollars.
e. Preliminary estimates.
Figures may not add up, due to rounding.

percent in 1981, and to over 75 percent in 1985; although this increase is somewhat overstated, given the drop in oil production. Despite a recent decrease in income, Saudi Arabia's nominal GDP per capita is still one of the highest in the developing world at US$8,000 in 1986, though it was only US$600 a decade and a half ago.

Saudi Arabia's exports, mainly oil, and, most recently, oil-related products, have also increased dramatically. Between 1970 and 1981, export revenues grew from US$2.1 billion to over US$110 billion in 1981, only to drop again to nearly US$40 billion in 1984, and US$20 billion in 1986. Non-oil exports have consistently accounted for only 2-5 percent of total exports over the entire period. Imports have kept pace with exports as far as the growth rate is concerned, but have clearly fallen far short of total exports over the period, resulting in a positive trade balance in most years (exceeding US$80 billion in 1981); the interest on foreign assets contributing to the buildup of the Kingdom's foreign assets. In 1982, foreign assets had reached US$140 billion and, despite recent drawdowns that were needed for tiding over budget deficits, foreign assets of the government and its agencies were estimated at around US$88 billion for 1986.

THE PETROLEUM SECTOR

Saudi Arabia possesses 24 percent of the world's proven crude oil reserves. At times, Saudi Arabia has accounted for up to 17 percent of the non-communist world's oil production, or an average production of 10 million barrels a day in 1980-1981 (see Table III.2). During this time, nominal prices have increased from US$3.00 per barrel in 1970, to US$33.50 per barrel in 1982; and, after a drop to US$9.40 per barrel in July 1986, have fluctuated, at around US$18.00 per barrel in 1987. Real oil-GDP, as a percentage of total GDP, was close to 60 percent during the 1970s, but had declined to less than 30 percent in 1986, largely as a result of the decrease in production and prices.

In order to reap benefits from downstream operations, Saudi Arabia has, over the past decade and a half, significantly expanded its oil—refining capacity to meet domestic and export demand for petroleum products. Through the Saudi Arabian Basic Industries Corporation (SABIC), Saudi Arabia has invested heavily to develop a significant petrochemical industry.

Over the past 10 years, SABIC has spent nearly US$12 billion on the development of 13 industrial projects in the area of petrochemicals, most of which are on stream. The industrial cities of Jubail and Yanbu were built for the express purpose of housing Saudi Arabia's primary and secondary industries. It was, and is, expected that by locating the primary industries in these two cities and by providing the necessary infrastructural support, secondary industries would be located nearby.

GROWTH IN THE NON-OIL SECTOR

Overall Growth

Saudi Arabia's accomplishments extend beyond the petroleum sector into the sectors of basic industries, construction, agriculture, and infrastructure. In the area of basic industries, beyond petrochemicals and refineries, SABIC's investments include factories for the production of steel (1 million tons/yr) and fertilizers (500,000 tons/yr). In order to support industry, the government had extended soft loans through the Public Investment Fund (PIF) amounting to US$13.4 billion by the end of 1984.[2] Such loans apply to large government-sponsored projects (e.g., SABIC) and carry a charge when the project is profitable. Another arm of concessionary financing is the Saudi Industrial Development Fund (SIDF) which had granted over US$4.1 billion by 1984 to help finance 830 factories. SIDF is expected to provide over 50 percent of the funds required for the offset projects to be implemented in the Riyadh area, with the primary stated objective of diversification of the Saudi Arabian economy away from hydrocarbon-related industries, as well as the introduction of high technology in association with export production.[3]

One of the most rapid and unexpected developments in the Kingdom was spurred by the generous incentives and subsidies provided to the agricultural sector. Saudi Arabia not only provides for its own wheat consumption, but exports some of its excess production. Wheat production grew nearly fifteenfold from 130,000 tons in 1970, to over 2 million tons in 1986. The agricultural subsidies and loans necessary for such growth have been administered by the Ministry of Agriculture and Water, the Saudi Arabian Agricultural Bank (SAAB), and the Grain Silos and Flour Mills Organization (GSFMO). Agricultural loans increased from US$35.6 million in 1970, to US$1.2 billion in 1983. Total loan facilities granted by SAAB exceeded US$4.9 billion by the end of 1984.

Growth in Infrastructure

The government of Saudi Arabia decided that, during this period of extraordinary gains in revenues and general economic surplus, one avenue of ensuring the future growth of the Kingdom would be through the development of a substantial physical infrastructure base. It was hoped that by putting in place part of the foundations of a modern economy in the form of infrastructure, private sector participation would be increased. Large-scale development projects have been carried out in many areas, ranging from education and health care to physical infrastructure. In Table I.2 some representative statistics on Saudi Arabia's development in the area of infrastructure are presented.

Table I.2. Selected Statistics on Saudi Arabia's Development

Year	*Generated Electricity (million kwh)*	*Paved Roads (length/km)*	*Desalinated Water Supply (million gal/day)*	*Port Handling*[a] *(thousand tons)*	*Airpassenger Arrivals (millions)*	*Telephone Lines (thousands)*	*Schools (number)*	*Hospital Beds (number)*
1970	1,825	8,021	4.6	—	0.8	76.6	3,107	7,165
1973	2,908	8,976	4.6	—	1.2	76.6	4,254	8,870
1975	4,270	11,243	10.6	6,102	2.5	131.6	5,634	8,250
1978	9,713	17,200	17.8	21,530	5.3	215.0	8,695	10,412
1980	18,909	20,238	37.7	37,800	8.4	587.3	11,070	11,968
1981	25,061	22,496	49.7	41,300	9.8	741.0	11,379	13,066
1982	31,014	23,794	98.3	46,700	10.7	970.7	12,619	14,333
1983	33,010	26,042	330.6	48,800	11.7	1,123.0	13,426	16,990

Note: a. Based on capacity at 70 percent.
Source: Ministry of Planning (1984).

In transportation and communication, the Kingdom's asphalt roads have quadrupled from approximately 8,000 kilometers (km) in 1970, to 30,000 km in 1984. The total number of telephone lines has increased seventeenfold to over 1.1 million lines. In order to accommodate the influx of goods and services for now and for the foreseeable future, seaport capacity was increased from 27 operating piers, in 1973, to 133 in 1984. This enabled the handling of an aggregated 38 million tons of trade in 1983, with approximately 7 million tons a year to spare. The Kingdom's 23 airports handled a total of 11.5 million passengers a year in 1983, compared to a mere 800,000 passengers in 1970. Electricity generation has grown seventeenfold, from 1.8 billion kilowatt/hours (kwh/hrs) to 31 billion kwh/hrs. Desalination planet capacity increased to 500 million gallons in 1984, a hundredfold increase in nearly 15 years.

In the area of housing, the government has provided soft-term loans for the construction of private residences as well as rental units. From 1975 to 1984, the Real Estate Development Fund (REDF) has provided loans in excess of US$20.9 billion to the public at large; this effort has also been supported by loans from individual ministries and defense organizations for the construction of residential dwellings throughout the country.

All along, Saudi Arabia has also given prominent attention to fostering the education and well-being of its citizens. While not quite comparable to physical infrastructural achievements, the development of human capital has been one of the major ingredients of Saudi Arabia's long-term development. To that end, the number of schools in Saudi Arabia was increased from 3,000 in 1970, to nearly 14,000 by the end of the Third Development Plan (1984). Special attention was given to the expansion of female education. Over the past three development plans, the ratio of female students increased from virtually zero to over one-third of the student populace. In the area of higher education, 51 colleges and 7 universities offer over 400 courses to the 85,000 registered students. The government has also been increasing its commitment to technical and vocational training. The number of technical schools has increased from 7 to over 38, between 1970 and 1985, and vocational schools have grown from 4 to over 30, during the same time period.

In order to meet the health needs of the Kingdom's populace, beds at the Ministry of Health hospitals were increased from 7,000 in 1970, to nearly 17,000, in 1983. Some of these specialty health clinics are unique in the Middle East (Ministry of Planning, 1984; Ministry of Information, 1985).

THE BUDGET

Saudi Arabia's achievements have not come cheaply.For the past three development plans, Saudi Arabia has spent US$12.3 billion for the First

(1970-1975), US$120 billion for the Second (1975-1980), and US$223.7 billion for the Third Development Plan (1980-1985), for a cumulative expenditure of US$356 billion. During the same period, Saudi Arabia has been able to accumulate a substantial amount in foreign reserves. In Table I.3, budgetary statistics pertaining to the Saudi Arabian economy are presented. Over the period of time under consideration, budgetary revenues increased by leaps and bounds, from US$1.8 billion at the beginning of the First Development Plan, to nearly US$110 billion at the beginning of the Third Development Plan. Budget revenues at the start of the Fourth Development Plan (1985-1990) had fallen to US$36 billion. As can be seen from column 2 in Table I.3, the largest factor contributing to budget revenues was the sale of oil, as nearly 90 percent of all revenues emanated from oil. With a decrease in oil exports and the gradual development of other economic sectors, the contribution of oil to the budget decreased to 56 percent in 1986-1987, the most current year for which actual figures are available.

The difference is split almost evenly between investment income (23 percent) and other revenues, largely consisting of taxes, fees and charges, and the sale or rental of property (27 percent). It should be noted, that although the share of investment income has increased, overall investment income has declined over the past five years, due to a decline in international interest rates, and to a decline in the size of foreign assets.

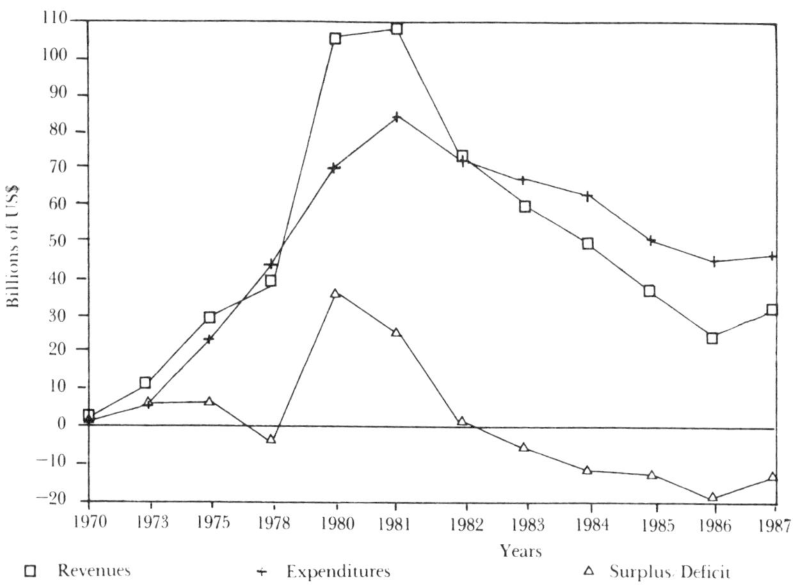

Figure I.2. Saudi Arabian Budget

Table I.3. Summary Statistics on the Saudi Arabian Budget
(In US$ Billions)

Year	*Budgetary Revenues*		*Budgetary Expenditures*			*Budget Surplus or (Deficit)*	*Budget Revenues (% of GDP)*	*Budget Expenditures (% of GDP)*
	Total	*Oil (%)*	*Total*	*Proj. Exp. (%)*	*O&M[a] (%)*			
1970-1971	1.8	86.3	1.4	25.5	—	0.4	34.9	27.5
1973-1974	11.0	92.4	5.0	43.3	—	5.9	40.9	18.7
1975-1976	29.5	90.7	23.4	41.9	—	6.2	62.8	49.7
1978-1979	38.7	88.9	43.0	33.1	—	(4.4)	52.7	58.6
1980-1981	105.5	89.9	69.8	53.4	—	35.7	66.9	44.3
1981-1982	108.2	89.3	83.7	51.2	—	24.5	70.1	54.2
1982-1983	72.4	75.5	72.0	50.8	—	0.4	59.3	59.0
1983-1984	59.0	70.3	65.8	47.6	11.6	(6.8)	55.6	62.0
1984-1985	49.0	69.4	61.8	48.8	11.9	(12.8)	50.6	63.8
1985-1986	36.0	66.7	49.7	41.8	12.5	(13.7)	45.5	62.9
1986-1987[b]	24.1	56.3	44.1	30.3	14.3	(20.0)	35.1	66.9
1987-1988[c]	31.3	67.6	45.3	30.7	11.8	(14.0)	—	—

Notes: a. Operation and Maintenance.
b. Preliminary.
c. Budgetary.

Sources: Saudi Arabian Monetary Agency (various years) and International Monetary Fund (various years).

Budget expenditures increased in line with the rise in budgetary revenues, from US$1.4 billion in 1970, to US$83.7 billion in 1981. A major part of the budget outlay was devoted to investment or capital expenditures (including loans to the private sector), as opposed to current expenditures, and accounted for over 53 percent of total expenditures in 1980-1981. Since then, the share of capital expenditures has declined to 30 percent in 1986-1987. Current expenditures, in turn, increased from 28 percent to 55 percent of total budget expenditures over the same period. A decline in capital expenditure was anticipated as major infrastructural commitments were being completed. The legacy of infrastructural expenditure is also reflected in a new category of data that is listed as a separate item in official statistics: Expenditure on Operations and Maintenance (O&M). For the three years since these figures have become available, expenditure on O&M has accounted for over 2 percent of the annual budget. A potentially disturbing element of O&M expenditure is the decline of nominal expenditure from US$7.6 billion in 1983-1984, to US$6.4 billion in 1986-1987. As the number of projects subject to O&M has increased over the same period, this drop either indicates greater efficiency in O&M through contracting and better management, or an increasing level of neglect in O&M.

The drastic increase in budget deficits over the periods of 1983-1984 and 1986-1987 demonstrates the extent to which an actual decline in expected revenues could not be matched by cuts in budget expenditures, since major projects were near completion and as a too sudden drop in government spending would have been unsettling for the entire economy. In addition, some expenditure is very difficult to cut, such as subsidies, defense, and security. Over the period 1980-1986, expenditures on defense and security rose from 23 percent to 36 percent of total expenditure, or, in 1986-1987, defense expenditure exceeded oil revenues (see Chapter III).

SCOPE OF STUDY

Saudi Arabia's enormous achievements in social services and rapid growth have been well-documented and have been the subject of a number of studies and reports.[4] Our purpose is not to merely repeat these facts or to present another version of Saudi accomplishments. Rather, it is to look beyond the statistics and determine what has actually been accomplished and whether development policies have been efficient in the context of the Saudi economy. As can be seen from all the available statistical information, Saudi Arabia has made major financial commitment toward its development, but what has it in turn received? As Saudi Arabia is entering a new phase of its development—with substantial physical infrastructure in place, current revenue constraints relative to historical government expenditure levels, and a less promising outlook for oil revenues—past policies regarding domestic economic development, as well as those policies dealing with Saudi Arabia's depletable natural resource (oil), need to be reviewed. Such a review may be helpful both for Saudi decision makers and for those who follow the progress of the Saudi Arabian economy to assess the likely course of Saudi oil policy.

Has Saudi Arabia's oil policy served the Kingdom's long-run self-interest? Has the tremendous expenditure on infrastructure been appropriate? Have the oil resources used in the development effort produced new productive capacity of equal value? Has the economy been put on the intended track of diversification away from exports of oil- and petroleum-related products? Have the expenditures on education and health care substantially increased literacy rates and reduced infant mortality?

What is the extent, nature, and viability of private sector development? Is the private sector able to accomplish its role as envisaged in the Fourth Development Plan? What are some of the manifestations of the large expenditures and subsidies on industrial projects, construction, and agriculture?

As thousands of graduates are leaving the Kingdom's universities and returning from their education abroad, what are some of their opportunities for gainful employment either inside or outside of the government? Has the economy provided for adequate employment and to what extent are current graduates ready and qualified to fill the available jobs?

What are some of the general issues that have been learned along the way? And, most importantly, should Saudi Arabia continue to implement its present policies or are there other meaningful alternatives?

In order to assess the existing economic situation in Saudi Arabia and to address some of these questions, it is essential to examine several factors:

1. *Nature of the Saudi Arabian Economy:* The underlying basis of Saudi Arabia's GDP is the depletion of a non-renewable resource. If the proceeds of the sale of this resource are not prudently spent or invested, they are, in essence, wasted and unrecoverable. The implications for managing such an economy are critical to an evaluation of Saudi Arabia's achievements and future options.
2. *Oil Policy:* Saudi Arabia's policy regarding exports and the sale of its predominant resource is another critical component of the overall picture. The sale of this resource fuels the entire economy. Although there are external constraints, an oil policy geared toward long-run maximization of discontinued oil revenues will increase Saudi Arabia's flexibility and provide more leeway in deciding on its future development and disposition of its natural wealth.

3. *External Investments:* One of the avenues that can be used to diversify Saudi Arabia's income-base is to invest some of its oil revenues abroad, in various financial and nonfinancial instruments. The quality and quantity of its investments and management could clearly play a key role in Saudi Arabia's future ability to rely on non-oil sources of income.
4. *Domestic Economic Policies:* Given the pivotal role of government as the sole recipient of oil revenues and because of its predominant size relative to the overall domestic economy, government economic decisions are critical in determining sectoral economic growth. Diversion of resources into one area is necessary at the expense of other areas. The critical question is whether past policies have resulted in the diversification of the economy to compensate for oil depletion. Is the resulting economic and institutional structure appropriate for long-term development and what are the lessons to be learned?

It is of particular interest to analyze the general approach of the government toward developing a domestic non-oil sector. The government has followed three broad policies to encourage this development: first, it has built a large physical infrastructural base; second, it has provided incentives for the private sector to take the lead; and third, the government itself has undertaken investments, in the very capital intensive sectors, such as petrochemicals and export refineries.

It is our intention to review and analyze each of the four areas critical to the Kingdom's economy: the nature of the economy, its oil policy, its policy on external investments, and, most importantly, its domestic economic policies.

NOTES

1. Over a span of about 15 years, enormous strides have been made in the availability of medical care, housing, education, telephone service, electricity service, road networks, and the like.

2. The exchange rate of Saudi Riyals (SR) per US$ ranged from 4.5 to 3.3, between 1970-1985. For most of this period (since 1973), the exchange rate was between 3.4 and 3.5 SR/US$. Currently, the rate is 3.75.

3. Offset investments have been recently required of the Boeing Aircraft Company as an integral component of its winning the bid, in 1985, to build an air defense system for the Saudi Air Force. Offset investments are also incorporated into Saudi Arabia's purchase of Toronado jets from the United Kingdom.

4. For one of the most recent and comprehensive books documenting Saudi Arabia's economic growth, see Johany, Berne, and Mixon (1986).

Chapter II

The Nature of Saudi Arabia's Economy

INTRODUCTION

The heavy reliance of an economy on a depletable resource such as oil, differentiates it from other economies. In an oil-based economy, the interpretations of national product, savings, and other important economic variables are unique. This, in turn, has fundamental implications for economic policy.

The fact that the economic base of a country is almost entirely dependent on the extraction of an exhaustible natural resource has little precedent. Thus, in this chapter a discussion of what may be correctly called a national product in an oil-based economy, and its implications for economic policies, is presented. An examination of some of the related economic characteristics of Saudi Arabia follows and, in conclusion, some general economic policies based on these observations are discussed.

THE MEANING OF NATIONAL OUTPUT IN SAUDI ARABIA

The standard method of including oil production in national product is to simply add the market value of the crude oil extracted at the earliest stage of production.[1] This procedure has some peculiar ramifications. If, for instance, Saudi Arabia increases oil production from 8 to 12 million barrels per day, the national product originating in oil production immediately increases by half. At the extreme, if Saudi Arabia produced all of its oil in one year (a technical impossibility and an economic absurdity), then given standard national income accounting procedures, its national product would be a large number; more realistically, Saudi Arabia could obtain a high national output by selling all of its oil reserves underground, getting a lump sum payment, and having no economic ties to the production of the oil in this foreign "enclave." But in the second year, its national product would be relatively low. The actual size of the national product would depend on the proportion of the national product that is invested, and on the rate of return on this investment; the larger these numbers are, the larger the national product is.

In essence, the national product of an extractive economy is not comparable to the national product of a diversified, nonextractive economy. Conventionally calculated national product in an extractive economy embodies a great proportion of asset transformation, as opposed to economic production. This arbitrariness goes against some rather basic notions about what net national product ought to represent. In an economy that is dependent on the depletion of an exhaustible resource, economic production (i.e., oil depletion) results in the reduction of a capital asset (i.e., oil in the ground). Thus, it is essential to separate that part of the net national product (NNP) that corresponds to the reduction of the capital asset.[2]

To determine the contribution of oil extraction to NNP, we have to ask what NNP is supposed to represent. In a dynamic economy with reproducible capital, but no depletable resources, the most reasonable and commonly-accepted interpretation of NNP is the largest permanently maintainable amount of consumption. To determine NNP, a thought experiment is performed. As if the aim were to enjoy a constant stream of consumption: What is the largest possible value of steady consumption given the resources of this economy? Such a thought experiment can be transformed into a simple model to assess the appropriate interpretation of "measured" or traditionally calculated output for a country such as Saudi Arabia.

For a country totally dependent on oil, the ratio of conventionally measured (i.e., as reported in government statistics) to theoretically correct (i.e., a sustainable level of product) NNP is dependent on the inverse of the real rate of return on capital investments multiplied by the expected life of proven oil reserves (see Appendix I for details). The ratio is an indicator of the relative size of the theoretically correct NNP for an economy totally based on oil, if comparisons are to be made with other economies that have little or no extractive industries.

An idea of the extent by which Saudi Arabia's reported national product exceeds what may be labeled as its "true" national product (i.e., comparable to that of countries with small extractive sectors) can be gauged by examining likely values of the real rates of return on capital and the expected life of proven oil reserves. In Table II.1, the expected life of proven oil reserves is calculated and in Table II.2, the ratio of actual national output to theoretically correct output is calculated for two assumed values of the real return on capital.[3]

Table II.1. Expected Life of Proven Oil Reserves

Year	*Estimated Proven Oil Reserves (bb)*[a]	*Estimated Oil Production (mbd)*[b]	*Expected Life of Proven Oil Reserves (years)*
1981	164.80	9.81	46
1982	168.30	6.48	71
1983	169.00	4.54	102
1984	169.00	4.08	113

Notes: a. Denotes billion barrels.
b. Denotes million barrels per day.
Sources: SAMA (1988); Ministry of Petroleum and Mineral Resources.

Table II.2. Ratio of Actual National Product to Theoretically Correct National Product

		Real Rate of Return
Year	*1%*	*3%*
1981	1.81	0.80
1982	1.64	.66
1983	.99	.66
1984	.94	.69

From Table II.2, it can be seen that the computed NNP overstates the sustainable NNP for Saudi Arabia if a real rate of return of 1 percent is assumed in 1981 and 1982. However, and as is to be expected, as the real rate of return on investment goes up, or as the expected life of proven oil reserves goes up (as oil extraction is reduced), the computed NNP no longer overstates the sustainable NNP, but in fact understates it. This fact, and it sensitivity, points out the dramatic need for sound investment policies to transform oil resources into projects and investments with an adequate real rate of return.

These results are quite intuitive. The longer the life expectancy of proven oil reserves, the longer the period over which Saudi Arabia has to establish alternative sources of NNP and a larger proportion of the current NNP can be considered as output from a sustainable base. At the same time, the higher the real return on investments, the less the government has to invest today in order to receive a given flow of income in the future, and thus a larger proportion of the current NNP can be considered as output from a sustainable base. Because, the higher the rate of return, the higher the income stream of the capital assets. But the point is that the country must still earn a real rate of return from investments. Although this basic point is well-taken for Saudi Arabia, it is even more important for countries in which oil is of great significance to current economic output, but where the expected life of proven reserves is very limited, countries such as Egypt, Algeria, and the Cameroun.[4]

The extent that the computed NNP overestimates sustainable output turns on the real rate of return on investments and on the future of oil prices. Regarding foreign investments, the real rate of return on U.S. government securities over the long term, since the 1930s, has been close to zero. However, the real return on the Standard and Poors (S&P) index has been much higher. The real rate of return on domestic investments in Saudi Arabia is anybody's guess, but it is unlikely to be a positive number. If there is no positive rate of return, capital will not produce income and will thus be gradually used up in consumption.

Compensating for the depletion of oil has important implications for future generations of Saudis. Oil reserves should be seen as the birthright of all generations of Saudis. To the extent that the current generation depletes oil, without compensation through productive investments, it is effectively living off of the assets of all future generations and reducing the standard of living of future generations in its own favor. It should, however, be pointed out that savings can also take the form of keeping oil in the ground. Thus, if oil is being extracted at the optimal rate (i.e., where the increase in the price of oil net of extraction cost is equal to the social rate of discount), then the issue of how much should be saved does not arise.[5]

The basic point made here has been obseerved by others as well. For instance, Stauffer (1981) has made two points in this regard:

1. The standard national income accounting understated the role of oil in the economy of Kuwait.
2. The source of the national product in Kuwait is based more on exhaustible resources, or on depletion of capital, than is the case in industrialized countries.

Amuzegar (1983), in his treatise of oil-exporting countries, has also discussed the implications of oil for oil-based economies.

The implication of the exhaustibility of oil for an economy can be looked at from a somewhat different angle. That is, given an estimated real rate of return on investments (0.5 percent), one can calculate what the savings rate has to be while oil lasts and is being depleted (see Appendix I). The result is that the savings rate today should be about 58 percent.[6]

The lesson from optimal growth theory is clear: in order to achieve reasonable savings rates in the future, when oil is depleted, Saudi Arabia should start (at least with the parameter values assumed here) saving at extremely high rates *now*. If Saudi Arabia has a utility function consistent with eventually saving 20 percent (after oil has run out), the optimal policy is to now save approximately 60 percent of the national product in *productive* capital and/or in foreign assets (financial or real) with the same rate of return.

Whatever the duration of oil extraction, an optimal savings policy will smooth consumption over time, by accumulating capital during the oil-producing years in sufficient quantities to guarantee satisfactory consumption levels after oil runs out. In industrialized economies whose economic base is primarily reproducible capital, consumption rates of 80 or 90 percent are reasonable. But, for an economy based on a depletable resource, it would be unwise to think in terms of such consumption rates. However, it should be recalled that oil extraction rates can be reduced, increasing savings in the form of oil in the ground.

The figures for Saudi Arabia should, in turn, be compared to actual savings rate to determine whether they are in the neighborhood of what is required to compensate for the depleting nature of oil. For Saudi Arabia, recent savings rate have been 59 percent (1981), 56 percent (1982), 31 percent (1983), and 30 percent (1984) (World Bank, 1983, 1984, 1985, 1986). From these figures, it is clear that actual savings rates were roughly consistent with calculations presented here for 1981 and 1982; the later decline is, in part, explained by the fact that oil production decreased (thus increasing the expected life of proven oil reserves and reducing the required rate of savings). A word of caution is called for regarding the adequacy of savings rates in Saudi Arabia. The savings rate is derived as a residual; thus, whenever the national product is overestimated, so is the savings rate. As a result, given that the conventionally measured national product may be an overestimate of the theoretically correct national product, then the savings may embody such an upward bias.

Uncertainty has not been discussed because it is technically difficult to incorporate. But, almost surely, the presence of uncertainty would argue against keeping so much of a country's wealth in one particular type of asset (oil in the ground), and in favor of diversifying by extracting at higher rates than are appropriate, and by spreading out the proceeds in a variety of assets. However, it should be noted that as far as uncertainty is concerned, the decision as to whether to keep oil in the ground or to extract it and to invest in other assets for diversification, also depends on the relative uncertainty of oil prices and on the returns on investments. If it is most profitable to pump oil out of the ground slowly, in a certain world, the diversification effect would argue in favor of pumping it out somewhat more rapidly in an uncertain world. Moreover, in an uncertain world, specifically in regard to oil prices and oil revenues, aversion toward risk would, with everything else the same, dictate even a higher savings rate while oil lasts.

Finally, because of the importance and exhaustibility of oil in the Saudi economy, economic conditions look better than they really are when oil revenues decline abruptly.[7]. On the one hand, when oil revenues increase, Gross National Product (GNP) per capita, current account, and the like, improve dramatically. But it should be understood that such improvements are not permanent; they are only permanent if the revenue increase lasts and is compensated for by non-oil revenues as oil revenues decline. On the other hand, when revenues so decline, the same economic indicators worsen substantially. But again, conditions are not as bad as they appear unless oil revenues stay at low levels permanently, and unless non-oil revenues do not increase. In short, sudden changes are normally a temporary divergence from the long-run path of revenues, but permanent economic conditions are determined by whether current oil revenues are employed to generate alternative sources of income and by the long-run price of oil.

ECONOMIC MANIFESTATIONS OF AN OIL-BASED ECONOMY

Measure of Dependence on Oil

Most exhaustible resource-based economies, such as that in Saudi Arabia, have certain economic characteristics, that distinguish them from other developing countries. In this section, these distinguishing features are discussed.

Exhaustibility of Oil. As was discussed in the previous section, the depletable nature of oil is the critical distinguishing feature of these economies. This means that each barrel of oil extracted, today, reduces the number of barrels to be extracted in the future. This distinguishes oil exporters and exporters of all depletable resources, from exporters of agricultural or manufactured products, since the income or output of the latter is derived from a *sustainable* economic base. Current oil production, in a sense, reduces the aggregate national capital stock or wealth of oil-producing countries and, in turn, the future flow of oil income. Future income and consumption levels can only be protected from declining if adequate amounts of the revenues derived from oil wealth are transformed into equivalent income-generating, domestic or foreign, assets. This view of oil resources as wealth or capital raises important questions for the choice of savings, investment, and development strategy for Saudi Arabia.

Dependence on Oil. A second distinguishing characteristic of Saudi Arabia lies in its degree of dependence on a single product, namely oil. Not

Table II.3. Dependence on Oil
(In the Kingdom of Saudi Arabia)

Year	*Ratio of Oil Exports to Total Exports*	*Ratio of Oil Exports to GDP*	*Ratio of Oil Revenue to Government Revenues*
1979	99.8	59.9	91.2
1980	99.9	87.8	91.7
1984	96.5	45.3	69.4

Source: SAMA (1984, 1988).

only does oil provide the bulk of foreign exchange earnings, but it also generates most budgetary revenues and, through government expenditures, supports much of the economic activity in the domestic non-oil private sector. This dependence makes Saudi Arabia potentially more vulnerable to factors affecting market conditions in a single product than is the case for most other developing countries with a more diversified economic base (see Table II.3).

In assessing dependence, there are a number of measures that can be used. One is the ratio of exports of the exhaustible commodity to total exports. For Saudi Arabia, oil represents over 96 percent of its export earnings.

Dependence on oil is also illustrated by the high ratios of oil exports to GDP. In some respects, this statistic is more significant since it reveals not only the high ratio of oil exports to total exports, but also the high ratio of the value of export production to other outputs. For Saudi Arabia this figure was 87.8 percent in 1980.

A more limited measure of dependence is provided by the ratio of oil revenues to total government revenues. For Saudi Arabia, over 90 percent of government revenues were derived from oil before the enormous drop in oil revenues, an indication of a limited tax base. But although Saudi Arabia is heavily dependent on oil and thus appears to have little diversification in its ability to earn foreign exchange and to have a limited tax base, the accumulation of foreign assets provides an effective method of addressing these twin problems.

In the more recent years (1986-1988), Saudi Arabia's dependence on oil has declined. Non-oil exports have accounted for about 10 percent of the total, oil exports to GDP has declined to about 30 percent, and oil revenue to total government revenues has been on the order of 50 percent. Such reduced dependence on oil is temporary and is a function of lower oil prices, reduced oil output, and thus of the increasing relative importance of investment income.

Diversification of Exports. A country is better off, the more diversified its export structure, provided that diversification is a result of comparative advantage. Although the measures presented suggest that a higher degree of dependence is to be found for Saudi Arabia than for other developing countries, Saudi Arabia has, in the past, had large current account surpluses, resulting in the accumulation of foreign assets: US$94,619,000 (1973-1979), US$42,000,000 (1981), and US$12,000,000 (1982). Hence, its vulnerability to fluctuations in receipts from oil, provided it is not prolonged, may not be as great as that of countries whose measured dependence is less, but that do not have such a large cushion of reserves.

Implications of Revenue Dependence on Oil

As was mentioned in the previous section, the government derives a high proportion of its revenues directly from oil. As a result, the external adjustment process and domestic development will depend almost exclusively on the nature and quality of the government's decisions.

In a world free of capital transactions, when international transactions are undertaken predominantly by the private sector, balance of payments (BOP) surpluses (or deficits) can be expected to set in motion forces that will tend to cause their elimination. In a Keynesian world, a trade surplus yields an increase in domestic real income that prompts an increase in aggregate demand. This increases imports directly and also puts upward pressure on the domestic price level that causes the substitution of foreign for domestic sources of tradable goods. Viewed in a monetarist framework, a BOP-induced increase in domestic liquidity creates a temporary excess supply of money. Efforts to restore real balances to the desired level then lead to increases in expenditure (part of which falls on imports), increases in prices (for nontradable goods), or to capital outflows—the joint result of which is to produce a deterioration in the balance of payments.

When export revenues accrue directly to the government, the same equilibrating change in money supply and factor incomes can take place, but the distinction is that they will only do so when the government takes the active decision to expand expenditure on the basis of the new higher level of revenues. For most governments this may be politically more feasible as revenues expand. The direct accural of oil revenues to the government does not afford the economy with automatic linkages to stimulate economic development. Instead, because oil revenues accrue to the government, the speed and dimensions of domestic economic development will depend on when and how the government transforms oil revenues into government expenditures.

The accrual of export revenues to the government means that it has a readily available source of savings and foreign exchange with which to finance investment. This fact makes savings decisions easier for these countries by avoiding the pains of taxation and its collection. This is in contrast to many other developing countries where the domestic savings and foreign exchange constraints retard growth and development. In this connection, however, it should be noted that the removal of constraints on savings and foreign exchange does not mean there will be an absence of resource constraints on development. All investment projects require complementary domestic, as well as imported resources, and the government's overall investment strategy has to take into account the need for domestic resource mobilization. In Saudi Arabia, skilled labor and agricultural land are a binding constraint. All in all, the direct accrual of oil revenues to the government gives it added flexibility as well as increased responsibility in the nature and direction of the development process.

If the government wishes to influence the pattern of investment, either for social or economic reasons, it is easier to do so when investment decisions are under its direct control, than when it has to use indirect methods such as fiscal and credit incentives. A dominant role for government in investment planning and implementation does not, of course, guarantee that investment decisions will be conducive to efficient development. One danger with government involvement in resource allocation decisions is that it could allow a large weight to be given to politically strong interest groups, at the expense of efficiency, and to take a short-run view in order to insure its own immediate survival.

The Nature of Oil Export Revenues

There are two characteristics of oil revenues that are of special concern to Saudi Arabia. The first concern is uncertainty in the future size of revenues, especially those associated with the price of oil. While the price of oil has increased since 1971, it has also fallen dramatically since 1982. The demand for oil depends on a number of unpredictable factors: the growth of the world economy; new policies to limit energy consumption and the success of conservation; oil discoveries in the rest of the world; competition from existing non-oil energy sources; and technological progress in exploiting alternative energy sources, such as solar, shale, tar sands, fusion, fission, biomass, and wind. This suggests that Saudi Arabia should diversify its export base, not only because reserves of oil are finite and declining, but also because the demand and price of oil is uncertain. There is, therefore, a short-run as well as a long-run case for diversification. But a policy of diversification is faced with a variety of difficulties in its implementation.

A second concern, and a problem for diversification, is that the receipt of substantial oil export revenues today, could have an undesirable impact on the real exchange rate (relative price of nontraded to traded goods), limiting the development of competitive non-oil exports necessary as oil is depleted over the long run (commonly referred to as Dutch Disease).[8] Revenues from the extraction of exhaustible resources normally rise at the early stages, reach a maximum, and then decline steadily as the resources near depletion. The exchange rate effect, resulting from the revenue boom, is derived from two sources. The higher level of domestic income results in higher expenditures on both traded and nontraded goods. The price of traded goods does not rise as the price of these goods are internationally determined, while the price of nontraded goods increases. The lower relative price of traded goods, in turn, reduces the incentive for the production of traded goods and thus lowers its output. Secondly, if both the traded and nontraded goods sectors employ common factors of production, the expansion of nontraded goods tends to increase the price of these factors, increasing the price of nontraded goods, and thus resulting in an appreciation in the real exchange rate. The real exchange rate normally follows this revenue path, appreciating in the early stages of resource exploitation, and then depreciating in the later stages. However, such an exchange rate appreciation may make non-oil tradable goods industries uncompetitive, or prevent such industries from developing in the first place. The real exchange rate would normally decline again at a later stage in the cycle; but if at this time there was no non-oil economic base, the adjustment process would be much more difficult, unless the government adopts countermeasures to achieve an appropriate real exchange rate to encourage the development of the non-oil sector.

A booming resource sector, besides affecting the structure of production through real exchange rate effects, may also cause unemployment; if the increase in the price of nontraded goods necessitates a reduction in real wages but real wages are heading downward and/or if real incomes increase and thus the real demand for money, causing unemployment if real money supply does not increase. Thus, a booming resource sector has been used as the basis for *selective* industrial subsidies. If learning-by-doing is an important input in industrializaiton, then subsidies can be justified on a selective basis in sectors where learning-by-doing is important. To the extent that real exchange appreciation negatively impacts on these industrial sectors (tradables) in the short-run, the optimum level of subsidies could be justifiably increased.

Finally, it should be noted that diversification, through the acquisition of foreign assets, avoids the problems associated with Dutch Disease.

Diversification from Oil

Given Saudi Arabia's heavy dependence on oil, an all-important objective has been diversification of its economic and revenue base away from oil. The underlying reasons for diversification are many.

The most direct reason for diversification is the fact that oil reserves will eventually be depleted, necessitating an alternative economic base of production. In the absence of a non-oil economic base, domestic economic activity and revenues will decline with oil depletion. Such a development will not only adversely affect domestic economic activity, but also export and government revenues and other economic indicators directly or indirectly linked to oil extraction. Moreover, diversification away from oil will reduce the risk or exposure associated with dependence on one export commodity, as opposed to a diversified export base. Such a diversification can be expected to result in more stable revenues, benefiting the planning process and, in turn, economic development and growth.

The oil industry cannot directly generate enough diverse employment opportunities. The oil industry, especially modern oil refineries and petrochemical plants, are highly capital intensive. Labor requirements are minimal, and require relatively high skills. To create increased employment opportunities and opportunities for different professional and skilled categories of manpower, diversification away from oil is required. Similarly, since the oil sector uses advanced foreign technology, it does not provide training opportunities for the indigenous labor force. Thus, in a sense, the dominance of the oil sector forces Saudi Arabia into a vicious circle, whereby the necessary demand for human capital does not exist, and whereby the supply cannot be forthcoming as the required training channels are not available. The demand for factors of production is derived from the demand for goods and services. Oil production does not directly increase the demand for domestic goods significantly and for nontraded services substantially but largely through government expenditures.

In Saudi Arabia, human and social considerations play a dominant role in the objective function of the policymakers. However, the oil sector, with its direct linkage to the government, does not directly provide a mechanism for distributing income and purchasing power to citizens. As a result, the government itself is required to use direct and indirect channels to distribute income. But, Saudi Arabia has discovered that this is a very difficult task; diversification from oil and the development of a large private sector would reduce the dimensions of this problem. Diversificaiton from oil and the resulting linkages can be expected to create new investment opportunities for the private sector, expand the participation of the private sector, and reduce capital exports by creating increased domestic investment possibilities. Moreover, diversifications would simultaneously reduce the existing and potential social and economic problems associated with a dualistic economic structure that has been promoted by the high technology and high wage oil sector.

Potential for Diversification

The normal path to diversification for most developing countries has been out of agriculture and into some form of labor-intensive manufacturing. Such a strategy is consistent with their low capital/labor ratio and with the observed higher income and price elasticity of manufacturers in world trade. If a developing country has a large internal market, this diversification might be primarily aimed toward import substitution, although most success stories among devleoping countries have relied on export promotion.

Even if capital is abundant, Saudi Arabia is not guaranteed a competitive advantage in exporting petroleum-based processed goods. Where raw materials and semifinished and finished products are all transportable, which country has a comparative advantage in processing depends on much more than the location of the raw material. Among the factors to be taken into account are relative transport costs of finished and unfinished products, capital construction costs in processing industries, relative costs of financial capital, relative labor costs, and external economies. Since construction costs and labor costs for technical personnel in Saudi Arabia have tended to be extremely high, resource-based industrialization may be most profitable if proximity to the energy source is an important factor. Recently, relative construction costs have been changing in favor of Saudi Arabia. Early in the decade of the 1970s, the construction costs of petrochemical plants in the region were 2 to 3 times that of Japanese and European locations. Currently, the construction costs of some plants are about 1.5 times that of Japanese and European plants, and, in the most recent case of a plant constructed by SABIC, this factor has averaged 1.35. In the case of a second plant, this factor is further reduced by 25 percent as compared with the first plant.[9]

A program of industrialization based on energy sectors, that is, refined products and petrochemicals, does not provide the necessary diversification. The markets for refined products and petrochemicals are closely linked to that of energy, and to oil in particular. In addition, these energy-related sectors have many of the same undesirable properties for the domestic economy, such as a low level and lack of diverse employment opportunities, lack of channels for distributing income, and a low level of linkages to the private sector. Further, the avialable world capacity in petrochemicals and petroleum refineries is already too large to allow additional entry into the market, unless there are substantial competitive advantages for Saudi Arabia to make inroads in these industries.

While noting these potential negative consequences of industrialization based on petrochemicals, some of the positive elements should be recognized. Petrochemical development enables the integration of oil and gas production into the domestic economy. Moreover, diversification based on petrochemicals and energy industrialization may be considered a bridge between total dependence on the exports of primary products to exports of value-added manufactured goods. Finally, this process should help in the development of technical and managerial skills.

Social and International Factors

The rapid inflow of financial resources from oil has resulted in great expectations on the part of the domestic population. Such a high level of expectation has put pressures on the government to increase current and capital expenditures at rates that have been inflationary, in part due to bottlenecks and structural problems, and have at times resulted in economic waste.

On the international side, the higher oil prices, the larger accumulation of reserves, and the solidarity with other developing countries have all placed a great deal of pressure on Saudi Arabia to provide increased assistance to developing countries.

GENERAL ECONOMIC POLICY IMPLICATIONS

Given the nature of the Saudi Arabian economy, and the role and implications of a large oil sector, what should be Saudi Arabia's general economic policies? Two policy implications stand out.

First, given that oil reserves are by far the largest component of the wealth or assets of Saudi Arabia, a rational oil policy is of paramount importance. The essential feature of a rational oil policy would have as its prime objective, maximizaiton of discounted oil revenues. This obvious point can be stated differently. The larger the discounted value of oil revenues, the more leeway the government will have to develop a source of large non-oil income or NNP.

Second, Saudi Arabia should invest a large portion of its current NNP, or oil revenues, in areas yielding a high real return to compensate for the depletion of oil. By real return, it should be understood that one does not mean an artificial return that does not incorporate explicit and implicit subsidies such as low energy prices, an overvalued exchange rate, and tariffs. For the purpose of compensating for the depletion of oil, however, the return need not be necessarily from domestic investments alone. But given that in Saudi Arabia oil revenues accrue to the government, it places more responsibility on the government to pursue sound economic and investment policies; and given the overwhelming role of the government, this is even more critical than in most other developing countries.

In addition to the two policy objectives just mentioned, which are the most critical, the examination of the Saudi Arabian economy also points to other policy objectives. The heavy reliance on oil—contribution to the GNP, export earnings, and government revenues—necessitates a series of policies aimed at diversification in order to reduce the impact of a downturn in oil revenues.

NOTES

1. This section draws on Appendix I.
2. There are two components to the income generated from the sale of extracted oil—factor payments and scarcity rent. In the case of Saudi Arabia, a low-cost producer, it is the latter component that is large. Thus, as oil is extracted, the value of national wealth declines. The inclusion of all revenues (the rent component) as national product is, therefore, incorrect because it does not take into account the depreciaiton of national wealth resulting from oil depletion.
3. In Appendix I, the model assumes that the oil sector is the only sector of the economy. An adjustment can be made by calculating the weighted ratio of 1 (i.e., assuming that actual output for the non-oil sector is all sustainable) for the non-oil part of the economy. The share of non-oil sector GDP has been 30.4 percent (1980-1981); 35.3 percent (1981-1982); 49.9 percent (1982-1983) and 57.0 percent (1983-1984).
4. In the derivation of the ratio of the actual to the theoretically correct national product, it is assumed that the real rate of return on capital investments equals the rate of oil price increase. If, however, the rate of oil price increase is higher than the return on capital, it would be optimal to slow down the rate of depletion, extending the life of reserves, in which case a larger fraction of NNP can be attributed to output from a sustainable base.
5. This statement assumes that the chosen social rate of discount by the planners is "fair" or "just," reflecting "appropriately," the welfare of future generations.
6. Again, an adjustment should be made for the relative size of the oil sector to the equation derived in Appendix I.
7. We are grateful to Vahid Nowshirvani for this observation.
8. For a discussion of various aspects of Dutch Disease, see Neary and Winjnbergen (1985).
9. For a detailed study of downstream projects, see Turner (1979).

Chapter III

Saudi Arabia's Oil Policy

INTRODUCTION

The impact of Saudi Arabia on the world oil market can be gauged by a glance at simple statistics.[1] In 1986, Saudi Arabia possessed 24 percent of the world's proven crude oil reserves, over 55 percent of the Gulf Cooperation Council (GCC)[2] reserves, and in excess of 35 percent of OPEC's reserves (see Table III.1). Saudi Arabia, at times, has accounted for up to 17 percent of the non-communist world's oil production, up to 43 percent of OPEC production, and over 73 percent of GCC's production (see Table III.2). In recent years, OPEC and GCC oil production, as well as Saudi Arabia's share of OPEC's and the non-communist world's production, have decreased markedly. Nevertheless, the relative importance of Saudi Arabia in the future of the world oil market is largely a function of its extensive share of proven and potential oil reserves.[3]

BACKGROUND OF THE INTERNATIONAL OIL MARKET

Oil was discovered in the United States in 1859. Until 1875, oil prices were quite volatile. Between 1875 and 1911, the oil market in the United States was effectively regulated by the Standard Oil Trust, with reduced price volatility (standard deviation).[4] After the breakup of the Standard Oil Trust in 1911, the market was much more volatile for the next 22 years. In 1933, the Texas Railroad Commission was formed to regulate production and thus stabilize prices; it was quite successful in performing its mandate during the 1930s as the oil industry was not yet internationalized. Finally, from the 1940s until the early 1970s, the majors in the form of the "Seven Sisters," tightly controlled oil production and prices.[5]

Table III.1. Saudi Arabia's Proven Oil Reserves

	Barrels (billions)	*Ratio of Saudi Arabia's Reserves (%)*
Saudi Arabia	168.8	100.0
GCC	303.7	55.6
OPEC	474.4	35.6
World	707.6	23.9

Source: *BP Statistical Review of World Energy* (1986).

The impact of the actions of the major oil companies was one of the main contributing factors to the oil price increases of the 1970s and to the rising importance of OPEC. Specifically, the majors kept oil prices at what may be considered artificially low levels in the sense that it resulted in unprecedented growth in oil consumption, while simultaneously reducing exploration activity,[6] (see Table III.3) and, in time, resulting in shortages and thus inducing price volatility and higher prices.

OPEC was formed in 1960 in response to nominal declines in the price of oil, and thus in the producer countries' revenues, or take from a barrel of oil. During most of the 1960s, OPEC was, by and large, an unnoticed bystander as opposed to an organization affecting, much less controlling, oil prices. However, the actions of the international oil companies were laying the foundation for OPEC's rise to prominence during the 1970s.

The government take per barrel of oil for OPEC countries was roughly US$0.78 in 1960, and stood at only US$0.85 in 1968 (Exxon Corporation, 1984).

This price structure encouraged oil consumption and discouraged oil exploration and development of alternative energy sources. The results were dramatic; oil consumption in the non-communist world grew from 26.5 million barrels per day in 1965, to 47.6 million barrels per day in 1973 (*BP Statistical Review,* 1985); an increase of about 80 percent in eight years—a rate substantially higher than the growth of the world GNP. Over the same time period, OPEC's share of the non-communist world output increased from 44 percent in 1960, to 67 percent in 1973;[7] this was because of low levels of exploration activities outside of the Middle East, and because outside of the Middle East region, the highest quality reserves had already been found (see Table III.4).

During the period 1960-1971, many independent oil companies (independents) entered the international oil market, resulting in a loss of control for the majors. The independents, unlike the majors, did not have diversified sources of crude. In 1971, for example, around 90 percent of Occidental's worldwide crude came from Libya. The independents did not

Table III.2. Oil Production
(In thousand barrels/day)

	1974	*1975*	*1976*	*1977*	*1978*	*1979*	*1980*	*1981*	*1982*	*1983*	*1984*	*1985*
Saudi Arabia	8,350	6,970	8.525	9.235	8,315	9,555	9,990	9,985	6,695	5,225	4,760	3,600
GCC	13,680	11,785	13,725	14,230	13,340	15,020	14,405	13,570	9,625	8,340	8,145	6,965
OPEC	31,055	27,530	31,090	31,690	30,275	31,470	27,450	23,390	19,935	18,475	18,345	17,225
Total World	58,620	55,700	60,085	62,560	63,050	65,775	62,745	59,375	57,020	56,705	57,800	57,340
Percentage Share of:												
Saudi Arabia GCC	61.0	59.1	62.1	64.9	62.3	63.6	69.4	73.6	69.6	62.6	58.4	51.7
Saudi Arabia OPEC	26.9	25.3	27.4	29.1	27.5	30.4	36.4	42.7	33.6	28.3	25.9	20.0
Saudi Arabia World	14.2	12.5	14.2	14.8	13.2	14.5	15.9	16.8	11.7	9.2	8.2	6.3

Source: *BP Statistical Review of World Energy* (1985).

Table III.3. Real 1972 Dollars and Nominal Oil Prices in the United States

	Nominal Dollars	*Year-Year Percent Change*	*Real Dollars*	*Year-Year Percent Change*
1944	1.21	1	3.27	(1.5)
1945	1.22	1	3.22	(1.5)
1946	1.41	16	3.20	(0.6)
1947	1.93	37	3.90	21.9
1948	2.60	35	4.91	25.9
1949	2.54	(2)	4.84	(1.4)
1950	2.51	(1)	4.68	(3.3)
1951	2.53	1	4.43	(5.3)
1952	2.53	—	4.37	(1.4)
1953	2.68	6	4.56	4.3
1954	2.78	4	4.66	2.2
1955	2.77	—	4.55	(2.4)
1956	2.79	1	4.44	(2.4)
1957	3.09	11	4.75	7.0
1958	3.01	(3)	4.56	(4.0)
1959	2.90	(4)	4.29	(5.9)
1960	2.88	(1)	4.19	(2.3)
1961	2.89	—	4.17	(0.5)
1962	2.90	—	4.11	(1.4)
1963	2.89	—	4.03	(1.9)
1964	2.88	—	3.96	(1.7)
1965	2.86	(1)	3.84	(3.0)
1966	2.88	1	3.75	(2.3)
1967	2.92	1	3.69	(1.6)
1968	2.94	1	3.56	(3.5)
1969	3.09	5	3.56	0.0
1970	3.18	3	3.48	(2.2)
1971	3.39	7	3.53	1.4
1972	3.39	—	3.39	(4.0)
1973	3.89	15	3.68	8.6
1974	6.74	73	5.87	59.5
1975	7.56	12	6.02	2.6
1976	8.14	8	6.16	2.30
1977	8.57	5	6.12	(0.6)
1978	8.96	5	5.96	(2.6)
1979	12.51	40	7.66	28.5
1980	21.59	73	12.10	58.0
1981	31.77	47	16.24	34.2
1982	28.52	(10)	13.62	(16.1)
1983	26.19	(8)	12.16	(10.72)
1984	25.88	(1)	11.58	(4.8)
1985	24.03	(7)	10.41	(10.1)

Source: Salomon Brothers Inc. (1986).

Table III.4. OPEC Crude Oil Production, 1960-1983
(In thousand barrels/day)

	Middle East Members	*% of OPEC*	*Other Members*	*Total OPEC*	*OPEC as % of Non-communist World*	*Middle East OPEC Members as % of Non-communist World*
1960	5,028	64	2,846	7,874	44	28
1961	5,577	66	2,920	8,497	45	30
1962	6,110	61	3,844	9,954	49	30
1963	6,701	62	4,164	10,865	50	31
1964	7,358	61	4,724	12,082	52	32
1965	7,996	61	5,191	13,177	53	32
1966	8,876	62	5,341	14,217	53	33
1967	9,837	63	5,794	15,631	54	34
1968	10,855	61	6,805	17,660	55	34
1969	11,893	58	8,448	20,341	59	34
1970	13,229	60	8,905	22,134	58	35
1971	15,594	62	9,498	25,092	63	39
1972	17,301	65	9,410	26,711	64	41
1973	20,599	66	10,390	30,989	67	45
1974	21,234	69	9,513	30,747	68	47
1975	18,904	70	8,296	27,200	65	45
1976	21,309	70	9,249	30,558	67	47
1977	21,805	69	9,612	31,417	67	47
1978	21,013	69	9,358	30,371	64	45
1979	21,016	68	9,895	30,911	64	43
1980	17,913	67	9,028	26,941	59	40
1981	15,221	67	7,459	22,680	55	37
1982	12,137	64	6,754	18,891	49	31
1983	10,965	62	6,584	17,549	46	29

Source: Exxon Corporation (1984).

have the same leverage over producing countries that the major oil companies had enjoyed, thus further increasing OPEC's bargaining position.

In short, OPEC achieved little in increasing its revenues per barrel of oil over the period 1960 to early 1971 (the Teheran Agreement of February); rising from US$0.78 per barrel in 1960, to only US$0.86 in 1968, and it was only at the February Agreement (Teheran) of 1971, which resulted in an increase of up to 50 percent in government take (or an increase of between US$0.25 and US$0.65 per barrel). The actions of the majors resulting in OPEC's increased market share, the entrance of independents into the international oil market, and OPEC's enhanced organization in pursuit of similar goals, gave OPEC stronger bargaining power. This ultimately resulted in the fact that by the early 1970s, in the short run, the marginal barrel of oil demanded had to come from OPEC sources. As a result, while OPEC did little up to February 1971, it was poised to play an active role for the next decade.

As a result of these forces, oil prices increased in 1971, 1972, and more substantially during 1973-1974, cutbacks in production by Saudi Arabia (and some other Arab oil producers) also played a key role in the price increase (see Quandt, 1982). OPEC's oil production peaked in 1977. But, thereafter, OPEC production and OPEC's share in the output of the non-communist world declined. Oil prices again increased over the period 1979-1981, largely due to political (the Iranian revolution and the Iran-Iraq war) events in the region; but thereafter, prices declined and OPEC output continued its decline to a level of about 15-16 million barrels per day in 1985, compared to an average of around 30 million barrels per day during 1973-1979.

It is helpful to explain in more detail the reasons underlying the behavior of oil prices and OPEC production levels.

Over the period 1971-1978, the oil market was driven by demand. Although prices had increased during 1973-1974, it took time for the impact to be reflected on demand. Similarly, exploration outside of OPEC increased, but it took time for it to impact supply. As a result, OPEC's share of crude oil sales increased. The reason why prices in nominal terms moved very little between 1974 and 1978, and declined in real dollar terms, was that OPEC maintained and/or increased output. The obvious should be stressed. If over the period 1974-1978 OPEC had cut back output (either undertaken by a major producer besides Saudi Arabia, or by OPEC as a whole with individual quotas) then prices would have soared. The point should also be clear that by the early 1970s the gap between world consumption and potential world output had narrowed, resulting in little excess capacity in the world relative to the 1960s. Under these conditions, if OPEC or individual OPEC countries reduced output, the impact on prices would have been greater than in a situation where there was large excess capacity. In a sense, as excess capacity is reduced, there is more potential for prices to increase as output reductions in one or more countries may not be matched, in the short run, by increases in other countries. Individual OPEC countries, especially those with relatively large reserves, did not reduce output because higher prices may not have been in their long-term interests as demand for OPEC oil may have declined even more rapidly.

During the period 1978-1981, prices again increased due to panic buying that ensued over the forced production cutbacks in two OPEC countries (Iran and Iraq) which in turn was due to political events. The reason why prices did not rise evern more, was because Saudi Arabia increased its output substantially to meet supply shortfalls and thus to meet the needs of the international economy.

During the 1970s, OPEC's experience might be summed as an "easy" phase. It was easy for OPEC because:

- each OPEC country was producing at its desired, or physically possible, levels;
- Saudi Arabia, Kuwait, and the United Arab Emirates each could have produced more, but this might have resulted in declining revenues given their large market share, especially in the case of Saudi Arabia;
- although the demand for OPEC oil declined, excess capacity in OPEC was affected moderately because of events in Iran and Iraq; and
- no production quotas were necessary within OPEC.

It should be noted that neither OPEC, nor a subgroup of OPEC, tried to coordinate production levels to support a particular price. OPEC price decisions basically confirmed market developments with a lag; OPEC official prices consistently lagged behind Rotterdam spot prices. Saudi Arabia, unilaterally, but not as a part of a coordinated policy, increased output to moderate price increases. Thus, OPEC did not fix prices but Saudi Arabia's unilateral policies had substantial effect in moderating price increases. All of this was possible because effective excess capacity worldwide was low, resulting in a tight market.

In recent years, an important factor in the international oil market has been exchange rates. Oil prices are quoted in dollars by OPEC. Therefore, if the dollar rises in value relative to other currencies, then the effective price of oil rises for the world as a whole. This simple mechanism has been largely ignored by most followers of the oil market. But in recent years, especially since 1979, exchange rate influences have had a substantive impact.

In Table III.5, the dollar price of crude oil, an index of the price of oil in different currencies and a composite weighted (by the shares of each country's imports) price index are given for the period 1979-1986 (monthly for 1985-1986). Although the dollar price index of oil increased, reaching its highest level in 1982, the price in other currencies continued to increase substantially thereafter and peaked in 1985. As a result, the price of oil in other currencies and as reflected in the composite (by import shares) index increased substantially more than the dollar index. This higher increase in the composite price of oil was, of course, due to the sharp appreciation of the dollar. And similarly, beginning early 1985 (February/March) the decline in the nondollar price of oil and in the composite index has been much more rapid than in the dollar index, as the dollar has sharply depreciated.[8]

Table III.5. Oil Price Indices for Selected Oil-Importing Countries

	Oil Price		Price Index Per Barrel in Local Currency									
Year	*(US$ barrel)*	*(Index)*	*Belgium*	*Canada*	*France*	*Germany*	*Italy*	*Japan*	*South Korea*	*The Netherlands*	*Spain*	*Composite Index*
1979	17.26	100	100	100	100	100	100	100	100	100	100	100
1980	28.67	166	166	166	165	165	171	172	207	165	177	169
1981	32.50	188	238	193	241	232	258	189	265	234	259	214
1982	33.47	194	302	204	300	257	316	220	293	258	317	248
1983	29.31	170	296	179	304	237	310	184	272	242	363	232
1984	28.47	165	325	182	339	256	349	179	275	264	395	242
1985	27.95	162	328	189	342	260	372	176	291	268	410	246
Jan.	27.95	162	350	183	369	280	380	188	278	289	385	260
Feb.	27.72	161	362	185	380	288	392	191	278	299	369	263
Mar.	27.69	160	364	189	381	290	402	189	281	299	357	266
Apr.	27.62	160	339	186	354	269	380	184	284	278	358	245
May	26.93	156	333	183	347	265	373	181	280	274	358	237
Jun.	26.81	155	327	181	341	260	365	176	280	267	358	237
Jul.	26.97	156	313	180	326	249	360	172	282	256	375	232
Aug.	27.38	159	306	184	318	241	357	172	289	248	389	238
Sep.	27.61	160	313	187	326	248	366	173	295	255	405	237
Oct.	27.79	161	294	188	305	232	346	158	297	239	413	231
Nov.	27.98	162	290	190	301	229	342	151	298	236	405	227
Dec.	27.90	162	283	192	292	222	334	150	298	228	413	219
1986												
Jan.	27.53	160	272	192	281	213	320	154	293	219	416	213
Feb.	16.50	96	156	115	161	122	183	81	175	126	259	121
Mar.	15.19	88	139	105	144	109	163	72	161	112	240	110
Apr.	11.03	64	101	76	108	79	120	51	117	82	164	82
May	12.17	71	110	83	118	86	130	54	129	88	184	72
Jun.	11.40	66	103	73	111	81	120	51	121	83	172	84
Jul.	9.36	54	82	64	88	64	96	39	99	66	136	66
Aug.	11.54	67	97	79	106	75	114	47	122	78	163	80
Sep.	11.95	69	100	82	109	77	117	49	126	79	174	83
Oct.	12.05	70	99	83	107	76	117	50	126	79	168	82
Nov.	12.65	73	105	87	114	81	124	54	132	84	174	87
Dec.	12.68	73	104	87	113	80	122	54	131	82	171	87

Notes: The composite price index is calculated by multiplying import shares of individual countries with their respective price indices. The reference oil prices are spot prices for Arab Light f.o.b. Rotterdam.

Sources: IMF (1988); *Platt's Oilgram Price Report* (various years); *The Wall Street Journal* (various years).

What do all of these dollar exchange fluctuations portend for the oil market? Essentially, the sharp dollar price increases of 1979-1980, which stimulated exploration outside of OPEC and dampened demand, were further reinforced on a world scale as the dollar, the currency of denomination for oil, appreciated. As a result of the appreciation of the dollar, OPEC difficulties to allocate shares in a declining market, were accentuated as demand for OPEC oil fell even more sharply than might have been expected. Beginning in early 1985, the appreciation of the dollar, was sharply reversed. This, in turn, will stimulate demand for OPEC oil by more than what most observers believe by looking purely at the dollar price. Therefore, if the dollar stays at its level of early 1987 or depreciates further, it will be easier for OPEC to allocate shares as demand can be expected to increase by more than that if the dollar had not depreciated.

All of these dollar and composite oil price fluctuations besides directly affecting demand and supply, have more subtle and indirect effects. These price fluctuations (especially in nondollar currencies as these movements are further magnified by exchange rates) induce conservation, production, and increase uncertainty in forming price expectation for oil. Conservation and production effects are in large part irreversible. If prices rise, expenditures in equipment and machinery are made, technical changes are made, habits are changed, and the like; but these are not totally reversed when prices fall by the same amount as the increase; demand does not go back to where it was as conservation measures are in place; and supply does not decrease, as marginal cost of production is now the determinant of output, as capital expenditures have already been made. These irreversible and overtime effects and thus price fluctuations, are clearly to the detriment of an expanding market for OPEC oil. On the other hand, price fluctuations also increase uncertainty in forming price expectations and may thus work to impede capital expenditures outside of OPEC, which is to OPEC's advantage.

In short, pricing of oil in dollars by accentuating effective price changes was clearly working to OPEC's long-run disadvantage over 1979-1985, by adversely affecting the long-term market for oil. However, it is true that the real price of oil (in terms of internationally traded goods) was increasing further as the dollar appreciated, but what good is high oil prices if little oil can be sold?

SAUDI ARABIA'S OIL POLICY

Oil policy in Saudi Arabia is determined at the highest levels of government. The king, the crown prince (deputy prime minister), and the second deputy prime minister, are the ultimate decision makers. Some input is solicited from the Higher Petroleum Council, composed of selected members of the cabinet. As a result, Saudi Arabia's oil policy has been historically motivated by broad political and economic considerations, as opposed to purely technical factors. The major political considerations have been Arab solidarity, the Arab-Israeli conflict and regional politics, cohesiveness within OPEC, and Third World and Western (especially U.S.) support. Economic factors include long-term diversification from oil and short-term revenue needs to meet both domestic and external financial obligations.

Regarding political motivations, Arab solidarity and the Arab-Israeli conflict are closely related. In the aftermath of the October War (1973) and the helplessness of the Arab world, oil was seen as the only "weapon" available to show Arab anger at U.S. support of Israel. If oil became the weapon, it was Saudi Arabia that led the charge, playing a key leadership role in cutting back oil production by 5 percent a month, and by raising prices by approximately 70 percent. This "oil as a weapon" concept is still alive today in the minds of many Arabs, and consequently Saudi Arabia is mindful of how its oil policy is perceived in the Arab world. If oil prices are seen at a level that only serves Western interests, the Saudis will be open to Arab criticism and resentment.

Although Saudi Arabia is stable and has a well-equipped military force, it still must take into account regional considerations, like its two powerful neighbors, Iraq and Iran. Consequently, Saudi decision makers consider the impact of their oil policy on these two adversaries. Given that Iraq, and to a greater degree Iran, are not as well endowed with oil on a per capita basis as is Saudi Arabia, a drop in the price of oil has a greater effect on their economies. And, in the case of Iran, with its production capacity at a low level and with its recent war expenses being paid in cash, it was imperative that oil brought in as much revenue as possible.

Saudi Arabia's political influence in international affairs is derived from various sources. In part it comes from its position as the protector of the two holiest cities in Islam: Mecca and Medina (beginning in 1986, the king has asked to be referred to as the "Custodian of the Two Holy Mosques"). But Saudi Arabia's power flows mainly from its economic position. As the giant among oil producers, Saudi Arabia is important to the economic well-being of oil exporters and importers alike. Through its wealth and its ability to render assistance to Third World countries, it has gained significant influence. In the late 1970s and early 1980s, its financial assets made it an important voice in international capital markets.

As a country that has such diverse areas in which its influence is felt, there are naturally aspects of its policies that will be in conflict with one another. For example, to the extent that some of the other oil exporters demand a higher price for oil, and powerful oil importers desire a lower price, Saudi oil policies cannot please everyone. However, cohesiveness within OPEC and the interests of powerful Western countries, especially the United States, are given priority.

Saudi oil policy is, of course, also motivated by economic considerations. They truly have an oil-based economy, and as such, its actual Net National Product (NNP) cannot be correctly compared to the NNP for industrial countries. That is, it is not correct in the sense that Saudi Arabia's NNP does not represent maximum long-run sustainable consumption. A large portion of the actual NNP must be saved and invested in order to generate alternative (sustainable) sources of income as oil is depleted. In such a setting, Saudi Arabia's long-term interests are clear. They need to maximize discounted oil revenues (a technically difficult task but necessary to attempt anyway) and to save and invest a significant portion of their revenues in profitable investments, foreign or domestic, to compensate for oil depletion.

These long-term economic interests at times conflict, however, with their short-term needs. With high government expenditures, Saudi Arabia in the short run, has high revenue needs, needs that must be met by oil exports since other sources of income are inadequate. As will be shown, short-run revenue needs are substantial, arising from two main expenditures: military and subsidies (see Chapter VI).

To the extent that Saudi Arabia's financial reserves are depleted or are expected to be depleted, the Saudis are influenced by considerations that may maximize short-run revenues. Politically, given the importance and size of military and subsidy expenditures, short-run requirements become at times, the overriding consideration.

In addition to domestic revenue requirements, Saudi Arabia has substantial financial commitments to Arab neighbors and other Islamic countries. GCC member states, Iraq, Syria, Pakistan, the Mujahedeen in Afghanistan, and others, receive substantial amounts of aid from the Kingdom. These financial commitments play an integral part in Saudi Arabia's political clout in its region of influence.

Finally, the availability of natural gas in Saudi Arabia is limited by oil production since most of it is in the form of associated gas; as such, the Kingdom needs some minimal amount of oil production to satisfy its gas needs. In the future, this problem will be somewhat ameliorated due to the discovery of unassociated gas in Saudi Arabia and the acquisition of gas from Qatar. This never has been a major motivator of Saudi oil policy, but it has contributed to their domestic oil consumption needs.

During the last 15 years, all of these factors have come into play at one time or another, contributing in varying degrees to the formulation of Saudi oil policy.

From an *economic* view, Saudi Arabia's oil policy can more precisely be broken down roughly by different time periods—prior to 1981, 1981-1985, and since 1985.

Table III.6 Crude Oil Production, 1973-1983
(In thousand barrels/day)

	1973	*1974*	*1975*	*1976*	*1977*	*1978*	*1979*	*1980*	*1981*	*1982*	*1983*	*1984*	*1985*
Iran	5,861	6,022	5,350	5,883	5,663	5,242	3,168	1,662	1,380	2,214	2,465	2,195	2,225
Iraq	2,018	1,971	2,262	2,415	2,348	2,563	3,477	2,514	1,000	972	1,105	1,225	1,435
Qatar	570	518	438	497	445	487	508	472	405	329	310	425	310
Saudi Arabia	7,596	8,480	7,075	8,577	9,245	8,301	9,532	9,900	9,815	6,470	5,225	4,760	3,600
United Arab Emirates	1,533	1,679	1,664	1,936	1,999	1,831	1,831	1,709	1,474	1,214	1,175	1,200	1,280
Kuwait	3,020	2,546	2,084	2,145	1,969	2,131	2,500	1,656	1,125	827	900	985	910
Algeria	1,097	1,009	983	1,075	1,152	1,161	1,154	1,012	805	710	980	1,075	1,040
Libya	2,175	1,521	1,480	1,933	2,063	1,983	2,092	1,787	1,140	1,158	1,110	1,105	1,090
Gabon	150	202	223	223	222	209	203	175	151	155	155	150	155
Nigeria	2,054	2,255	1,783	2,067	2,085	1,897	2,302	2,055	1,433	1,295	1,235	1,385	1,475
Indonesia	1,339	1,375	1,307	1,504	1,686	1,635	1,591	1,577	1,605	1,339	1,345	1,410	1,310
Ecuador	209	177	161	188	183	202	214	204	211	210	240	255	280
Venezuela	3,366	2,976	2,346	2,294	2,238	2,165	2,356	2,168	2,102	1,891	1,875	1,875	1,745
Total	30,988	30,731	27,156	30,737	31,298	29,807	30,928	26,891	22,646	18,784			
World Total	55,674	55,582	52,880	57,312	59,685	60,057	62,535	59,538	55,900	53,162			

Sources: U.S. Department of Energy (1973-1982); *BP Statistical Review of World Energy* (1983-1985, 1986).

Table III.7. OPEC Crude Oil Productive Capacity

	Year-End (Mbd)			
	Installed Capacity[a]	*Maximum Sustainable Capacity*[b]	*Available or Willing Capacity*[c]	*Limiting Assumption or Condition*
Kuwait	3.0	2.5	1.3	Policy
Saudi Arabia	12.5	11.0	8.5	Policy
United Arab Emirates	2.6	2.5	1.5	Policy
Neutral Zone	0.7	0.6	0.6	Policy
Iran	6.0	4.0	1.5	War limitation
Libya	2.5	2.1	1.0	Short-term technical problems and policy
Iraq	4.0	3.8	1.5	War limitation
Venezuela	2.6	2.4	2.2	Revenue and availability
Nigeria	2.5	2.4	2.2	Availability
Algeria	1.2	1.1	1.2	Availability
Qatar	0.6	0.6	0.5	Historical trend
Indonesia	1.8	1.7	1.7	Availability
Ecuador & Gabon	0.5	0.5	0.5	Availability
Total	40.5	35.2	25.2	

Notes: a. Installed Capacity, also known as nameplate or design capacity, includes all aspects of crude production, processing, transportation, and storage. Installed Capacity is generally the highest capacity estimate.

b. Maximum Sustainable Capacity (MSC), or operational capacity, is that part of Installed Capacity that can be sustained for several months. It takes in the implications of operating the total system and may be 90-95 percent of installed capacity. This capacity concept may, however, be higher than the maximum production rate sustainable without damage to the fields, and does not reflect external limitations such as the current hostilities between Iran and Iraq.

c. Available or Willing Capacity is the lowest capacity estimate reflecting:

- the fact that, on an annual basis, availability is likely to be below the maximum capacity that can be sustained over a few months;
- that Abu Dhabi, Kuwait, and Saudi Arabia have, more or less, firm production ceilings. These are, however, sometimes interpreted on an annual basis, resulting in the probability of production exceeding the ceiling in a given month;
- pipeline and shipping limitations, due to the Iran/Iraq hostilities.

Source: International Energy Agency (1983).

Prior to 1981

The period prior to 1981 can be characterized as a period when Saudi oil policy focused on short-run considerations and on the absence of a long-run policy. As can be seen from the production figures in Table III.2 and from comparative statistics on excess production capacity (Table II.8), production was essentially demand driven. Saudi Arabia acted as a "swing

Table III.8. Comparative Statistics on Oil Production: Capacity,[a] Output, and Excess Capacity
(In thousand barrels/day)

	1976	*1977*	*1978*	*1979*	*1980*	*1981*	*1982*	*1983*	*1984*	*1985*
OPEC										
Capacity	39,225	39,300	40,215	35,235	34,435	34,435	32,135	32,220	28,230	27,425
Output	30,461	31,137	29,881	31,470	26,799	22,491	18,445	17,581	17,490	16,063
Exc. Cap.[b]	8,764	8,163	10,335	3,765	7,636	11,944	13,690	14,639	10,740	11,362
Mideast-OPEC[c]										
Capacity	28,050	28,225	29,315	25,035	24,235	24,235	22,135	22,170	18,860	18,625
Output	21,226	21,545	20,541	21,375	17,874	15,054	11,706	11,021	10,708	9,546
Exc. Cap.	6,824	6,680	8,774	3,660	6,361	9,181	10,429	11,149	8,152	9,079
GCC-OPEC[d]										
Capacity	19,320	18,275	18,325	16,735	17,235	17,235	17,235	17,670	14,060	13,725
Output	13,751	13,617	12,711	14,725	13,761	12,841	8,838	7,590	7,318	5,921
Exc. Cap.	5,569	4,658	5,614	2,010	3,474	4,394	8,797	10,080	6,742	7,804
Saudi Arabia										
Capacity	11,840	11,840	11,840	10,500	11,000	11,000	11,000	11,000	9,000	8,500
Output	8,579	9,206	8,300	9,249	9,659	9,985	6,295	4,893	4,444	3,209
Exc. Cap.	3,261	2,634	3,504	1,251	1,015	1,015	4,705	6,107	4,556	5,291

Notes: a. Maximum Sustainable Capacity.
b. Excess Capacity.
c. Includes Saudi Arabia, Kuwait, Qatar, United Arab Emirates (UAE), Iran, and Iraq.
d. Includes Saudi Arabia, Kuwait, Qatar, and the UAE.

Sources: *Petroleum Intelligence Weekly* (various years); *BP Statistical Review* (various years).

producer," filling any gaps in demand, to the extent possible, by increasing output and thus moderating price increases.

Excess capacity for Saudi Arabia was at its lowest in the period 1979-1981, largely as a result of the decline of production in Iran and Iraq. Saudi Arabia was producing close to 10 million barrels per day (mbd) for the period 1979-1981. Saudi Arabia's share of OPEC production increased from 25.3 percent in 1975, to 42.6 percent in 1981. In effect, Saudi Arabia did prevent a further price rise during the 1978-1979 period. It was clearly in Saudi Arabia's interests to prevent a severe shock to the world economy and to keep the oil-market intact. Official government statements (Quandt, 1982, 8), however, convey a concrete Saudi oil policy and a definite goal:

> As far as Saudi Arabia is concerned, our interests are clear. First, we do not intend to exhaust this wealth quickly and deprive our future generations of it. On the other hand, we do not want to shorten the life span of oil as a source of energy before we complete the elements of our industrial and economic development, and before we build our country to be able to depend on sources of income other than oil. In this respect the kingdom's interests might differ from those of its OPEC colleagues.
>
> And the government's admission of past mistakes is also apparent:—in 1979-1980 we made a mistake. We raised prices without regard for actual demand.

It is difficult to reconcile these statements with actual Saudi policy.

1981-1985

Demand for oil in the non-communist world declined after 1979; world consumption decreased from 51.2 mbd in 1979, to 45.7 mbd in 1985, or by about 11 percent. Concurrently, non-communist world oil production decreased by 17 percent over the same period, OPEC production decreased by 42 percent, and Saudi Arabia's production dropped even further. Again, the major contributing element in this production decline was the role of Saudi Arabia as a "swing producer." Saudi Arabia acted as a swing producer because it was unwilling to accept a quota. Saudi Arabia curtailed its output to maintain higher price levels. And in reality, as was mentioned earlier, world prices were even higher in view of the appreciation of the dollar.

The strategy of acting as a swing producer had its consequences. Export levels of the swing producer are much more volatile. Just as an increase in world demand implies a large export increase for the swing producer, a downturn implies a large export reduction. The policy implication for swing producers, from a long-run perspective, is quite significant. Within OPEC, swing producers lose relatively more revenue during a phase of production contraction and gain disproportionately from a production expansion. The question is: Will other OPEC members allow the swing producers to take the lion's share of any expansion? As can be witnessed in the case of Saudi Arabia, the production differential between the highest and lowest level was 6.5 mbd during 1980-1985. Such fluctuations in production translate into similar swings in export revenues, and in the case of a highly oil-dependent economy such as Saudi Arabia, on its government revenues. Worst of all, this strategy does not allow for the implementation of a consistent policy to maximize long-term disocunted revenues, as it only serves to satisfy short-term world oil market needs and to maintain short-run cohesiveness within OPEC.

This strategy cost Saudi Arabia dearly. Saudi Arabia's share of production within OPEC decreased from 42.7 percent, in 1981, to 20.9 percent, in 1985. Among OPEC countries, Saudi Arabia and other GCC members of OPEC were the only countries in the aggregate where excess production capacity exceeded oil production between 1982 and 1985.

The results of this policy for Saudi Arabia were as follows:

1. A significant loss in market share (even though the 1981 share for Saudi Arabia was artificially high);
2. Proportionally lower export and government revenues than other OPEC countries due to the Kingdom's high degree of reliance on oil exports;[10]
3. Current account and budget deficits that are being financed from earlier savings.

Although not a result of Saudi policies, these losses were aggravated further by the 1985-1987 depreciation of the U.S. dollar.

It is difficult to give rational economic reasons for Saudi Arabia's oil policy during the period 1981-1985. The only economic explanation is that government officials felt that the downturn in demand was temporary and had resulted from the world economic downturn. They, therefore, believed that the market would soon turn around. This expectation was clearly erroneous. Most oil analysts also did not foresee the dramatic and sustained downturn in the market between 1981 and 1985.

There are, however, as indicated earlier, several political motivations. First and foremost, has been the Saudi desire to maintain political cohesiveness among other Arab oil producers and also among OPEC members. Saudi Arabia's political importance and prestige emanates from accumulated financial reserves, oil policy, and the location of Islam's two holiest cities. Saudi Arabia has consistently used these three assets to gain political support. As a result, Saudi Arabia has been reluctant to use its oil policy in ways that might lose support among countries, especially among countries in its region and sphere of influence. Second, Saudi Arabia had hoped that if it led the way, other oil-producing countries, within and outside of OPEC, might also reduce output. This was a clear miscalculation, which was not based on economic realities for other countries. What is even more difficult to comprehend, is that it took Saudi Arabia four years to see its policy shortfalls. But even this has its roots in the Saudi approach to decision making. Decisions are reversed slowly and only when other options are no longer available.[11]

Recent Policy 1985-Present

Given the aforementioned changes in the world oil market, the impact on the economy of Saudi Arabia, and public opinion, which was opposed to the swing producer role, Saudi Arabia decided to abandon its role as a swing producer and increase output up to its OPEC quota by instituting a policy of pricing its oil on a "net-back" basis. This did not occur until after Saudi Arabia had tried all possible avenues unsuccessfully to get other OPEC countries to produce within their quotas. Consequently, world crude oil prices dropped for a while, to below US$10 per barrel. Was such a strategy in Saudi Arabia's best interests?

Before looking into the results of the shift in Saudi policy, it may be useful to discover what motivated Saudi Arabia to make a change in 1985. When oil production hit a low of 2 mbd for a brief period in 1985, and external reserves began to decline more rapidly than envisaged under the budget, a general sense of panic emerged. The root of the panic was twofold. Economically, the situation was disastrous if continued, as Saudi Arabia's budgetary deficit was increasing. Government subsidies and military expenditures could not be significantly reduced in the short run. Politically, Saudi Arabia was losing influence with no tangible appreciation from countries that were benefiting from Saudi oil policy. At the same time, Iran was making some headway in its war efforts and Iraq was unable to reduce Iran's oil exports. Finally, the Saudis felt that a temporary increase in production would soon bring OPEC countries in line and more importantly, they felt that important non-OPEC producers, especially Mexico, Norway, the Soviet Union, and the United Kingdom, would also cooperate to reduce output. As the policy was instituted, they saw that their revenues did not decrease substantially, but most importantly, lower oil prices had more seriously affected Iran's ability to finance its war efforts (selling its restricted amount of oil output at lower prices) than anything Iraq had been able to do.

In December 1985, OPEC's announced objective, proposed by Saudi Arabia and the GCC, was to increase market share. This implied that OPEC's aggregate share was the target. However, if OPEC tried to attain this through collusive behavior, allocations disputes would have again arisen within OPEC regarding the appropriate level of individual shares or quotas. The December 1985 OPEC meeting may have had as its target OPEC's aggregate share, but all indications were that each member would try to get some "appropriate" market share for themselves, resulting in a larger aggregate share for OPEC. What would have exactly motivated each country's decision regarding its share and the resulting aggregate share was, in practice, unclear.

In August 1986, OPEC reached what might at best be characterized as a "temporary" agreement. The agreement was to set an aggregate quota of 16.8 mbd. This agreement was made possible by other OPEC members, especially Iran's suggestion to exclude Iraq from any output limitations.[12] The October 1986 OPEC meeting extended this fragile agreement with a slight production increase for the rest of the year. But an important question still remained—while the agreement may have been helpful in the short run, was it in the best long run interest of Saudi Arabia?

In our opinion, the agreement will be detrimental to Saudi Arabia if it does not tend toward long-run revenue maximization. Realistically, it is unlikely that OPEC can agree for long on individual shares. Additionally, expanding the membership of OPEC will again fail, because then it will be even more difficult to come to any agreement. Past experience may be useful in determining how OPEC and Saudi Arabia might emerge from its present crisis, despite its prior agreements.

First and foremost, Saudi production policies appear to have been in error after 1981. Saudi Arabia's oil production was too low after 1981, resulting in an inappropriately high price, especially high for many non-dollar currencies as the dollar started a period of long and sharp appreciation. This high price level induced further (to what had started in 1974) conservation, the development of alterative sources of energy, and increased exploration and production of oil outside of OPEC. Over time, these developments resulted in a continual reduction in OPEC's share of world oil output, and especially Saudi Arabia's role in the crisis of 1985-1986. Second, since OPEC is unable to effectively allocate shares in a shrinking market for a long period of time, an implicit enlargement of OPEC to new members will also—in the long run—fail. Third, pricing in dollars adds an inherent instability to the market as movements in the exchange value of the dollar will substantially change market demand and also impact on the real value of revenues to OPEC members. In short, Saudi Arabia and, in turn OPEC, must be more market oriented if it is to succeed in the future. Market orientation for Saudi Arabia implies realistic long-term production or pricing policies. How does this translate itself into practice, and how will OPEC and Saudi Arabia emerge from the present situation?

In our opinion, Saudi Arabia should pick a production level that would result in a price that would tend toward maximization of discounted revenues (actual revenue maximization is theoretically desirable, but practically impossible), as opposed to focusing on short- and medium-run results, and on market shares that should not be an end in themselves. Whether or not this approach will work will depend on the convergence or divergence of the economic interests of individual OPEC members. At one extreme, a country such as Ecuador, with little impact on the overall oil market (thus with little power), is producing close to its sustainable capacity and its desire is for prices to be as high as possible, implying that other OPEC members curtail their production. At the other extreme, Saudi Arabia's oil production policies have a significant effect on the oil market, thus, with a great deal of power in OPEC and its interest diverging from Ecuador, an artificially high price today will be against its long-term interests. Saudi Arabia could clearly use its power within OPEC to attain a solution that is closer to its economic goals. However; the Saudis do not appear to have followed such a policy, at least effectively, during the period 1981-1985.

Long-run revenue maximization should clearly be the overriding economic objective. However, though the goal can be simply stated, it is difficult to implement. Such a policy requires a great deal of future information, which is hard, if not impossible, to predict:

- long-run demand function for oil (which is in part, determined by world economic growth, price of alternative energy sources, and individual country energy policies)
- oil production policies of non-OPEC oil producers
- reaction (production) of other OPEC countries to any given Saudi production policy
- exchange rate developments
- real rates of return in Saudi Arabia and on foreign assets
- size of recoverable OPEC oil reserves and its distribution among members and
- oil production policies (keeping to individual quotas) of individual OPEC countries.

Revenue maximization does not seem to have been the objective of Saudi decision makers since policies did not even tend toward this goal.

A simple calculation will illustrate OPEC's long-run interests, the interests of individual members, and especially the interests of Saudi Arabia. In the calculation, two extreme alternatives for OPEC behavior are examined: OPEC increasing its output at a constant price to satisfy increasing demand and OPEC maintaining a constant output and allowing prices to rise. In reality, OPEC would pursue a policy in between the two extremes. The purpose of such an exercise is to determine whether OPEC policy is likely to be closer to the first or second alternative.

The results will depend on demand for oil, which in turn depends in large part, on world economic growth, income elasticity of demand for oil, price elasticity of demand for oil, and supply of oil and other sources of energy in OPEC and non-OPEC countries. Projected world economic growth from International Monetary Fund (IMF) Statistics and from other sources, would indicate optimistically, an annual figure of around 2.8 percent through 1995. Estimates for average income and price elasticities of demand for oil are given as follows: the income elasticity for developing countries is 0.5-0.6 in the short run, and 1.3-1.9 in the long run. For industrial countries, a uniform income elasticity of 0.8 is indicated. The price elasticity for developing countries is around -0.1 in the short run, and -0.25- -0.35 in the long run; for industrial countries these are -0.16 and -.40, respectively.

The other element is oil production. As a reasonable scenario, we could assume zero increase in production outside of OPEC. OPEC has roughly an additional 18 million barrels maximum sustainable capacity (see Table III.7). Of this, it is estimated that an additional 2 to 3 mbd would go to domestic consumption by the year 2000, leaving 15 to 18 mbd (18 in 1986 and going down to 15 in the year 2000) for exports (see Table III.9).

The question, therefore, becomes: How much should OPEC produce for exports? To answer this, we can examine two simple alternatives for OPEC behavior. Table III.10 gives the necessary background information to assess OPEC behavior and prices. We have made the following simplifying assumptions: (1) average income growth of 2.8 percent in the world economy for the period 1986-1995, (2) constant world oil prices, (3) average long-term income elasticity of roughly 1.0 and, (4) average price elasticity of -0.3.

Table III.9. Maximum Sustainable Crude Oil Production Capacity (In million barrels/day)

	1985	*1990*	*2000*
OPEC	31.6—33.0	29.1—34.3	27.8—33.5
Mideast-OPEC[a]	22.6—24.0	22.1—25.4	21.4—25.2
GCC-OPEC[b]	15.1—16.4	14.5—16.9	14.4—16.7

Notes: a. Includes Saudi Arabia, Kuwait, Qatar, UAE, Iran, and Iraq.
b. Includes Saudi Arabia, Kuwait, Qatar, and UAE.

Sources: *Petroleum Intelligence Weekly* (various years); *BP Statistical Review* (various years); International Energy Agency (1983).

Table III.10. OPEC Oil Output and Revenues—Two Simple Scenarios to the Year 1995[a b]

	1985	*1986*	*1987*	*1988*	*1989*	*1990*	*1991*	*1992*	*1993*	*1994*	*1995*
1. World oil demand (million barrels/day)	57.6	59.2	60.9	62.6	64.3	66.1	68.0	69.9	71.8	73.9	75.9
2. OPEC production (million barrels/day)	16.0	17.6	19.3	21.0	22.7	24.5	26.4	28.3	30.2	32.3	34.3
3. Increase in OPEC oil revenues relative to 1985 at constant price of: US$17.00/barrel (million US$/day)	—	27.4	55.6	84.6	114.4	145.0	176.5	208.8	242.1	276.3	311.4
4. Oil prices if OPEC does not increase output but allows prices to rise (US$/barrel)	—	18.6	20.3	22.2	24.3	26.6	29.0	31.7	34.7	38.0	41.5
5. Increase in OPEC oil revenues relative to 1985 at constant level of production but with rising prices (US$ million/day)	—	25.4	53.1	85.5	116.7	152.9	192.6	236.0	283.4	335.2	391.9
6. Difference in revenue increase—scenario, row 5—scenario, row 3 (US$ million/day)	—	2.0	2.5	-1.1	2.3	8.0	16.1	27.2	41.3	58.9	80.5

Notes: a. This approach was first applied by El-Kuwaiz (1986).
b. This scenario was assumed in 1987. As a result, some of the facts on oil demand, output, and oil production are somewhat outdated but the direction of the results are similar.

Based on these assumptions, we have derived the world demand (Table III.10). In this scenario (with no extra output outside of OPEC), all the 1986-1995 increase in demand would be satisfied from OPEC sources. In the third row, the implied extra revenues to OPEC are calculated, assuming a constant price of $17 per barrel. In row 4, we estimate a price level (using a price elasticity of -0.3) that would develop if OPEC did not increase output. In row 5, the addition to OPEC revenue is calculated. Should OPEC follow the dictates of revenues of rows 3 or 5? In row 6, the difference in the respective increase in revenues due to each policy are calculated.

Before discussing the results, it is noted that the two outcomes, that is, rows 3 and 5, are intended as extreme cases. Clearly, through 1988, OPEC revenues would be slightly higher if output was increased as opposed to letting prices rise (see row 6). Beginning in 1988, OPEC behavior would depend on whether *individual* members would benefit more by increasing output or increasing prices. Given the high levels of excess capacity in some OPEC countries, the future of oil prices depends on the relative benefits of the two scenarios for individual member countries. Taking rough production figures available for the end of 1985, one can see that roughly 11.5 mbd, or around 70 percent of the extra capacity, was in three OPEC countries—Saudi Arabia, Kuwait, and the United Arab Emirates—while about 35 percent of OPEC exports at that time (a low of 2 mbd for Saudi Arabia) was in these same countries.

The issue then becomes: Is it to the advantage of these countries to get 70 percent of the scenario presented in row 3, or 35 percent of the scenario presented in row 5? Clearly, prior to 1988, revenues in row 3 are higher than in row 5, so that the Saudi Arabia and other GCC countries in OPEC are better off exporting more oil, as opposed to letting prices go up, even if the percentages were 50-50. However, given their low level of exports (resulting in a total share of only 35 percent of OPEC exports), they would be better off every year by getting 70 percent of row 3, as opposed to 35 percent of row 5. Additionally, it should be noted that the scenario represented in row 5 is a much larger overestimate than that of row 3 because in the former scenario, a substantial extra energy output should be forthcoming from non-OPEC sources, thus moderating price increases and OPEC revenues. This further supports the likelihood of the scenario represented in row 3. In reality, if the first scenario is pursued, prices will also rise somewhat as excess capacity is reduced. All of this would indicate less volatility in oil prices, with prices increasing gradually, but at an increased rate as excess capacity is reduced.

In the 1979-1981 period, the reverse of this situation existed. The financial incentive was to let prices increase. These calculations are illustrative and simplistic, but the basic point is evident, assuming any reasonable price elasticity, a few members that have the lion's share of excess capacity (Saudi

Arabia and other GCC member states of OPEC), but have a minority of current output, are better off, in both the short and long run, by increasing output as opposed to letting prices increase as demand expands.[13]

These results lead to one inescapable fact—OPEC can be divided into at least two groups with divergent interests. One group—with little or no excess capacity, or with policy reasons not to increase output—would like to maintain the OPEC share prevailing in 1985 and let prices rise over time. The other group—with substantial excess capacity—would like to increase its output, and thus its share over time. For the long run, these differences are even more important as the members with more capacity and reserves would like to pursue policies today that preserve a future market for their oil (i.e., a low discount rate); while the countries with low capacity and reserves would like to sell their limited oil at a high price in the short-run (i.e., a high discount rate) and have less interest in the long-run market outlook. OPEC's overriding dilemma is to reconcile these two divergent interests or discount rates.

For Saudi Arabia/GCC the (December 1985-October 1986) strategy of expanding output makes sense also for the following reasons:

1. It will, in the medium-term, increase Saudi/GCC revenues, despite the drop in price.
2. The long-run benefits of this strategy to Saudi Arabia/GCC is that lower oil prices will not only make production less feasible for some new entrants into the world oil market, but will also dissuade further exploration and development of alternative sources of energy in the future.
3. It will stimulate demand over the medium and long term.
4. At the end of the Iran-Iraq war, due to the high absorptive capacity of both their economies, they are likely to argue for higher production shares in OPEC. With a higher relative share of production to begin with, Saudi Arabia/GCC would be in a better bargaining position than if negotiations began from a lower production level.
5. Although a temporary agreement was reached in August and October 1986, it was made possible because of the hardships that increased Saudi/GCC oil production had caused for other OPEC countries and non-OPEC producers such as Mexico, Norway, and the Soviet Union.
6. One cannot ignore the devastating impact that lower oil prices had on Iran's oil revenues and therefore on Iran's ability to finance its war efforts.

Table III.11. Saudi Defense and Security Expenditure in Relation to Government Budget (In US$ Millions)

	1980	*1981*	*1982*	*1983*	*1984*	*1985*	*1986*[a]
Defense and security	16,423	19,387	19,390	18,494	19,293	16,702	16,419
Total budget expenditure	71,042	84,215	71,403	66,721	61,467	50,138	45,946
Oil revenues	95,887	97,217	54,229	42,065	29,511	17,630	11,510
Total government revenues	104,540	108,878	71,773	59,832	48,724	36,325	24,089
	Defense and Security as Percentage of:						
Total expenditures	23.1	23.0	27.2	27.7	31.4	33.3	35.7
Oil revenues[b]	17.1	19.9	35.8	44.0	65.4	94.7	142.7
Total revenues	15.7	17.8	27.0	30.9	39.6	46.0	68.2

Notes: a. Preliminary figures.
b. Excludes transfers from the petroleum sector.
Source: Ministry of Finance and National Economy (annual budget announcements).

The reversal of Saudi policy in 1986, to allocate quotas to support a price of US$18 was in the first instance motivated by short- as opposed to long-term economic considerations. In the short run, given their quota, a price of US$18 and the expectation that other countries would not cheat on production levels, their revenues would have been higher than if they expanded outputs to say, 8 mbd. The level of short-run revenues are important given the fixity of some expenditures; military expenditures (see Table III.11) and cash outlays for subsidies (see Chapter V) account for over 50 percent of the budget. Second, some observers have argued that the Saudis felt that a stable price of roughly US$18 was a "wish" of the United States, as indirectly indicated by former Vice President Bush during his visit to Saudi Arabia in 1986. And third, the Saudis claimed that this was being done to support Iran! But all in all, this policy was again motivated by short- as opposed to long-term economic considerations. However, given the level of the dollar in late 1987, the price of oil in terms of a composite unit may still allow OPEC to expand its total output slowly over time and thus allocate shares easier; especially if the dollar stays at its 1987 levels or depreciates further.

Future of Saudi Oil Policies

Where does this leave us? It is evident that Saudi Arabia did forego its long-run share by following a production policy that sustained high prices and was subsequently forced to continually reduce production in order to maintain prices. The motivations behind the swing producer role were largely due to political considerations and miscalculations of the impact of high prices on demand, mentioned earlier. The abandoning of the swing producer strategy in 1985 appears to have been to the benefit of Saudi Arabia and of other GCC members, both economically and politically—at least within the Gulf region. If anything, Saudi Arabia/GCC can afford to produce even more in order to regain a larger share of the market, also resulting in higher medium- and long-run revenues. The importance of a sound, international oil policy for Saudi Arabia cannot be overemphasized. The overwhelming importance of oil to its economy has been established in Chapter II, this will continue for years to come. In short, the nature of the Saudi economy continues to indicate one dominant sector for the foreeseeable future—oil. A sound oil policy, therefore, is of paramount importance.

In the past, Saudi Arabia has not given due emphasis to its special economic interests within OPEC. Several OPEC countries have relatively little or no excess capacity and would like to maintain the OPEC shares prevailing in 1985 and let prices rise. Saudi Arabia and the rest of the GCC on the other hand—with large reserves and substantial excess capacity—should increase their output and thus their share, even if it results in a lower price; as this would still increase revenues in the medium term. For the long run, these differences are even more important as those OPEC members with more capacity and reserves should pursue policies that preserve a future market for their oil; while countries with low capacity and reserves would like to sell their limited oil at a high price in the short run and have less interest in a long-run market outlook. Saudi Arabia's and OPEC's policies have in large part created the difficulties for OPEC today, especially for Saudi Arabia itself. These policies resulted in a price that was too high in relation to the long-run equilibrium price; reducing demand and inducing high levels of oil exploration and the development of alternative sources of energy.

Instead of pursuing policies that would have tended to maximize discounted long-run revenues, Saudi Arabia/GCC, but especially Saudi Arabia, basically went along with OPEC decisions and acted largely as swing producers. This policy, while benefiting Saudi Arabia/GCC in the period from 1979 to 1981, has had several negative medium- and long-term manifestations; that is, a dramatic and disproportionate decline in:

1. oil output after 1981,
2. market shares,
3. oil revenues,
4. excess capacity.

Given this historical perspective on Saudi oil policies: What should be the fundamentals of a Saudi oil policy? A coherent oil policy should include the basic principles and actions outlined below.

Long-run Revenue Maximization. Saudi Arabia should pursue more forcefully, policies within OPEC that broadly maximize discounted long-run revenues for Saudi Arabia. If this means increased output, so be it. Revenues, not prices or output, should be the target. Although revenue maximization is difficult to implement in an uncertain world, it should at least be the moving target for Saudi Arabia's oil policy.

Oil Quota. Once Saudi Arabia pursues discounted revenue maximization as its objective in OPEC, Saudi Arabia and the GCC could establish a combined GCC quota as opposed to maintaining individual country quotas within OPEC. This would allow representation of a group of countries with similar objectives, while affording the GCC the opportunity to internally determine each of its members' quota. This would be beneficial to Saudi Arabia and to the GCC because it would afford member countries internal flexibility regarding production levels, while keeping overall production high enough to preserve market share. For example, if one of the members wishes to produce less than its share, another country can produce more, so as to prevent a loss in the overall GCC market share. The existence of such an overall GCC quota would have been beneficial during the 1986 meetings of OPEC.

Capacity Development. The situation of excess production capacity is expected only to last into the mid-1990s. The general prognosis is for the oil market to tighten thereafter. In order to continue to have an important impact on the international oil market into the 1990s, Saudi Arabia could usefully invest in capacity expansion so that it can prevent the mistakes of the late 1970s; namely, letting prices increase too rapidly, thereby reducing demand and encouraging exploration in other parts of the world. By always maintaining some level of excess capacity, and by satisfying demand while letting prices increase slowly, Saudi Arabia can prevent another price shock and thus discourage new oil exploration and investment in alternative energy sources.[14]

Denomination of Oil Prices. In order to reduce significant price fluctuations (as the impact of a price increase on the demand for OPEC oil is largely irreversible) and to stabilize the real purchasing power of revenues, Saudi Arabia could try to persuade the rest of OPEC to denominate oil in terms of a basket of currencies with appropriate weights reflecting

OPEC's (Saudi Arabia's) import denominations. Although such a pricing scheme has been intermittently under consideration in OPEC since the mid-1970s, the time for its implementation is overdue.

OPEC Membership. Saudi Arabia should not argue for enlarged OPEC membership as it would further polarize OPEC. However, if Oman and Bahrain could qualify, it would be in the interest of Saudi Arabia/GCC for these two countries to join OPEC, resulting in added bargaining power for the GCC. If the implementation of these policies is not workable within an OPEC context, then Saudi Arabia/GCC should seriously consider withdrawing from OPEC. Non-GCC OPEC countries have more to lose economically than Saudi Arabia/GCC from such an eventuality, since any reduction in GCC output is beneficial to non-GCC OPEC members. The big stumbling block to Saudi/GCC withdrawal from OPEC is political in nature—Arab and Third World solidarity.

If Saudi Arabia pursues the indicated oil policies, what will be the likely course of oil prices? Oil prices should, at most, increase slightly between now and the mid-1990s; at about the rate of the general price level. Thereafter, and in the absence of unforeseen external shocks, prices should increase at a rate somewhat above the general price index, and at an increasing rate toward the end of the decade. The expectation would be that prices would also be much less volatile than during the period 1978-1986. Finally, success for Saudi Arabia in the economic field will be largely measured by success in its oil policy.

As was proposed in Chapter II, the key to success for Saudi Arabia is two-fold—sound oil and investment policies. The actions of late 1985 constitute a step in the right direction. However, the agreements of August and October 1986 might be a step backward because it is questionable whether the production levels agreed to are in the long-run interests of Saudi Arabia and are likely to tend toward revenue maximization. For the future, Saudi Arabia could usefully give added emphasis to economic motives in developing its internal oil policy, as opposed to short-run economic and political considerations; this change of policy should be expected, given Saudi Arabia's financial needs and requirements over the next 10-15 years.

NOTES

1. This chapter draws on an earlier paper by Askari and Dastmaltschi (1987).
2. The GGC includes Saudi Arabia, Kuwait, Bahrain, Oman, Qatar, and United Arab Emirates.
3. For an excellent exposition of Saudi oil policy, see Quandt (1982). For strategic importance of Middle East oil, see Yorke and Turner (1986) and Meir (1986).
4. For further detail, refer to Salomon Brothers Inc. (1986).
5. For a history of the major oil companies, refer to Sampson (1975).

6. Prices in this table are the U.S. prices that were higher than the world price, given U.S. import quotas. OPEC governments received only a fraction of the world price in the form of royalties and taxes up until the early 1970s.

7. Clearly, OPEC's share of world exports was an even higher percentage.

8. This composite index is clearly very crude, as it does not incorporate government policies (taxes) in response to changes in the domestic price of oil.

9. This statement is attributed to the Saudi oil minister, Ahmed Zaki Yamani (1984).

10. But it should be recognized that lower oil production means that savings have been achieved in the form of oil in the ground (i.e., not produced).

11. In a volatile world, at times it is clearly desirable to react prudently and deliberately to events as contrasted with sudden changes in policies toward what could be temporary developments.

12. This statement may at first glance appear to be inconsistent as Iran was implicitly supporting, or endorsing, potentially higher revenues for its enemy, Iraq. But given Iran's production limitations, revenue needs, and limited ability to pay for imports through credit, a doubling of oil prices then, was more beneficial than the negative effects of higher Iraqi revenues in the future.

13. This simple exercise could be logically expanded to include different rates of social discounts for individual OPEC countries and to present discounted revenue maximization to determine the different solutions that are available to OPEC as a whole.

14. In late 1989, Saudi Arabia announced a substantial effort to expand oil production capacity. This is envisaged to occur in two stages. In the first stage, repair and maintenance to existing wells should bring capacity to 9-10 mbd. In the second stage (mid-1990s), capacity will be increased beyond 10 mbd.

Chapter IV

Saudi Arabia's External Investment Policies

INTRODUCTION

For Saudi Arabia, economic success is measured by two basic criteria: a successful oil policy and the development of a viable, or competitive, non-oil sector to compensate for oil depletion.

There are, in turn, two basic choices in developing a non-oil sector. One approach is that of Kuwait. Kuwait has relied heavily on external investments to compensate for the depletion of oil, in the form of both portfolio investments and direct foreign investments (i.e., where control is exerted). This policy has afforded Kuwait economic diversification (in revenues), it has ameliorated difficulties associated with Dutch Disease, and these foreign assets can be used any time to finance domestic economic development. The other approach is to more rapidly promote domestic economic development, that is, the development of a viable domestic non-oil sector, through domestic investments. Saudi Arabia has largely relied on the latter approach, with external investments serving as a temporary depository for oil revenues.

From the discussions in Chapter II, one message comes across loud and clear; Saudi Arabia must try to get a high, or at least a positive, real rate of return on its investment, whether domestic or external, if it is to adequately compensate for the depletion of oil. External investments provide one viable channel to achieve this goal.

External investments have some obvious advantages over domestic investments. Even if Saudi Arabia's goal is ultimately to develop the domestic economy, external investments may provide an attractive temporary outlet, especially if domestic absorptive capacity is low in the near term. During the period 1972-1982, Saudi Arabia's accumulated current account surplus exceeded US$190 billion (IMF, various years; Mattione, 1985).[1]

Acquisition of foreign assets by Saudi Arabia affords an alternative to domestic investments if attractive investments could be found abroad. The option of foreign investments offers an unusual degree of flexibility. Saudi Arabia can base its oil production decisions on factors other than domestic absorption rates. Foreign investments give added flexibility to the domestic decision-making process as these investments may be used to finance consumption or investment, now or at any date in the future. Foreign investments afford a ready source of diversification across sectors, giving Saudi Arabia a diversified source of income on a global scale. Such a strategy may be sound in itself for Saudi Arabia and may eventually serve as the basis of relationships to develop a diversified economic productive capacity.

Foreign investment also avoids some of the incidental costs involved in a rapid increase in domestic spending. To the extent that oil export revenues are invested abroad, rather than translated into government domestic expenditures, the induced inflation and relative price effects that can adversely affect the profitability and international competitiveness of non-oil exports are minimized. To the extent that it is in financial assets, foreign investment can be converted relatively easily into real resources, when import needs increase. Thus, absorption can be more closely fitted to the economy's absorptive capacity, including the constraint on labor availability.

The major challenge or drawback to a sound program of acquisition of foreign assets may be a higher risk (especially expropriation and the like) associated with such assets and the fact that foreign assets may do little to employ Saudis seeking jobs. What has been Saudi Arabia's approach to managing its external assets?

ALLOCATION OF EXTERNAL ASSETS

The bulk of Saudi Arabia's external assets were earned and invested during the period 1972-1982, a figure of roughly US$190 billion. However, accurate figures for the disposition of these assets are not readily available. For selected oil-exporting countries, available estimates are shown in Tables IV.1, IV.2, and IV.3 (see also Mattione, 1985, 11 and Stoga and Bennett, 1981).

Somewhat more than one-fourth of Saudi Arabia's gross foreign assets is estimated to have been held by commercial banks and by the nonbank private sectors, while the remainder was held in the form of reserves and other public sector foreign assets. The share of the private sector's and commercial banks' in total foreign placements, showed a marked increase in 1979, reflecting rising outflows of private capital largely in response to

Table IV.1. Oil-Exporting Countries:
Estimated Disposition of Current Account Surplus, 1974-1981[a]
(In US$ Billions)

	1974	*1975*	*1976*	*1977*	*1978*	*1979*	*1980*	*1981*	*Total 1974-1981*
Current Account Surplus[b]	58	35	40	31	3	70	115	71	433
Plus: Oil sector capital									
Transactions[c] (outflow)	-12	1	-6	-1	2	-9	1	2	-22
Net borrowing[d]	2	3	8	10	16	10	7	8	64
Equals: Cash surplus available for disposition	58	39	42	40	21	71	123	81	475
Disposition of cash surplus									
Fund and World Bank[e]	4	3	2	—	-1	-1	1	3	11
Loans and grants to non-oil developing countries[f]	5	7	7	8	8	8	9	10	62
Bank deposits in industrial countries net[g]	30	11	13	13	5	40	42	6	160
Direct placements	7	2	1	2	2	8	6	-1	27
Eurocurrency deposits	23	9	12	11	3	32	36	7	133
Other Placements[h]	19	18	20	19	9	24	71	62	242

Notes: a. For country classification, see IMF (1982).
b. As shown in IMF (1982, Table 18).
c. Changes in accounts receivable from oil exports and in net direct investment of foreign-owned oil companies.
d. Total net increase in external liabilities of the public and private sectors (including banks). Includes small amounts of official transfer receipts, inward non-oil direct investment capital, and other miscellaneous capital items. Excludes borrowing from other oil-exporting countries.
e. Includes lending to the Fund, together with other changes in the reserve position in the Fund and direct purchases of World Bank bonds.
f. Includes contributions and capital subscriptions to regional and international development agencies (other than World Bank). Estimates are based on highly uncertain information.
g. Includes deposits in Eurocurrency markets.
h. Includes net acquisitions of government securities, corporate stocks and bonds, bilateral lending (mainly to governments), real estate and other direct investments, and prepayments for imports. Also includes unidentified placements and statistical discrepancies.

Source: IMF (1982).

Table IV.2. Selected Oil-Exporting Developing Countries: Estimated Disposition of Cash Surpluses, 1974-1981

	1974	*1975*	*1976*	*1977*	*1978*	*1979*	*1980*	*1981*	*Total 1974-1981*
Placements in industrial countries and in Eurocurrency markets (net)	84	74	79	80	70	90	92	84	85
Bank deposits	52	28	31	33	25	56	34	7	34
Direct placements	12	5	2	5	10	11	5	-1	6
Eurocurrency deposits	40	23	29	28	15	45	29	8	28
Short-term government securities[a]	14	—	-5	-3	-5	6	4		
Other capital flows[b]	19	46	52	50	50	25	54	77	51
Fund and World Bank[c]	7	9	5	—	-5	-1	1	4	2
Flows of funds to developing countries[d]	9	18	17	20	35	11	7	12	13

Notes: a. Mainly placements in treasury bills in the United States and the United Kingdom.

b. Includes net acquisitions of long-term governments securities, corporate stocks and bonds, bilateral lending (mainly) to governments, real estate and other direct investments, and prepayments for imports. Also includes relatively small amounts of placements in non-Fund members, as well as statistical discrepancies.

c. Includes investments in the Fund oil facility and supplementary financing facility, together with other changes in the reserve position in the Fund and direct purchases of World Bank bonds.

d. Includes bilateral grants and loans, as well as contributions and capital subscriptions to regional and international development agencies (other than Fund and World Bank). Also includes relatively small amounts of other capital flows to developing countries. Estimates are based on highly uncertain information.

Source: IMF (1982).

Table IV.3. Mideast Oil Exporters' U.S. Investments

Investment (US$ Millions)	*End 1979*	*End 1980*	*June 1981*	*End 1981*	*June 1982*
U.S. Government securities	15,770	24,943	32,537	38,993	44,105
Treasury bills and certificates	5,868	5,919	7,193	7,006	6,445
Treasury bonds and notes	6,954	14,626	19,856	25,782	31,381
Federal agency issues	2,948	4,398	5,488	6,205	6,269
Corporate bonds	2,788	4,837	6,075	6,495	6,274
Corporate stocks	6,702	7,908	8,297	9,049	9,559
Commercial bank liabilities	9,454	8,556	7,957	6,187	7,833
Nonbank liabilities[a]	1,048	931	998	933	856
U.S. Government liabilities[b c]	2,980	3,631	3,478	4,327	4,401
Direct investment[d]	321	520	559	3,353	—
Total	39,063	51,326	59,901	69,337	76,431

Notes: a. Iran, Iraq, Kuwait, Qatar, Saudi Arabia, UAE, Bahrain, and Oman.
b. Excludes Bahrain and Oman.
c. The position consists of cumulative flows from 1972.
d. First-quarter data.
When added, individual sums may not equal the total due to rounding. The total does not include US$17.6 billion on deposit in offshore branches of U.S. banks.
Sources: U.S. Department of the Treasury; U.S. Department of Commerce.

higher international interest rates. As more than 80 percent of the combined current account surplus in the period 1974-1981 was accounted for by four surplus countries (Saudi Arabia, Kuwait, UAE, and Qatar), the bulk of the stock of foreign assets has been concentrated in this group.

The limited data available indicate that most placements abroad have been made in industrial countries (including Eurocurrency markets) and that there has been an increasing diversification of asset holdings in recent years, with larger portions going into longer-term and less liquid placements. This trend is explained in part, by the increasing concentration of total foreign assets in a few countries with already strong liquidity positions. Other contributing factors have been the rising share of the private sector's foreign asset holdings (as government expenditures resulting from oil-revenues have resulted in highly profitable private enterprises in the past) and the development of more sophisticated investment policies in the major surplus countries. In addition to diversification among various types of assets, there has been a tendency toward geographical and currency diversification of total placements during the past few years, reflecting in part, the shifts of current account balances among the industrial countries. However, there do not appear to have been any major shifts among existing investments, and diversification has been sought mainly through new placements.

After the U.S. freeze of Iranian assets in 1980, it seems that Saudi Arabia became concerned about potential U.S. actions against its U.S.-held assets. Following this episode, Saudi Arabia slowly reduced its U.S. holdings because of the many laws in the United States which basically allow the U.S. government ot take any unilateral action against foreign depositors. Besides investment restrictions in sectors that are deemed sensitive in the United States, there are a host of potential restrictions that can be invoked; these depend on determinations by regulatory agencies that oversee foreign investments. Potential restrictions in the United States include:

1. Extraterritoriality (i.e., United States laws apply not only in the United States, but wherever a transaction abroad has an effect within the United States),
2. Foreign Sovereign Immunities Act (U.S. courts determine whether a foreign government enjoys a sovereign immunity),
3. Trading with the Enemy Act (assets of citizens of countries in undeclared war, with the United States may be seized),
4. The National Emergencies Act (allowing the president to take actions, such as freezing assets, without a war),
5. The International Emergency Economic Powers Act (giving further authority to the president).

Such laws are not unique to the United States, they also apply in different forms in other industrial countries. All of these have worried the Saudi authorities, encouraging the diversification of their assets.

SAUDI ARABIA'S MANAGEMENT OF EXTERNAL ASSETS

The first basic decision on the allocation of foreign assets is the choice between portfolio and direct foreign investment. Direct foreign investment is distinguished from portfolio investment by the fact that the investor exerts substantial control over direct foreign investment, making it more complex in nature than portfolio investment. The complexity of direct foreign investment has many dimensions; two components of this complexity have been particularly worrisome to Saudi Arabia—the limitation of Saudi personnel to implement and monitor direct foreign investments, and the potential political repercussions in host countries. Saudi Arabia seems especially concerned about political difficulties surrounding high profile foreign investments and has been reluctant to undertake any such investments. In fact, this reluctance is underscored by their policy to even limit the size of individual portfolio investments in order to avoid public disclosure and unwanted publicity. Kuwait, on the other hand, has made numerous direct foreign investments, for instance, in Santa Fe and in gasoline marketing in Europe (under the name of Q8). Saudi Arabia, given a more conservative approach, has limited the disposition of its foreign assets to portfolio investments.

In Saudi Arabia, the management of the surplus funds (liquid reserves and other foreign assets) is entrusted to SAMA, with the Ministry of Finance having ultimate control. SAMA has an investment department that is specifically entrusted with the task of managing all foreign assets and advising an international investment committee, chaired by the minister of finance. The Saudi component of this staff includes a handful of experienced managers. The investment department has for some years been supported in-house, by a few advisors supplied under contract by Merrill Lynch/White Weld and by Baring Brothers.

Saudi Arabia does not make a conscious decision on the proportion of oil revenues to save and invest in domestic and foreign assets. Instead, current and development expenditure decisions are made first, and any remaining surplus is allocated to SAMA. SAMA's goal in managing its external assets is liquidity, short-term accessibility, and safety. The government, in essence, justifies such a policy by stressing the fact that surplus funds may be needed at short notice to finance domestic development. As a result, SAMA's portfolio are virtually confined to short-term financial assets. This concentration in short-term financial assets, satisfies SAMA's liquidity objectives and the acquisition of liquid financial assets (bank deposits in the largest banks and government paper of industrial countries) requires less expertise and relieves bureaucrats of any blame for sour investments.

As a result of its policies, almost all the funds of the SAMA are held abroad. Around 30 percent of these funds are held in bank deposits, with a small proportion of this in bank trust funds. The remaining 70 percent is held in bonds—largely government securities of industrial countries, to a lesser extent capital and lending to international and regional institutions, and corporate bonds. In terms of geographical spread, historically about half of SAMA's investments have been in the United States, although about 60 percent of the total foreign investments were denominated (in 1982) in dollars and the rest largely in deutsche mark and yen. Of the investments in the United States, the bulk has been in Treasury bills and notes, and federal agency obligations (e.g., Federal National Mortgage Association); the value of Saudi holdings of these U.S. government obligations was estimated at roughly US$30 billion at the beginning of 1987.

A substantial purchase of U.S. obligations have been made directly from the market, in addition to purchases on a non-competitive basis. A much smaller part of the purchase of U.S. government securities has been handled through the secondary market, generally through correspondent banks. It is also largely these same banks that manage much of SAMA's portfolio of American corporate bond and stock holdings—the value of these were estimated to have been around $5 billion in 1982, and around $12 billion at the beginning of 1987, largely due to capital gains. The investment managers of banks act on a discretionary basis within guidelines set by SAMA. A fundamental feature of these guidelines is that at no time should SAMA's investment reach 5 percent of the voting stock of any company. This practice confirms SAMA's intention not to take control, or exert management responsibilities, in any U.S. company. At the same time, this self-imposed limit allows greater confidentiality, for only ownerships amounting to 5 percent or more must be reported to the Securities and Exchange Commission.

SAMA has also placed some funds in the private placement market in the United States with maturities up to 7 years. Because of its no-risk approch, SAMA has so far, limited its corporate loans to AA companies or better.

SAMA's investments outside of the United States are mainly in dollars, in West European banks and European branches of American banks as well as in dollar bonds of Canada, West European countries, and Japan. SAMA has made repeated loans to Canadian provincial governments. SAMA has also made substantial loans to the World Bank, the International Monetary Fund (IMF), various agencies of the United Nations, and international regional agencies such as the African Development Bank. In 1981, loan commitment to the IMF was its single largest loan amounting to roughly US$10 billion. Saudi Arabia's loans to international and regional institutions, and especially to Third World countries, are heavily motivated by noneconomic considerations. SAMA owns 50 percent of the equity of the Saudi International Bank in London, sharing it with Morgan Guaranty Trust (20 percent) and other Western banks.

Until the 1980s, any inclination by SAMA to diversify out of the dollar was dampened by the reluctance of hard currency countries like West Germany and Switzerland to allow the purchase of securities denominated in their own currencies. This reluctance stemmed from fear that their currencies could develop into international reserve assets and create domestic economic management problems. SAMA has preferred government issues and was, therefore, reluctant to acquire substantial amount of nondollar denominated Eurobonds.

However, as the West German mark and the Swiss franc began to lose value relative to the dollar in late 1979, many of the psychological and legal barriers to foreign investment in these countries began to be removed. In early 1980, West German Finance Ministry officials obtained an agreement in principle, for the sale, to the Saudi government, of some 5.2 billion marks (nearly $3 billion) of short-term promissory notes at rates slightly below prevailing money market rates. A West German law eased limitations on promissory note sales to foreigners by allowing foreigners to hold notes that would mature in less than 2 years, rather than the previous 4. In early 1980, SAMA made an agreement with the government of Japan to buy up to $2.4 billion of Japanese government bonds annually.

Saudi diversification into nondollar assets has always been a lot less than might be expected. Whenever the dollar has been low on the exchange markets, the Saudis have been hesitant to shift into stronger currencies, not only out of fear that they might exacerbate the problem, but that they would begin losing when the dollar started to rise again, as they have always been confident it would. On the other hand, when the dollar has been strong, the Saudis have had a tendency to stick with it because of the confirmation of their faith in the stability of the United States and its economy; in fact, when the dollar is high relative to historic levels is precisely the time to diversify out of dollars.

In 1974, SAMA dealt with only half a dozen international banks. Now, however, SAMA's bank deposits abroad are placed in about 85 major internationl "approved" banks. Although well over half of these deposits are outside the United States, dollars on the Euromarket are effectively in the United States.

ASSESSMENT OF EXTERNAL INVESTMENT POLICIES

Accurate figures for Saudi Arabia's external assets are difficult to obtain. Mattione (1985, 60) estimates that government and private sector foreign holdings amounted to US$145 billion at the end of 1983. Current account deficits for the period from 1984 to 1988 are estimated at US$45 billion. Thus, external assets are estimated at roughly US$100 billion as of the end of 1988. Of this amount, roughly one-fourth are in loans to Iraq, which are at best illiquid. Another one-fourth is estimated as private sector holdings, leaving half as liquid government foreign assets.[2]

Several features of the managment and disposition of Saudi Arabia's foreign assets should be noted. First, it should be emphasized that Saudi Arabia does not take a conscious decision on how much to save out of oil revenues or NNP in order to compensate for the depletion of oil, and does not then, in turn, allocate the savings between domestic and foreign investments to reflect rates of return and economic externalities. Instead, domestic consumption and investments are funded and the residual is invested by SAMA. Second, these foreign assets are managed by a very small staff with in-house support from expatriates and reliance on some bank managers (trust departments) from large banks. Some investments are handled through institutions in association with other Arab governments, such as the Gulf International Bank and the Gulf Investment Corporation. There is no comprehensive and integrated worldwide system in place for the management of SAMA's assets. Third, the lion's share of SAMA's assets are in short-term financial investments. The high proportion of short-term assets is not a function of market conditions at any time, but is instead a stated policy.

Whether such an approach to external investments by Saudi Arabia makes economic sense depends on one's view of the role of external surplus in an oil-based economy. Before addressing this question, it is useful to assess the historical rates of return on categories of assets. Ibbotson and Sinquefeld (1986) provide a most comprehensive analysis of calculated return for the U.S. market on common stock, small stock, long-term corporate bonds, long-term government bonds, Treasury bills, and the rate of inflation. Their results demonstrate an inescapable fact. Over the long run (since 1926, but the base year makes little difference if it is around 25 years or more), small stocks and common stocks have had substantial positive real rates of annual return (accompanied by a higher variance or risk), while bonds and bills have performed at about the rate of inflation, thus affording little or no positive real yield.

If Saudi Arabia's view of external assets is to compensate for the depletion of oil, then it may be taking an overly cautious approach over the long run. But, even if it views external assets as a temporary outlet, because of domestic absorptive capacity limitations, still its approach may be too conservative. Stocks are as liquid as corporate bonds and almost as liquid as Treasury bills and bank deposits, although the risk or the variance of the return on stocks is higher. The point is that even if external assets are eventually intended to finance domestic development, still the government should develop a strategy that maximizes expected long-run return on external investments, with the additional requirements of reasonable liquidity and diversification. Otherwise, if Saudi Arabia's external investment policy cannot yield a real rate of return as high as expected real oil price increases, then the appropriate policy may be to deplete oil reserves at a pace needed to finance "appropriate" domestic consumption and sound domestic development.

Saudi Arabia has not aggressively used the avenue of investing abroad (direct or portfolio) as a method of diversification. Given the short-run difficulties with rapid domestic diversifications—Dutch Disease, inflationary pressures, and identification of sectors of comparative advantage—investments abroad could have provided the Kingdom with a source of temporary and long-run diversification (as in the case of Kuwait). For the future, Saudi Arabia should re-examine its foreign investment polices and take a more aggressive approach. Although this may present some political and logistic problems, the success of Kuwait should serve as an example.

There are several reasons for SAMA's unwillingness to pursue a more aggressive investment strategy to attain higher return and diversification. First, SAMA has been unwilling, or unable, to develop the required organization and staff to pursue such a policy; the organizational requirement for acquiring government bills and bonds and bank deposits is more limited. Second, the bureaucracy has not been willing to expose itself to the possibility of any blame being placed at its doorstep in case of a "bad" investment. Third, SAMA has always pursued a low profile policy, which is inconsistent with an aggressive investment policy and unfavorable publicity that could arise. Fourth, there is a feeling that investment in stocks and direct investments could result in charges of stock manipulation and corruption. Fifth, Saudi Arabia has always, but especially after the freezing of Iranian assets, been afraid of political motives, in the guise of legal actions, blocking their foreign assets; because of this, they have felt more comfortable with the most liquid financial investments but unfortunately these are just as likely to be blocked and ironically they are more easily identified. There is also a genuine aversion to risk and illiquidity.

Saudi Arabia has clearly diversified its currency holdings since 1980. The speed of this diversification was in part affected by Saudi concerns for global financial and exchange rate stability. But the diversification that has occurred has been among currencies as opposed to types of assets.

Saudi Arabia's approach to its external asset management is clearly nonaggressive and, unlike Kuwait, Saudi Arabia does not appear to view these investments as compensating for the depletion of oil. Unfortunately, one of the implications of the Saudi policy is that they are unlikely to earn a high return on these assets while they are invested abroad, implying negative consequences for their overall economic development and diversification to compensate for the depletion of oil. Saudi Arabia should develop a longer-term approach for the role of its external assets and to expand its institutional capabilities to manage external assets aggressively. This may be especially important if later in the 1990s Saudi Arabia again experiences large current account surpluses. The accumulation of foreign assets provides a desirable vehicle for diversification. Given what might be termed the government's passive approach to external asset management, the performance of domestic investments becomes even more critical to compensate for the depletion of oil.

NOTES

1. Mattione (1985, 11) has estimated the cumulative current account surplus for the period 1974-1982 as US$160.1 billion.

2. It should be noted further that, of this, roughly US$50 billion in liquid foreign assets, roughly US$15-20 billion is managed by SAMA on behalf of autonomous government agencies such as the Saudi Fund for Development (SFD) and General Organization for Social Insurance (GOSI).

Chapter V

Domestic Policies to Promote Growth to Compensate for Oil Depletion: Physical Infrastructure

INTRODUCTION

In the early 1970s, the government of Saudi Arabia decided that a requirement for promoting the Kingdom's future development was the provision of adequate infrastructure. It was hoped that with infrastructure in place, the emerging private sector would not be constrained by bottlenecks that typically limit the development process in other countries (e.g., lack of transportation, telecommunications, and utilities). The tremendous increase in government revenues during 1971-1981 provided a seemingly infinite source of financing for such ambitious projects.

In this chapter, the extent of infrastructureal achievement is presented, along with an assessemnt of their adequacy, the impact on the economy, and an examination of the rationale upon which this undertaking was based. For the purposes of this discussion, infrastructure will include the provision of:

- Utilities: electricity, water, sewage, desalination, and telecommunications;
- Transportation: airports, ports, and roads

ACCOMPLISHMENTS

Electricity

The government of Saudi Arabia has assisted private sector companies in building and operating its electricity network through concessionary capital loans and continuing operating subsidies.[1] There are over 10 independent electricity companies; four are regionally consolidated (into the Saudi Consolidated Electric Company or SCECO) in the western, eastern, central, and southern regions. The remaining companies operate in the northern region. The dual purpose power/desalination plants of the Saline Water Conservation Corporation (SWCC) supplement electricity supplies.

Installed capacity has increased from 418 mw in 1970, to 13,316 in 1983, or at an average annual rate of 30.5 percent. In 1987, installed capacity reached 14,909 mw. At 80 percent of installed capacity, usable capacity reached 10,704 million kwh in 1983. Nearly 30 percent of the 29,150 million kwh of power sold was used for industrial purposes. Over 75 percent of the population in Saudi Arabia was served by electricity in 1983.

The approximate breakdown of energy sales by region (1983) are provided in Table V.1. With over 47 percent of electricity sales and over 40 percent installed capacity, the eastern region is the most saturated region in the country where practically 100 percent of the population is already served; and the major demand is industrial (65 percent of energy sales). The central and western regions account for another 48 percent of electricity sales and 52 percent of installed capacity; electricification of these areas is nearly complete with 85 percent of the population connected to electricity. Here, a combination of residential/commercial/industrial demand prevail. The southern and northern regions' rural demand are reached with a combined

Table V.1. Electricity Data (1983[a] and 1987[b])

	Energy Sales		*Installed Capacity*	
Region	*(Million kwh)*	*(%)*	*(mw)*	*(%)*
		1983		
Central	6,347	21.6	3,243	24.4
Western	7,656	26.2	3,631	27.2
Eastern	14,066	47.9	5,429	40.7
Northern	400	1.5	380	2.9
Southern	833	2.8	633	4.8
Total	29,150	100.0	13,316	100.0
		1987		
Central	12,090	24.7		
Western	12,281	25.1		
Eastern	20,833	42.6		
Northern	1,129	2.3		
Southern	2,033	4.2		
Total	48,906	100.0	14,909	

Sources: a. Ministry of Planning (1984).
b. SAMA (1988).

installed capacity of nearly 8 percent, and electricity sales amounting to nearly 4.3 percent of national consumption. It is estimated that only about 43 percent of the population in these two regions is reached by electricity. By 1987, there had been some minor shifts in regional consumption.

The growth in electric power generation capacity was facilitated by government subsidies (see Chapter VI). Over the period 1976-1985, under the Electric Utility Lending Program, the Saudi Industrial Development Fund (SIDF) lent over US$11 billion to induce the dramatic growth mentioned earlier. The level of subsidies has grown to such an extent, that it not only costs the government a great deal to maintain this system but it has also encouraged waste. In order to start the process of rationalization, the government increased electricity tariffs in late 1984, only to roll them back in 1985. It was officially announced (Middle East Economic Digest, 1985, 2) that the reduction in price was aimed at "relieving the financial burdens of the people." It is estimated that the cost of producing one kwh of electricity in Saudi Arabia is over four times the average revenue for the electricity companies per kwh;[2] this is because of the low tariffs. Considering the existing level of electrification, future areas of improvement include the following:

1. Reduction of the various subsidies to electricity companies to reduce distortionary effects in electricity production.
2. Increase of tariffs to encourage conservation in addition to introducing non-price conservation measures.
3. Provision of greater coordination and standardization between electricity generating companies in the Kingdom, such as SCECO, SWCC, Electrico, and the Royal Commission for Jubail and Yanbu.

Water, Desalination, and Sewerage

Saudi Arabia's water is supplied from three different sources: surface water (10 percent), underground aquifers (83 percent), and desalination plants (5 percent) (see Table V.2). The nonrenewable resources have provided nearly 80 percent of total consumption, and due to the rapid increase in demand over the past 5 years, they are being depleted at an alarming pace. Between 1980 and 1985, water consumption more than tripled from 2,362,000 cubic meters (m^3),[1] to 8,830,000 m^3. Most of this increased consumption has been in agriculture, already accounting for 84 percent of total consumption, and supplied free of charge. This policy is clearly surprising, given the fact that water is a highly scarce resource in Saudi Arabia, whose economic use should entail a price in line with the marginal cost of production and its intertemporal opportunity cost in the form of a "scarcity rent" (for further discussion of this point, including the government's perspective, see Chapter VI). Saudi Arabia has spent considerable resources on drilling wells,

Table V.2. Water Consumption

	M^3 Per Year		% Share	
	1980	*1985*	*1980*	*1985*
Demand				
agriculture	1,860	7,430	79	84
domestic, industrial, other	502	1,400	21	16
Total	2,362	8,830	100	100
Resources				
surface water	485	900	20	10
groundwater	660	950	28	11
renewable	1,154	6,480	49	73
nonrenewable	63	400	3	5
reclaimed wastewater	—	100	—	1
Total	2,362	8,830	100	100

Source: Ministry of Planning (1985).

building dams, and installing pumps. The desalination plants are constructed and operated under the supervision of the SWCC. Daily desalination plant capacity reached 500 million gallons in 1984 (up from 5.12 in 1970) and estimated desalinated water supply is around 400 million gallons a day. In 1988, desalinated water consumption production reached 509 million m^3.

Sewage collection has not been well-planned. With the exception of the industrial cities of Jubail and Yanbu and the city of Damman, all major cities have inadequate facilities.

The major issues that confront the government in the area of water are the rate at which irreplaceable water sources are being depleted and the cost of providing desalinated water. Considering that only 20 percent of the Kingdom's water supply is subject to tariff, it seems imperative for the government to reevaluate its water policy (water policy is discussed in greater detail in Chapter VI). Elements of this new policy should include:

- installation of recycling systems (plants) for industrial and agricultural use,
- levying of appropriate user fees to reflect opportunity cost,
- leakage detection and correction programs,
- irrigation management techniques in agriculture.

Telecommunciations

Over the past decade and a half, Saudi Arabia has installed one of the most modern telecommunications networks in the world. This has afforded

Table V.3. Selected Data on Communications: Telephones (In thousands of units)

Year	*Number of Operating Telephones*	*Exchange Line Capacity*
1970	29.4	76.6
1975	90.1	131.6
1980	319.6	587.3
1985	903.0	1,216.0

Source: Ministry of Post, Telegraphs, and Telephones (1986).

Saudi Arabia the capacity to handle its communication needs in the area of local and international telephone, telegraph, maritime, and television distribution services, via cable, satellite, and terrestrial transmission systems.

In Table V.3 the increase in telephone services is indicated. Since 1970, the number of exchange line capacity has increased fifteenfold, from 77,000 lines to 1.2 million in 1985. The telex network has also been growing rapidly; the available capacity is nearly 60,000 lines (1985), with nearly 17,000 subscribers.

Despite these developments, it is understood that Saudi Arabia intends to further improve its telecommunication system and that the rate of growth in telecommunications will remain strong through the Fourth Five-Year Plan, as past growth was not designed to reach villages and outlying areas.

The policy issues regarding telecommunication can be divided into two categories:

1. The need to introduce greater levels of efficiency in the management and operations of existing capacity as current operating costs reportedly exceed international norms; and
2. expansion of existing network to inadequately serviced areas.

Airports

In order to accommodate the influx of passengers and cargo associated with rapid development, the Kingdom has built numerous domestic, and three international, airports in Jeddah, Riyadh, and Dhahran. The size and the aircraft capacity of each of these airports is expected to suffice well into the next decade, and the only additions that can be conceived are to passenger-handling capacity. In Table V.4, the aircraft capacity utilization rates for the three major airports are given. It appears that demand for the time being is more than satisfied. For example, the King Fahd Airport in

Table V.4. Per Hour Aircraft Operation Capacity Utilization Rate, 1985 (In Percent)

King Abdul Aziz International Airport (Jeddah)	44
King Khalid International Airport (Riyadh)	32
Dhahran International Airport	50

Source: Presidency for Civil Aviation.

Table V.5. Selected Data on Civil Aviation

Year	*Incoming Cargo (thousand tons)*	*Arriving Passengers (millions)*
1970	10.3	0.8
1975	42.4	2.3
1980	63.4	8.1
1983	225.0	12.1

Source: Central Department of Statistics.

the eastern province, now under construction, will have the capacity for 6 million passengers, with the potential of expanding capacity to 12 million passengers. The passenger load for that area peaked in 1983 at 4.3 million passengers, and has subsequently decreased to 3.5 million in 1985.

In Table V.5, the dramatic increase in passenger and cargo traffic is presented. The number of incoming passengers rose more than tenfold, from 800,000 in 1970, to 12.1 million in 1983. Passenger traffic has subsequently decreased somewhat. The volume of incoming cargo increased twenty-two fold over the same time period. The issues that confront planners and administrators in the future are:

- the apparent overcapacity in airport construction and its concomitant burden on maintenance and operating costs and
- the lack of revenue generation ability of underutilized airports.

Ports

During the First Development Plan, Saudi Arabia faced a situation where, due to high import levels and operational and physical problems, the rate of ship arrivals began to exceed discharge rates. Ships had to wait longer and longer to unload their cargoes. Needless to say, this created bottlenecks due to delays and resulted in costly demurrage charges. The Saudi Port Authority (SPA) was formed in 1976 to alleviate these problems, a task successfully accomplished. Today, Saudi Arabia possesses some of the most modern ports in the world. These include:

Table V.6. Selected Data on Ports

Year	*Handling Capacity*[a] *(thousand tons)*	*Berths (Number)*	*Volume of Imported Cargo (thousand weight tons)*
1970	—	—	1,837
1975	6,102	27	6,084
1980	37,800	101	27,480
1985	48,800	133	37,845

Note: a. Calculated at 70 percent capacity.
Sources: Central Department of Statistics; Saudi Ports Authority (1986).

1. 5 major commercial ports (Jeddah, Dammam, Jizan, Jubail, and Yanbu),
2. 11 minor commercial ports, and
3. 3 petroleum-related ports dedicated to the movement of crude and refined oil products.

The five major commercial ports represent nearly 90 percent of total port capacity, with Jeddah Islamic Port and King Abdulaziz Port accounting for 70 percent of the total port capacity. In Table V.6, some pertinent statistics on Saudi Arabia's ports are presented. The commitment to port development is clearly demonstrated. Handling capacity grew eightfold in only 8 years, while import volume increased twenty-twofold, from 1.8 million tons in 1970, to 37.8 million in 1983.

Demand for port facilities had been expected to continue to increase just as rapidly as in the past, but with a slowdown of the economy it is now expected that, given additions to selected aspects of the port infrastructure (e.g., improvement of storage facilites) and procedural changes (e.g., diversion of traffic to others ports and institutions of a policy of random inspection containers), Saudi Arabia's port facilities will accommodate demand well through the Fourth and Fifth Development Plans. Indeed, in the Fourth Plan, the need to increase the efficiency of port handling is stated as a desired objective over increasing capacity. In addition, measures should be implemented that encourage the use of the underutilized ports of Jubail, Jizan, and Yanbu.

Roads

Saudi Arabia is a large and sparsely-populated country with great distances between its major cities. The government has been able to link major areas through a network of modern highways that are the envy of

Table V.7. Selected Data on Roads
(In thousands of kilometers)

	Unpaved Roads	*Paved Roads*	*Total*
1970	3,687	8,021	11,708
1975	8,510	11,243	19,753
1980	24,186	20,238	44,424
1983	38,644	26,042	64,686
1988	59,226	33,576	92,802

Source: SAMA (1974, 1978, 1980, 1988).

any nation's road-building and maintenance program. These include the express road connections—Medina/Mekkah/Jeddah, Riyadh/Damman, Riyadh/Quassim, and Riyadh/Makkah. Over a period of 15 years, the length of asphalt roads more than tripled, from 8,000 km in 1970, to over 26,000 km in 1983. The length of unpaved roads, serving the rural areas, was extended even more during this period, from 3.5 thousand to 38.6 thousand km (see Table V.7). By any forecast, it is expected that there will be only minor capacity problems in the forseeable future, with the exception of areas where paved roads have not yet been provided. One objective of the Fourth Development Plan is to integrate underserviced areas more fully with a more complete road network.

In conclusion, one can summarize the concerns relating to infrastructure in two broad areas:

1. introduction of a greater level of efficiency, through better coordination and management techniques resulting in better utilization rates (e.g., ports) or reduction in excessive utilization (e.g., electricity and water)
2. creation of a more balanced infrastructural network, with less emphasis on oversupplied major metropolitan areas, and greater attention given to reaching outlying, unserved areas in the Kingdom.

The Industrial Cities of Jubail and Yanbu

The development of the industrial cities of Jubail and Yanbu epitomizes the efforts of the government to provide infrastructure for economic development. These two projects, one located north of Jeddah on the Red Sea (Yanbu) and the other situated on the Gulf near the oilfields (Jubail), entail the provision of a complete infrastructure network for future industries. The provision of services extends beyond roads, port facilities, and communication, to housing, schools, and health care facilities. It is

Table V.8. Royal Commission for Jubail and Yanbu Program Expenditures

Program	Fourth Plan Total (US$ million)	Fourth Plan Total (%)
Mangement and Administration	131.1	1.6
Operation and Maintenance	3,545.7	43.6
Studies; Design; Consultancy	220.5	2.7
Public Works	1,241.1	15.2
Power and Water and Sea Water	1,213.8	15.0
Training, Health, and Education	454.0	5.7
Community Housing and Facilities	449.2	5.6
Serviced Plots, Railroad, Special Projects	577.5	7.2
Telecommunications and Computer Network	189.7	2.3
Ports and Materials Handling	85.4	1.0
Total	8,108.0	100.0
Expected Revenues	1,135.4	

Table V.9. Number of Industries in Operation at Jubail and Yanbu by Category, 1980-1990

Industry Category	1980	1985	1990
Jubail			
Primary	0	10	16
Secondary	0	0	46
Support and Light	9	70	100
Yanbu			
Primary	0	5	5
Secondary	0	0	25
Support and Light	7	19	75

Source: Information obtained from The Royal Commission for Jubail and Yanbu.

expected that with the accommodation of "primary industries" in the heart of the industrial cities, "secondary industries" and ancillary services will be established in the area. Needless to say, the government is also studying policies to promote private sector investment and to encourage Saudi firms to locate in these two cities.

In the accompanying Tables V.8 and V.9, some aspects of the overall effort in Jubail and Yanbu are highlighted. From Table V.8, it is obvious that a good deal of the remaining work (after the largely completed infrastructural network) deals with maintenance and operation. Indeed 43.6 percent of the

US$8.1 billion budgeted for the Fourth Development Plan for the Royal Commission for Jubail and Yanbu, is intended for operations and maintenance. More significantly, the budget also reflects the totality of the government's effort. From Table V.9, it can be gleaned that most primary industries are already in place, in addition to some ancillary businesses. But it is too early to expect the secondary industries to have made any headway. In total, over 120 such secondary businesses have been identified. Needless to say, overcapacity is a problem that has also affected this project. According to an earlier projection, the population of Yubail should be about 150,000 people (1986-1987), but in reality it was only about 40,000.

ASSESSMENT

Introduction

There are two broad approaches to promoting domestic economic development in an economy where the lion's shares of export revenues accrue directly to the government. First, government expenditure policies can be targeted to investments in productive sectors—such as industrial and agricultural projects, directly yielding output that may or may not be competitively produced. A second approach is for the government, through its expenditure policies, to provide the basis for the private sector to take the initiative to develop the domestic economy. A major component (besides education) of this basis for development is the provision of infrastructure. However, this approach to development requires many other complementary policies, such as a sound financial structure and conducive commercial policy, as government expenditure on infrastructure does not directly stimulate, but only reduces the constraints to private investment. However, this approach takes much longer to bear fruit because it may indirectly and only over time induce productive sector investments and gains in efficiency.

Massive investments in infrastructure to meet the long-term requirements of an economy are questionable. Infrastructure needs cannot be accurately predicted for the distant future. Government bureaucracies, with small experienced planning staffs and absence of profit incentives, have a tendency to undertake a few, large, showcase projects that are motivated by political and other types of incentives. Moreover, government expenditures targeted to infrastructure and social projects implicitly involve even more financial commitment than productive projects, because the former usually involve longer future outlays in the form of operation and maintenance (O&M) expenditures. In a sense, a bad infrastructure expenditure may turn out to be more costly than an equal expenditure on a bad productive sector project.

In evaluating the overall infrastructure provided in Saudi Arabia, a few issues need to be addressed. The questions that should be answered are: What was the objective in putting these infrastructures in place? Given such objectives, what would have been an adequate level of infrastructure?

It appears that the intention of the government was to put in place a level of infrastructure that would, by virtue of its existence, stimulate Saudi Arabia's economic development. It was felt that by establishing infrastructure systems ahead of the corresponding level of development, impediments to development would be removed. "Adequate" infrastructure was intended to cover all the basic areas of utilities and transportation requirements of a modern economy. To this end, the latest technology, the most spectacular airports, and a modern telephone system were installed over the shortest period of time.

But the question remains: What was the appropriate or adequate level of infrastructure, and how have the past and present infrastructural undertakings affected Saudi Arabia's economic development?

Evaluation of Policies

A review of infrastructural facilities in place reveals the following:

1. Most major infrastructural projects have been finished. Judging from reasonable projections of the Kingdom's future growth, major metropolitan areas will not encounter infrastructure-related shortages well into the Fifth Plan, except in the areas of water and sewerage.
2. There is significant concentration of infrastructural projects in the major metropolitan areas and provision of services to the hinterlands is still lagging. The notable exception is the development of the industrial cities of Jubail and Yanbu. For example, by reviewing the development efforts of the Ministry of Municipal and Rural Affairs (MOMRA), it becomes clear that most projects were concentrated in the major metropolitan areas of the eastern, central, and western regions. A glance at the statistics provided in Table V.10, and corresponding Figures V.1 and V.2, illustrate the nature of this development. The bulk of the 1,067 projects undertaken by MOMRA, over the span of the Third Plan, was concentrated in the central region (419) followed by the western region (208) and eastern (181) regions. As a percentage of total expenditures, 39.2 percent of all funds were spent in the western region, and on the average, each project in the western region cost more than twice that of an average project in either the central or the eastern regions. Altogether, over 90 percent of MOMRA's Third Plan expenditures were spent in the western, eastern, and central regions; of the remainder, the northern region received nearly 5 percent; on the average, more was spent for each of their projects (US$ 9.50 million) than in the southern region,

Table V.10. Expenditures of Third Development Plan (MOMRA)

Party/Region	*Number of Projects*	*Total Cost (US$ billons)*	*Share of Costs*	*Average Cost/ Project (US$ millions)*
Central region	419	8.29	0.37	19.79
Western region	208	88.8	0.39	42.71
Eastern region	181	3.51	0.15	19.37
Southern region	142	0.86	0.04	6.08
Northern region	117	1.11	0.05	9.50
Subtotal	1,067	22.65	1.00	21.23
Ministry and Directorates General	61	6.61		108.34
Total	1,128	29.26	1.00	25.94
Ministry and Directorates General	61	6.61	0.23	108.34
Metropolitan municipalities	155	10.28	0.35	66.30
Municipalities	785	6.27	0.21	7.98
Village cluster centers	54	0.20	0.01	3.70
Water departments	73	5.91	0.20	80.94

Notes: Total may not add up due to rounding.
Totals do not include projects for governors palace, diplomatic quarters, or premises of Ministry of Foreign Affairs.

Source: MOMRA (unpublished).

with 3.8 percent of total expenditures and the lowest average expenditure per project (US$ 6.08 million). On the surface, such disparity may appear significant. Yet, considering the concentration of population, the traditional importance of the western region, the economic role of the eastern region, and the presence of the capital of Saudi Arabia in the central region, it comes as no surprise that economic activity as well as accompanying expenditures have been concentrated in these three areas. In addition, expenditures within each of the regions themselves vary. A similar pattern can be discerned from all government and private sector budgets, whether in the areas of health, transportation, commerce, or construction. One of the objectives of the Fourth Development Plan is to address and rectify this imbalance.

3. This existing infrastructure can be used more productively and potential shortages can be thwarted by introducing more rationalized policies, such as planning coordination between the different electricity companies and reduction of subsidies to the suppliers of various services. The demand side can be influenced even more directly by gradually

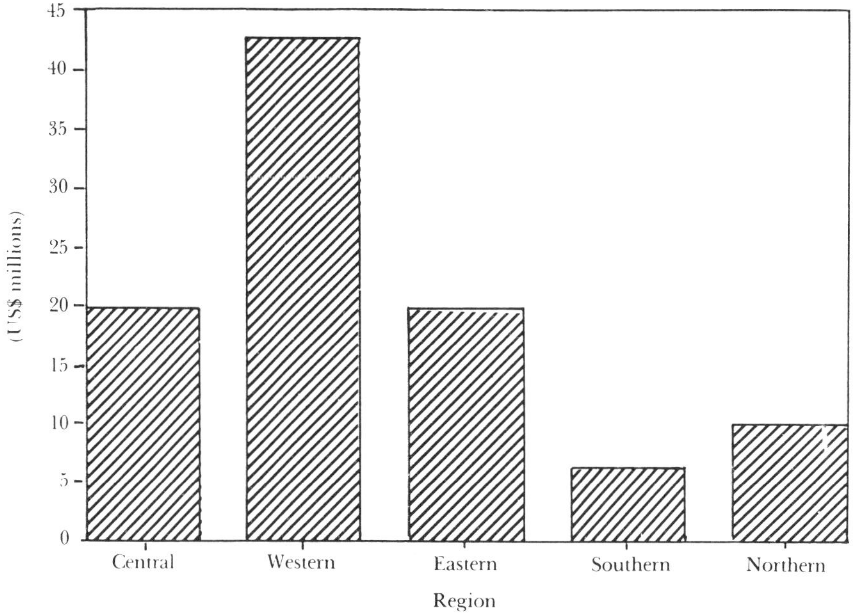

Figure V.1. MOMRA: Average Expenditure Per Project (Third Development Plan, 1980-1985)

introducing pricing measures that would reflect opportunity costs and moderate existing demand. The current pricing structure, despite recent improvements, still encourages wasteful consumption in addition to creating unrealistic user expectations that may be difficult to reverse.

4. By putting in place this extensive infrastructure, the government has put itself into a position of having to maintain and operate its facilities at substantial costs. The government has committed itself to maintenance costs that will have to be paid out of current revenues. The percentage of expenditure on operations and maintenance, which was never a line item in the past, has increased from11.6-12.5 percent of budget expenditures since 1983. Considering that only a fraction of these costs are currently offset by user fees, O&M expenses may represent a heavy burden on the budget in perpetuity. If the maintenance of the infrastructural support requires continued subsidies that are to be financed by oil revenues, it negates the original objective of putting this infrastructure in place.

5. The development of the infrastructure has also resulted in substantial capital costs. Expenditures on infrastructure were made but the facilities

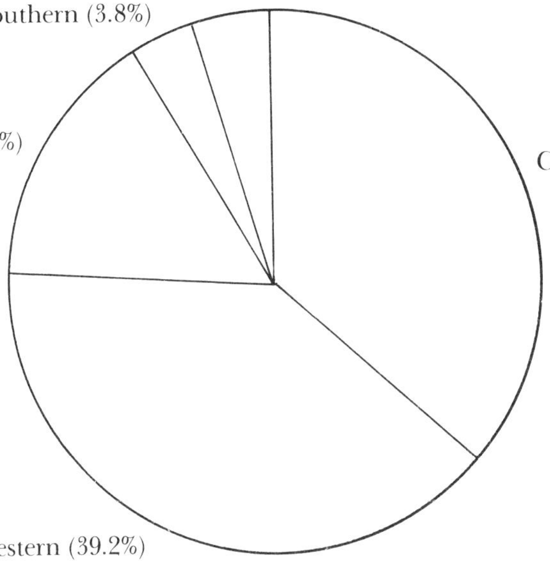

Figure V.2. MOMRA: Share of Regional Expenditure (Third Development Plan, 1980-1985)

were not fully utilized. Clearly these (excessive) capital expenditures could have been avoided and the capital used in more productive projects or invested abroad. Essentially, infrastructural development has entailed large capital outlays and continues to siphon current expenditures in the form of operations and maintenance. To the extent that the infrastructure is underutilized, the capital expenditures imply a continuing opportunity cost for the economy (as the capital cannot be recovered) and O&M represents an expenditure with no direct benefits (*Middle East Economic Digest,* 1985, 24-36).

6. Finally, a primary objective in providing infrastructure was to facilitate the development of a productive and competitive private sector. The private sector, by benefiting at little cost from such infrastructural services, was expected to play a dominant role in future economic development. This expectation has not yet materialized.

These are some of the more apparent facts of Saudi Arabia's infrastructural development. On a more fundamental level, other issues need to be considered that may appear less obvious but that are still important.

The speed with which this work has been performed has allowed little time to review and decide whether the level of commitment to infrastructural growth was warranted.

There is a problem with the manner in which the program was implemented. While planning ahead may have been a good decision, one may question what has been planned for. Infrastructural needs can be anticipated only to an extent. But the hope that by favoring one geographic area, or one kind of infrastructural installation (i.e., industrial as opposed to rural), in order to induce economic development, is at best questionable. Infrastructural needs are not static in nature and change with the level and the direction of a country's development. A more careful and selective program for infrastructural decisions (especially on the nature of the installations) would have given the government much more flexibility in meeting the needs of its developing economy and would have also saved future generations a good deal in national resources that have been unnecessarily spent on underutilized infrastructure. Today, over 17,000 vacant public housing units nationwide, such as the empty standing apartment complexes in Riyadh and Jeddah, attest to this fact. The third terminal at the Riyadh airport (KKIA), or the new airport in the eastern province, are other examples of underutilized capacity.

The requirements for industrial development change too rapidly for governments to be able to plan years in advance. Indeed, by the time such developments take root, the infrastructural facilities may be both outdated and inappropriate. It is also highly doubtful that the expense of building and operating the infrastructure can be amortized to the planned factories and concerns that will be using the facilities and still expect them to show a profit. Again, continued subsidies by the state will be needed.

Another negative development associated with rapid program implementation was that building the infrastructure, at times, appeared as an end in itself, as opposed to a means for insuring or expediting future development. Some systems, such as roads and ports, were expended in order to accommodate the erection of other facilities. The tremendous effort required an influx of foreign technical and manual support, whose steady increase in turn necessitated putting in place accommodation and related facilities (housing and airports). It therefore seems as if the building of the infrastructure was feeding on itself; the more that was being built, the more resources were required for infrastructure growth to support the construction of other infrastructure. One of the official explanations for the rapid buildup was that since working crews and equipment were already in place, one should proceed to build as much as possible now, rather than having to deploy these crews again in the future.

Since 1983, with substantially lower oil revenues, the government has tried to cut O&M costs by reducing the quality of maintenance. This may turn

Table V.11. Average Annual Sectoral Growth Rates Under the Four Development Plans, 1970-1971—1989-1990
(In constant 1970 prices/By percent)

	First Five-Year Plan 1970/71-1974/75	*Second Five-Year Plan 1975/76-1979/80*	*Third Five-Year Plan 1980/81-1984/85*	*Fourth Five-Year Plan 1985/86-1989/90*[a]
	Non-oil Sectors			
Producing sectors				
Agriculture	3.6	6.9	8.1	6.0
Other mining	21.1	9.6	7.3	3.0
Other manufacturing[b]	11.4	15.2	12.4	15.5
Utilities	10.9	21.9	18.6	5.0
Construction	18.6	15.8	-0.9	-2.8
Service sectors				
Trade	13.9	22.8	8.7	2.5
Transport	17.0	19.3	7.1	5.0
Finance	8.2	14.0	4.4	9.0
Other services	7.1	11.8	4.4	3.5
Government	7.8	6.5	6.4	0.0
Total non-oil sector	11.7	14.8	6.4	2.9
	Oil Sector			
	14.8	4.8	-14.2	5.6
Total economy	13.4	9.2	-1.5	4.0

Notes: a. Projected.
b. Includes petrochemicals.
Source: Ministry of Planning (1986).

out to be "halala wise but riyal foolish" as major replacements of infrastructural components may have to be accelerated. The government needs an infrastructural plan. There are many questions that must be addressed in this context. Are there infrastructural systems that are unlikely to be used in the future? If so, they should be abandoned and good money (O&M) should not be poured in after bad money; they should learn to cut their losses. Is the level of maintenance adequate in view of the usage rate? If it is not adequate, they should increase maintenance because in the long run the cost of insufficient maintenance is likely to be larger. Is the usage rate too high, resulting in deterioration and/or requiring new facilities? If yes, then government should study and implement appropriate user fees, as opposed to increasing subsidies.

One of the most tangible effects of the infrastructure effort was the private sector's capacity to service the needs of this growing component of Saudi

Table V.12. Employment by Economic Activity[a] (1979-1980, 1984-1985, 1989-1990)

	1979-1980		*1984-1985*		*1989-1990*[b]	
	(Thousand)	*(Percent)*	*(Thousand)*	*(Percent)*	*(Thousand)*	*(Percent)*
Producing Sectors	1,424.2	47.0	2,067.2	46.5	1,934.7	45.8
Agriculture	545.6	18.0	617.4	13.9	663.0	15.7
Other mining	2.3	0.1	5.1	0.1	5.2	0.7
Other manufacturing	170.4	5.6	411.4	9.3	538.2	12.7
Utilities	67.0	2.2	147.4	3.3	147.4	3.5
Construction	638.9	21.1	885.9	19.9	580.9	13.8
Service Sectors	1,157.0	38.3	1,844.6	41.5	1,773.5	42.0
Trade	323.1	10.7	556.1	12.5	493.0	11.7
Transport	180.0	6.0	303.4	6.8	310.7	7.4
Finance	51.8	1.7	136.3	3.1	140.2	3.3
Other services	602.8	19.9	848.8	19.1	829.1	19.6
Government	399.4	13.2	469.1	10.5	446.2	10.6
Subtotal: Non-oil sectors	2,981.3	98.5	4,380.9	98.5	4,154.5	98.4
Subtotal: Oil Sectors	44.7	1.5	65.1	1.5	66.0	1.6
Total	3,026 0	100.0	4,446.0	100.0	4,220.5	100.0

Notes: a. Excludes noncivilian employment, and includes daily wage workers not classified as civil servants.
b. Projected.
Source: Ministry of Planning (1986).

Arabia's economy. The private sector was primarily preoccupied with providing construction, transportation, and trade (import of goods and services) related to infrastructure, as opposed to entering into areas that the government was hoping to serve by installing infrastructural systems. Indeed, the demands on the economy and the devotion of the resources to this endeavor by the government, were so great, that it was inevitable for the private sector to be attracted to related businesses. In Table V.11, this trend is shown.

During the first two five-year plans, rates of growth for the construction, trade, and transportation sectors and later for utilities, each exceeded growth rates in other sectors, of the economy. Even during the third Five-Year Plan, the trade and transportation sectors were still experiencing growth rates in excess of 7 percent anually, while the construction sector clearly had stopped growing.

In Table V.12, the percentage of the workforce by economic activity is presented. It is apparent that after government employment (community and social service), the construction sector has had the highest (albeit declining) share in employment, followed by trade, manufacturing, and transportation. The fact that over a quarter of the population (including expatriates) was employed by the construction sector, is yet another indication of the degree of Saudi Arabia's effort in this area.

One consequence of this concentration of the Kingdom's limited human and entrepreneurial resources on the rapid provision of infrastructure systems was the diversion of these elements from other areas of development. An overriding objective of the Fourth Development Plan is to encourage private sector growth and diversification, to offset the omnipresent involvement of government in every facet of economic life and also to encourage the private sector to make longer-term commitments. In the aftermath of the great rush for infrastructural growth (in the early 1980s), economic activity, especially in the construction sector, fell precipitously, resulting in idle capacities, declining profit margins, and even bankruptcies. It is now again for the government to come to the rescue and to encourage development and diversification into other areas. So not only is the government burdened with the capital cost of infrastructure, but also with the cost of its maintenance. It also has the obligation to lead the effort to provide the private sector with alternative opportunities.

It can be argued that at least now, more than an adequate level of infrastructure is in place, and even with a rebounding of the economy, Saudi Arabia will not have to worry about bottlenecks due to the lack of infrastructure for some time. It will, however, be unfortunate if by the time economic diversification takes hold, it is discovered that the existing infrastructure is no longer appropriate, whether due to its age, inadequate maintenance, or geographical concentration. The development of physical infrastructure must be accompanied by other inputs, especially human capital; this component of the development process is addressed in Chapter X.

CONCLUSION

In sum, due to inadequate planning and rapid implementation, the development of infrastructure in Saudi Arabia has resulted in overcapacity in some components and areas, while others are still underserved. It would have been advisable to have implemented the policy toward infrastructure more slowly, as infrastructural needs are difficult to predict, especially in a rapidly changing economy subject to vast structural transformations. The cost of this policy has been the opportunity cost of capital associated with overcapacity, the cost of additional infrastructure to accommodate inflows of labor to work on infrastructure (infrastructure "feeding" on itself), the additional maintenance cost and in the future, the possibility that some of the infrastructure may be abandoned. At the present, the government should make a comprehensive assessment of the existing infrastructure to determine the specifics of several policy options. First, the government should establish the appropriate level of charges and fees to reflect opportunity costs and avoid excessive usage of facilities. Second, the government should determine which facilities, if any, should be abandoned before good money (in the form of maintenance) is thrown after bad money. Third, the government should decide on the appropriate level of maintenance, which may result in more costly replacement in the future. And finally, the government's approach to future infrastructure development should be more deliberate and incorporate the notion of user charges and fees at the planning stage to determine the appropriate level of infrastructure development.

NOTES

1. For further information, see Ministry of Planning (1986).
2. These estimates are based on discussions with officials of various ministries.

Chapter VI

Domestic Policies to Promote Growth to Compensate for Oil Depletion: Subsidies

INTRODUCTION

To be economically successful, Saudi Arabia should pursue a sound oil policy (discounted long-run revenue maximization) and investment policies, both external and internal, which adequately compensate for the depletion of oil (a positive real rate of return and economic diversification). The government has relegated a relatively minor role to external investments and has, instead, focused on the development of a domestic non-oil sector to compensate for oil depletion.

In domestic development, the role of the government has been pivotal given that oil revenues accrue to the government and that the size of the government in relation to the overall domestic economy is, by any standard, large. For instance, during the period 1972-1980, the percentage of gross fixed investments originating in the government sector was 58.9 percent (Johany et al., 1986, 24); or the oil sector's contribution to the GDP in 1980 was 64.8 percent (Ministry of Planning, 1984); or oil revenues (which accrue to the government) have consistently accounted for 90-98 percent of exports.

There is no doubt that the goal of the government is now, more than ever, to develop the domestic non-oil sector (Ministry of Planning, 1986):

> Despite the fact that oil represented the main source of income for the financing of development plans during the first phase, we were fully aware that it was a diminishing and unrenewable item and that it was inevitable, for our own good and for the welfare of future generations, to restructure our economy on solid pillars based on diversification of income.

The general approach for promoting a domestic non-oil sector has been threefold: to provide an adequate infrastructural base; to provide "incentives" or subsidies; and to make investments in capital intensive sectors, such as petrochemicals and export refineries.

Saudi Arabia's basic development strategy has involved the government undertaking projects requiring large investments that may be beyond the capacity of private sector, namely, basic (bulk) petrochemicals and export refineries. These projects have been largely housed at Jubail and Yanbu, where sophisticated infrastructure has been provided. The justification for these projects has been to increase the value of Saudi Arabia's crude oil exports. To encourage economic diversification, the government has provided infrastructure and a variety of input subsidies that have been made generally available, that is, without any specific sectoral focus with the exception of some special considerations for agriculture. Additionally, the government has felt that the growth of basic industries would provide further stimulus to downstream diversification.

Before elaborating on the role of subsidies in Saudi Arabia, its appropriate place in the framework of the Saudi Arabian economy should be kept in mind. Recalling the discussion of Chapter II, it should be emphasized that oil is a finite resource and thus it is the heritage of all generations. As a result, the government should employ oil resources to benefit all generations, through the accumulation of foreign assets or through domestic investments. This means that in the case of subsidies, either the government should target subsidies to generate alternative sources of income to compensate for oil depletion, or subsidies should be at a level that can be maintained for all generations. In other words, it is important to distinguish between investment subsidies (in the form of capital, raw materials, education and so on) and general production subsidies, and consumption subsidies. To the extent that profitable investments are included, this benefits all generations; but the extent that consumption is subsidized, only the present generation benefits.

SUBSIDIES IN THE SAUDI ECONOMY

Subsidies are, to differing degrees, a feature of all economies; and are employed by governments to attain social as well as economic goals. In the case of Saudi Arabia, subsidies play a more pervasive role than in most other economies; the coverage of subsidies has been very broad, for both social as well as productive goals, and their value is large by any measure. In the absence of targeted macro- and commercial policies, the use of subsidies have been the most important domestic economic policy.

There are many categories of subsidies. There are subsidies for social as well as productive reasons. There are capital subsidies and operating subsidies. There are subsidies that are direct payments, and subsidies that are in the form of subsidized prices. And these subsidies cut across almost all sectors of the economy. The broad categories of sectoral subsidies cover:

- utilities
- fuels
- agriculture
- essential commodities
- social services (private and public)
- industrial
- other

In this chapter, the mechanism for some subsidies are described by sector, estimates of the size of some of the major subsidies are calculated, and a discussion of the viability and desirability of major subsidies is provided. But first, it may be useful to provide a brief rationale, from the government's perspective, for subsidies.

RATIONALE FOR SUBSIDIES

The original reason for much of the subsidies in Saudi Arabia in the mid-1970s was the need to distribute oil revenues and purchasing power to the population at large. Given the fact that oil revenues, the major source of income, accrues in the first instance to the government, the government was looking for ways to distribute some of this income to all Saudis. It was logistically difficult to give each Saudi an annual grant; although this would have been the most efficient method as then the average Saudi could have spent the income in a way to maximize his utility, as opposed to benefiting in the form of specific subsidized prices. Government expenditure, per se, would take too long to trickle down and the distribution of benefits would be too skewed. Consequently, subsidies, through government expenditures and subsidized prices, were adopted as a major instrument for distributing the benefits of oil wealth; while general government expenditures, and later input subsidies were targeted for the longer-term framework of the same goal (largely the development of infrastructure) and the development of a viable non-oil sector.

With time, the role of subsidies expanded to promote the private sector's role in economic diversification and became a central feature of the Saudi economy. Currently, subsidies in Saudi Arabia are targeted toward a diverse set of objectives:

- enhancement of purchasing power
- improvement of income and wealth distribution
- promotion of economic development of basic industries
- promotion of the private non-oil sector
- achievement of diverse social goals
- promotion of social stability

Enhancement of Purchasing Power

Beginning in early 1971, with the explosion in oil revenues, the lion's share of demand for goods and services was in the hands of the government. The government started to explore all avenues for transferring demand to the private sector in order to stimulate the domestic economy. The economically efficient method would have been a direct annual transfer to each citizen. This was difficult. The government did not have an accurate census of all citizens, and most Saudis were not easily reachable through the mail and the like. Instead, the government opted for subsidies to transfer the benefits of oil to its citizens. Additionally, there were at times, other objectives, such as allowing the bedouins to stay in rural areas,which prompted the government to adopt sector specific subsidies as the simplest means to attain its goals.

Enhancement of Income and Wealth Distribution

General government expenditures in Saudi Arabia in the early to mid-1970s largely benefited in the first instance, a few well-established merchant families. First, government contracts, which were large, were awarded to established companies. From the early to the late 1970s, profit margins were high and as a result these same companies benefited. Second, given the large component of foreign labor (averaging around 50 percent) in the total economy and higher in the private sector, a large portion of most government contracts, and in turn the next round of expenditures, accrued to foreigners who also gained from most subsidies and saved a higher proportion of their income (than Saudis at the same income level) for repatriation. Third, the average Saudi's benefit from general government expenditures was most apparent at the retail level and in the provision of services. As a result, a mechanism was required to distribute oil income and wealth in a more effective manner.

Programs such as fuel, electricity, water, and food subsidies have played an important role in improving the social condition of the average citizen, while subsidized loans for housing have resulted in a better distribution of wealth.

Promotion of Economic Development of Basic Industries

To most observers, Saudi Arabia's comparative advantage would probably be in energy-intensive industries, and in particular, in energy-intensive industries for which proximity to the source of energy was critical. This view also appears to be the position of the government. If Saudi Arabia has indeed a comparative advantage in the production of energy-intensive goods, then a subsidy should be required. However, if for infant industry type arguments, some form of subsidy protection was necessary, then economically, the most efficient policy would have been production subsidies, not subsidized energy or capital that in turn would introduce distortions into the production process. Clearly, energy and capital should be priced at their opportunity cost, but coupled with production subsidies for a limited period of time, until the industry of comparative advantage could compete on the world market. Instead, Saudi Arabia subsidized energy and capital to contribute to economic development and to promote exports of products produced by such industries. SABIC is the major manifestation of this approach to Saudi Arabia's economic development.

Promotion of the Private Sector

Given that the oil sector, and thus the government sector, has been the dominant force in the Saudi economy, Saudi Arabia has used subsidies in order to promote a large role for the private sector. Cheap utilities and fuels, capital subsidies from the Saudi Industrial Development Fund, and a variety of agricultural subsidies, have all been disbursed to encourage a wider role for the private sector. Again, such subsidies tend to be distortionary as compared to direct production subsidies.

Achievement of Diverse Social Goals

Subsidies have been used to quickly realize certain social objectives. At one level, these objectives have included certain desired levels of health and education. At another level, these have included diversity of appropriate job opportunities for Saudis, as is the case in the agricultural sector for bedouins. At another level, the government wanted to achieve domestic self-sufficiency in agriculture. The rapid attainment of social goals and objectives has been a very important determinant of the types and magnitudes of subsidies employed. However, again as in the case of production subsidies, specific social consumption subsidies encourage excessive consumption of that service; a distortion free policy would entail direct income transfers to consumers for them to choose for themselves. But as mentioned earlier, direct-income transfers were logistically difficult.

Promotion of Social Stability

Subsidies, once disbursed by the government, are difficult, if not impossible, to terminate. The population at large get used to receiving government handouts, important constituencies develop around individual subsidies and fight against the removal of subsidies as if subsidies were a birthright. In Saudi Arabia, this phenomenon is, if anything, more entrenched than in other countries. Subsidies are all pervasive; they are large in magnitude and have a great impact on the daily life of the average Saudi; and given the nature of Saudi society, appeals against the removal of subsidies can be made by individual citizens directly to the royal family. As a result, the government has had difficulties in terminating, or even significantly reducing, many of the subsidies as in the case of electricity. Thus, subsidies are in part maintained to promote social stability.

Mechanisms and Modes for Transfer of Subsidies

It is useful to briefly outline the mechanisms and modes of subsidies in Saudi Arabia in order to assess their implications for the long-term economic development of the Saudi economy, their true cost to Saudi Arabia and thus, their long-run viability.

There are broadly three types of subsidies. First, there are direct cash subsidies, such as payments for crops to farmers and operating expenses to utilities. Second, there are subsidized prices, such as fuel prices below the world price; these do not appear in the budget. And third, there are what might be called capital subsidies, such as subsidized loans to utilities and to citizens for residential housing; many of these also do not appear in the budget. In what follows, the category of subsidies are discussed by the targeted sector.

Subsidies to Utilities

The two major utilities receiving subsidies in Saudi Arabia are electricity and water, and to a lesser degree natural gas supply and distribution.

Electricity is sold at a subsidized price; up to 1984, electricity was sold at 1.5 cents (5 halalas; SR 1 = halalas 100) per kwh. Between 1984 and 1986, certain tariff changes were made to raise electricity rates. Currently, as of late 1985, a rate of 1.9 cents (7 halalas) per kwh has applied to the first 3,000 kwh, rising to 2.7 cents (10 halalas) for usage in the range of 23,000 to 4,000 kwh, and 4 cents (15 halalas) per kwh for consumption over 4,000 kwh, for residential users; for industrial and agricultural users the rate is still 1.5 cents (5 halalas) per kwh. Even with the new, higher rates, the cost of producing and supplying electricity is roughly four times the average price charged to customers. To defray these explicit and implicit costs, the government gives the electricity generating companies two subsidies. First, there is a cash, operating and profit, subsidy to cover operating losses and to give a reasonable profit to stockholders. Second, there have been capital subsidies under the Electric Utility Lending Program, through SIDF. The charges on these loans are 0.5 percent annually and recently (since 1985) all new capital requirements have come directly from the budget with no charges. And there is an implicit fuel subsidy to electricity generation, discussed later in this chapter.

Water is sold to residential, agricultural, and industrial users at subsidized rates. Water for agriculture (currently roughly 80 percent of the water usage) is free of charge; water for residential and industrial use (the remaining 20 percent) has been supplied at prices below production costs. The water tariffs, still highly subsidized were revised upward in September 1985 from 7.1 cents (25 halalas) per m^3 from 1 to 50 m^3 of consumption, $0.3 (SR 1) per m^3 from 51 to 150 m^3 and US $1.15 (SR 4) per m^3 for all consumption over 151 m^3. Water is supplied from three sources—underground (about 80 percent), surface (15 percent), and desalination (5 percent). The government provides direct allocations (capital and operating) for the supply of water to the Ministry of Agriculture and Water, Ministry of Municipal and Rural Affairs and to the Al-Hasa Irrigation and Drainage Project Authority; the government gives direct allocation to the Saline Water Conversion Corporation (SWCC) to cover operating losses and budgetary allocations on an interest free basis for capital expenditures.

The provision of natural gas, through the National Gas Company, is subsidized in much the same way as that of electricity.

In the case of all three utilities, there is, therefore, a consumption subsidy (as they are provided at subsidized prices), input production subsidies (capital and fuels), and general production subsidies (losses and dividends). As discussed later, these subsidies are distortionary.

As a result of these policies, electricity and water consumption has expanded dramatically as can be seen in Tables VI.1 and VI.2.

Subsidization of Fuels

The Saudi government, through Petromin, sells crude oil and oil products within Saudi Arabia at prices substantially below world price levels. Domestic fuel prices were unchanged between 1978 and 1984; in April 1984, domestic prices were revised upward, by about 60 percent. The subsidy element is still large as premium gasoline had sold for about US$0.35 per U.S. gallon until November 1987, when the price of premium gasoline only was doubled. Fuel subsidies are both in consumption and as an input subsidy in various production processes.

Table VI.1. Electricity Generation Capacity and Number of Subscribers

Year	*Power Capacity (MW)*	*Peak Load (MW)*	*Subscribers (number)*	*Power Sold (million kwh)*
1978	3,210	2,161	581,806	8,466
1979	4,124	2,955	726,805	13,449
1980	5,904	3,986	872,054	17,437
1981	7,359	5,227	1,041,958	21,644
1982	9,001	6,309	1,212,314	26,630
1983	10,704	7,796	1,390,565	31,177
1984	11,853	8,503	1,584,095	36,986

Sources: SAMA (1984, 1988).

Table VI.2. National Water Resources—Demand Balance

	Million Cubic Meters/Year		*Share (%)*
	1980	*1985*	*1985*
Demand			
Agriculture	1,860	7,430	84
Domestic, Industrial, Other	502	1,400	16
Total	2,362	8,830	100
Resources			
Surface Water	485	900	10
Groundwater			
renewable	660	950	11
nonrenewable	1,154	6,480	73
Desalinated Seawater	63	400	5
Reclaimed Wastewater	—	100	1
Total	2,362	8,830	100

Source: Ministry of Planning (1985, 139).

Subsidies for Agriculture

While the motives and the mechanisms for utility and fuel subsidization are rather straightforward, those for agriculture are more complex. The major stated motives behind the promotion of agriculture in Saudi Arabia are threefold. First, there is a genuine feeling that much of the Saudi population would not be attracted to employment in cities and industrial zones but would instead prefer to work on the land. Therefore, agriculture was seen as an avenue to provide desirable employment opportunities to the wage earner, the small farmer, and especially to the bedouin. Simultaneously, this was seen as desirable for all sorts of other social reasons,

Table VI.3. Saudi Arabia: Area Planted and Production of Main Agricultural Crops[a] (1978-1979—1983-1984)

	1978-1979	*1979-1980*	*1980-1981*	*1981-1982*	*1982-1983*	*1983-1984*[b]
Wheat						
Production	147.0	142.0	187.0	412.0	817.0	1,402.0
Area planted	79.0	67.0	74.0	137.0	408.0	673.0
Yield	1.9	2.1	2.5	3.0	2.0	2.1
Sorghum[c]						
Production	194.0	110.0	92.0	78.0	37.0	35.0
Area planted	371.0	350.0	173.0	105.0	49.0	63.0
Yield	0.5	0.3	0.5	0.7	0.8	0.5
Barley						
Production	16.0	5.0	6.0	5.0	2.0	2.0
Area planted	7.0	4.0	7.0	6.0	0.9	1.0
Yield	2.4	1.3	0.9	0.8	2.2	2.0
Millet[c]						
Production	13.0	9.0	8.0	11.0	7.0	4.0
Area planted	20.0	18.0	13.0	21.0	19.0	27.0
Yield	0.3	0.3	0.7	0.3	0.7	1.3
Tomatoes[c]						
Production	212.0	200.0	232.0	238.0	264.0	328.0
Area planted	20.0	18.0	13.0	21.0	19.0	27.0
Yield	10.6	11.1	17.8	11.3	13.9	12.0
Dry onions						
Production	118.0	59.0	14.0	56.0	7.0	20.0
Area planted	5.0	3.0	1.0	4.0	0.6	2.0
Yield	23.1	19.7	14.0	14.0	11.7	10.0
Eggplant[c]						
Production	29.0	25.0	20.0	24.0	34.0	31.0
Area planted	15.0	16.0	13.0	20.0	21.0	16.0
Yield	11.9	20.8	14.8	18.0	21.3	20.8
Watermelon						
Production	170.0	332.0	193.0	361.0	447.0	333.0
Area planted	15.0	16.0	13.0	20.0	21.0	16.0
Yield	11.9	20.8	14.8	18.0	21.3	20.8
Dates						
Production	416.0	342.0	372.0	421.0	467.0	454.0
Area Planted	64.0	60.0	62.0	70.0	55.0	56.0
Yield	6.5	5.7	6.0	6.0	8.5	8.1

(continued)

Table VI.3. (continued)

	1978-1979	*1979-1980*	*1980-1981*	*1981-1982*	*1982-1983*	*1983-1984*[b]
Grapes						
Production	53.0	57.0	61.0	78.0	42.0	77.0
Area Planted	6.0	4.0	4.0	5.0	4.0	6.0
Yield	9.5	14.3	15.3	15.6	10.5	12.8
Citrus fruits						
Production	31.0	40.0	39.0	9.0	9.0	10.0
Area Planted	5.0	5.0	3.0	1.0	1.0	2.0
Yield	6.9	8.0	13.0	9.0	9.0	5.0

Notes: a. Area planted in thousand hectares; production in thousand tons; yield in tons per hectare (yield figures are computed on the basis of unrounded production and area planted data).
b. Provisional.
c. Includes both winter and summer crops.

Sources: Central Department of Statistics (1987); Ministry of Finance and National Economy (1987).

Table VI.4. Domestic Egg and Poultry Production

	1973	*1982*	*1983*	*1984*[a]
Broiler chickens (tons)				
Domestic production	8,105.0	81,619.0	118,825.0	137,680.0
Imports	11,412.0	196,271.0	181,951.0	164,508.0
Consumption	19,517.0	277,890.0	300,776.0	302,188.0
Ratio of domestic production to consumption	41.5	29.4	39.5	46.0
Eggs (million)				
Domestic production	114.4	1,244.0	1,748.0	1,852.0
Imports	94.4	173.4	39.2	—
Exports	—	—	5.2	6.6
Consumption	208.8	1,417.4	1,782.0	1,845.4
Ratio of domestic production to consumption	54.8	87.8	98.0	100.4

Note: a. Revised.

Source: SAMA (1985, 99).

such as retarding rural-urban migration. Second, as a result of the threats (though empty) by some countries in 1974 to retaliate against the Arab oil embargo with a food embargo, food security became a national goal in Saudi Arabia. Third, the promotion of agriculture was seen to contribute to more balanced geographical growth within Saudi Arabia. But again many of these goals could have been more efficiently achieved through direct

Table VI.5. Meat Production and Consumption

	1979	*1982*	*1983*	*1984*
Red Meat Production[a]				
Domestic Production	14,628.0	28,346.0	70,115.0	70,115.0
Imports (slaughtered and livestock)	175,056.0	270,650.0	220,473.0	182,717.0
Total Consumption	189,684.0	298,996.0	290,558.0	252,832.0
Domestic production as percent of consumption	7.7	9.5	24.1	27.7
White Meat Production[a]				
Domestic Production[b]	58,611.0	108,882.0	162,995.0	170,341.0
Imports	159,937.0	221,512.0	230,897.0	231,128.0
Total Consumption	218,548.0	330,394.0	393,892.0	401,469.0
Domestic production as percent of consumption	26.8	33.0	41.4	42.4
Total Meat Consumption	408,232.0	629,390.0	684,480.0	654,301.0
Domestic production as percent of consumption	17.9	21.8	34.0	36.7

Notes: a. Production figures are calculated in tons.
b. Includes fresh fish.
Source: SAMA (1985).

subsidies, as opposed to indirect subsidies that introduce additional distortions.

Saudi Arabia, therefore, embarked on an ambitious program to promote agriculture. But its small family agricultural sector has not been transformed; it has been, instead, supplemented and dominated by large commercial enterprises. This transformation has been determined by the size and type of government incentive. Although overall agricultural output has increased by nearly 60 percent over the 6-year period from 1979-1980 to 1984-1985, a major shift has also occurred toward wheat production at the expense of other crops, such as sorghum and barley. The output increase in agriculture has been impressive (see Tables VI.3, VI.4, VI.5), but the major increase in crop production has been in wheat, and, in the livestock sector, in eggs, broiler chicken, meat, and dairy. The Ministry of Agriculture is aware of these shifts and is in the process of rectifying the situation.

The increased output in agriculture and the shift toward wheat production, has been a direct result of a myriad of distortionary government subsidy policies. Again, agricultural subsidies may be loosely classified into direct cash subsidies and capital subsidies. The cash subsidies can be further broken down into those for main crops, animal production, and inputs. The capital subsidies are derived from two sources—the Saudi Arabian Agricultural Bank and the Ministry of Finance and National Economy.

Cash or production subsidies are targeted toward cereals and dates. The subsidy (price guarantee) for wheat has gone through several revisions: US$735 (SR 2,500)/MT in 1978-1979, US$1,029 (SR 3,500)/MT in 1979-1980, US$857 (SR 3,000)/MT in 1984-1985 for production in excess of 500 MT, and US$550 (SR 2,000)/MT for all production for the period 1985-1986—1988-1989. The reduction in the wheat subsidy has been motivated by the size of the wheat surplus and by the heavy use of water in wheat production. There are also production subsidies for rice US$82 (SR 300/MT), and US$14 (SR 50) per each palm tree planted. There is also a price support of US$960 (SR 3500)/MT for dates. However, the major share of subsidies (more than 50 percent in 1983-1984) has been provided for wheat production as wheat was the major import crop.

The subsidies for animal production were US$8.20 (SR 30)/head per annum for up to 300 heads of sheep and goat and US$22 (SR 80)/head per annum for up to 70 head of camels. But, at the end of 1979, these subsidies were replaced by a subsidy for maize and barley feeds for sheep in order to encourage sheep production.

The subsidy for agricultural inputs are as follows:

Category	*Coverage and Amount of Subsidy*
Agricultural machinery	50% of price
Agricultural equipment	45% of price
Irrigation machinery and pumps	50% of price specified by the Ministry of Agriculture
Chemical fertilizers	50% of value costs, (cif), port of destination
Concentrated feed	50% of value (cif) if imported or of sale price as determined by Grain Silos and Flour Mills Corporation
Poultry equipment	30% of equipment value (cif), port of destination **or** 10% of value if equipment is covered by an Agriculture Bank loan
Milk production equipment	30% of value (cif), port of destination **or** 10% of value if equipment is covered by an Agricultural Bank loan
Drought contingencies subsidy	US$27 (SR 100) per ton of feed
Transportation of high productivity cows	Total cost of transportation from the country of origin to the port of destination, by air freight
Improved seeds for wheat, barley and sorghum	Free
Potato seeds	Five tons free of charge to the farmer
Fishing boats and nets	Grant of up to US$2,740 (SR 10,000) per person engaged in fisheries
Protection of plants	All services and materials for maintenance and protection are provided free of charge

The capital subsidies are in the form of interest free loans from the Saudi Arabian Agricultural Bank (SAAB), and from the Ministry of Finance and National Economy for special projects. SAAB loans fall into three categories:

- *Short-term agricultural loans:* Not exceeding one year, these loans are used for growing and marketing seasonal crops, and to procure production inputs, including seeds, fertilizers, fuel, plowing, wages, fattening animals, poultry, and feeds.
- *Medium-term agricultural loans:* Not exceeding five years, these loans are used for the procurement of agricultural implements, machinery, pumps, drilling and repair of wells, and construction of canals. They are also allocated for establishing modern farms, for producing meat and laying chickens, for producing sheep and poultry feeds and their concentrates, for raising sheep, cattle, and bees, for utilizing fisheries, and for financing agricultural manufacturing projects such as the production and processing of milk or tomato paste, for packing dates or essential oils or constructing plants for preserving hides and pickling or warehouses for refrigeration and preservation.
- *Long-term agricultural loans:* Not exceeding 25 years, these loans are earmarked for the reclamation and development of extensive fallow lands.

The loans from the Ministry of Finance cover large agricultural projects in the private sector. For agriculture, there are both input production subsidies (capital, fuels, and water) and general production subsidies (for individual crops, e.g. wheat).

Subsidies for Essential Commodities

The essential commodities subsidies apply to wheat flour, rice, sugar, meat, oils, vegetable fats, milk, animal feed (maize and barley), and cement. Three methods of subsidies for these items have been applied.

1. Method of variable subsidy where subsidy varies with costs to keep the price to the consumer constant. This method is based on guaranteeing a specified profit for the importer fixed at 10 percent of the cif price of the imported commodity. This applies to flour, rice, sugar, and maize and barley animal feeds. The formula of subsidy under this method is:

Subsidy = cif price + 10 percent thereof as profit for the importer + port charges + US$8.20 (SR 30) per ton for transport expenses (including loading and unloading) up to importer's warehouse minus domestic sale prices fixed for the importer by the Ministry of Commerce.

2. Method of fixed or specific subsidy where a certain amount is paid to the importer for each unit of imported commodities regardless of their cif price. The subsidy of the following commodities are granted as shown below:

- Powdered milk packed in tins is granted a subsidy of US$0.70 (SR 2.5) per kilogram (kg).
- Imported vegetable oils are granted US$0.50-US$0.70 (SR 1.85-2.5) per kg, depending on the type of container used.
- Chilled and frozen sheep meat imported in the form of complete carcasses, are granted a subsidy of US$0.40 (SR 1.50) per kg.

3. Method of subsidy at specified percentage of import costs (i.e., *ad valorem)* where the following commodities are priced on cost data of expended subsidy in order to reach the domestic sale price.

- Liquid, infantile, and powdered milk imported in barrels or bags are granted a subsidy of 20 percent of import costs (cif)
- Margarine is also granted a subsidy at 20 percent of imported costs (cif).

The subsidy system allows importers to obtain subsidy payments after goods arrive and prior to the sale of such goods, after submitting an application accompanied by supporting documents to the concerned office.

Subsidies for Social Services

There are a host of private social subsidies to individuals and entities. These subsidies include rewards to students, private schools, health (payment for treatment, both domestic and abroad), the press, sporting clubs, cooperation subsidies, benevolent societies, pilgrimage, marriage, reconditioning of houses, and trade.

The subsidy for university students include free tuition, free room, payment by the student for 20 percent of the cost of board and 25 percent of the cost of books, US$300 spending money per month, and free airline tickets home. Public service subsidies include transportation (air, land, and sea), telecommunication, housing, and storage. The government pays, as a budget item, the operating losses of the Ministry of Post, Telephone and Telegraph (PTT) due to its telecommunication activities and has contributed the capital for the necessary infrastructure. In the case of Saudia (the national airlines) and the Saudi Railroad Corporation, the government again pays operating losses and has contributed a large part of the capital. For the Saudi Public Transport Company, the government pays the operating losses, an amount to render a profit to stockholders, and a large part of the capital.

Housing subsidies, regardless of income, are a substantial social benefit to all Saudis. There are two types of such subsidies. First, the Real Estate Development Fund (REDF) extends long-term loans for up to US$85,700 (SR 300,000) (one-time) depending on the location, per borrower, for the construction of owner-occupied houses. The loan is repayable over a 25-year period with a 20 percent discount for timely repayment in installments, or a 30 percent discount on timely repayment in one installment. The REDF also provides investment loans to help real estate developers construct residential buildings. Second, the government has constructed public housing, some of which is empty, to be rented at below market prices or for sale at subsidized prices.

In the area of storage, the government has paid for the construction and equipment costs of large storage facilities and has rented the space out at a nominal fee or for free in order to reduce storage charges.

Industrial Subsidies

The industrial subsidies consist of subsidized loans from the SIDF and from the Public Investment Fund (PIF), the exemption of imported equipment and raw materials for industrial projects from tariffs, tariff protection, tax holidays for foreign partner's share of capital in joint ventures, subsidized use of infrastructure in industrial estates, training subsidies for Saudi manpower, preferential purchase of Saudi products, and guaranteed profits for certain corporations.

SIDF lends 50 percent of the total financing required for a project for up to 15 years, after an evaluation of reasonable profitability. There is an additional provision that the Saudi-owned component of the capital be no less than 25 percent. The charges on SIDF loans are roughly 2.5 percent per annum. PIF loans apply to large government-sponsored projects, for instance, those of SABIC and carry a charge when the project is profitable; this charge ranges from 3-6 percent depending on the rate of return. The other major industrial subsidies are the use of infrastructure at nominal prices, tariffs, in some cases up to 20 percent ad valorem, and training subsidies. But the dominant components of industrial subsidies are the reduced cost of capital, infrastructure, fuel, utilities and water, which were addressed earlier in this chapter.

Other Subsidies

The major item under this category is subsidized loans to hotels up to $14.3 (SR 50) million from the Ministry of Finance and National Economy. There are also loan subsidies for Saudi contractors and bakeries. Annual subsidies are also given to the chambers of commerce.

VALUE OF SUBSIDIES IN SAUDI ARABIA

To assess how important subsidies are in the context of the Saudi Arabian economy, some rough idea of their size is necesary. The Ministry of Finance's figure for subsidies is only a partial list and excludes all nonbudget items and capital subsidies. The exclusion of capital subsidies is in part in deference to Islamic principles prohibiting interest. But for a modern-day economy, which must compensate for oil depletion and confront budgetary deficits in the mid-1980s, capital subsidies are equivalent to foregone profits, dividends, and interest income on foreign investments. Thus, in the first instance, subsidies result in both lower government income and higher expenditures. And second, if they are inconsistent with long-term goals of the Saudi economy, they result in economic distortions, and in reduced standards of living for future generations.

The Ministry of Finance subsidy figures for 1983-1986 are given in Table VI.6. It is not our intention to dispute these figures, but to approximate a more comprehensive figure for subsidies in order to assess subsidy policies later in this chapter. Also, we cannot quantify some of the subsidies. Therefore, the figures in the next section should be seen as a *partial* and *approximate* value of subsidies in Saudi Arabia; as such, they are rough underestimated figures.

Table VI.6. Saudi Arabia: Budgetary Subsidies (1983-1984—1985-1986) (In US$ Millions)

	Actuals		*Provisional Actuals*
Fiscal Years	*1983-1984*	*1984-1985*	*1985-1986*
Food subsidies	457	729	534
Wheat subsidies	722	616	712
Electricity subsidies	1,014	770	479
Agricultural subsidies	327	230	365
Social relief payments	430	416	433
Other subsidies[a]	235	223	334
Total	3,185	2,983	2,857

Note: a. Including subsidies for Chambers of Commerce, social and sport clubs, several educational institutions, and hospitals. These figures were converted to dollars using an exchange of US$1 = SR 3.5 (1983), SR 3.57 (1984), and SR 3.65 (1985).

Source: Ministry of Finance and National Economy (1985).

Calculation of Subsidies

The various subsidies can be classified in many different ways. For our purpose, subsidies are classified by the sector receiving the subsidy and into:

- noncapital (operating)
- capital.

Operating subsidies are those that require a cash outlay for current transactions, such as wheat, essential commodities, electricity operating and dividend, desalination operating, and Saudia-operating subsidies. Capital subsidies are loans at subsidized interest rates that the government could have invested (largely abroad) instead of having made loans at subsidized rates.

In Appendix III, tables are presented for the calculation of the amount of each subsidy by sector of the subsidy. In this chapter, the size of individual subsidies, the aggregate of all subsidies, and ratio of the size subsidies to various indicators such as oil revenues and population are presented.

A discussion of the method of calculating capital subsidies is called for. From the perspective of the government, if capital subsidies are not given, these funds can be invested, resulting in revenues (interest) and the repayment of principal at maturity. In the case of most capital subsidies in Saudi Arabia, there is little or no revenues generated for the government and the repayment of principal is uncertain. The calculation of the size of the subsidy is based on the difference between the 6 months Eurodollar rate (the "opportunity rate" for the government), as roughly 60-70 percent of Saudi Arabia's external assets has been dollar-denominated short-term deposits, and the charges on the loan. Basically, the argument being that if the government had not made the domestic loan, it would have made additional short-term Eurodollar deposits. This method is not intended to measure the *cost* of subsidies to society, as it ignores many relevant facets of such a calculation; instead, it is a more comprehensive measure of what is spent on subsidies in Saudi Arabia, as the government reports a very narrow figure for its subsidy expenditures. To calculate the cost (or benefit) of subsidies or the "true" size of subsidies, one should incorporate the multiplier effects of a dollar of dometic subsidies versus that of investments abroad, the true value of the resulting output (i.e., at shadow prices), and so on. However, foreign exchange effects (i.e., domestic loans or expenditures are riyal denominated, whereas foreign investments are denominated in foreign exchange) are not applicable. This is because foreign exchange has not been a binding constraint in Saudi Arabia, as it is in most other developing countries, and thus there is no premium to be attached to earnings in foreign exchange and vice versa.

At least two methods of calculating the capital subsidy could be used. In the first method, the present value (discounted at the difference between the Eurodeposit rate in the year of the loan and the rate of interest, or charges, on the domestic loan) of the loan and the rate of interest, or charges, on the domestic loan) of the loan principal at its maturity would be calculated; then this present value of the principal would be subtracted from the actual size of loan; this difference would be the calculated subsidy and would be all attributed to accrue in the year that the loan was made. There are at least two shortcomings to this approach. In this calculation, it is assumed that the government has transferred all of the subsidy in one year, the first year of the loan. But from the government perspective, the foregone interest, which in turn is the subsidy, is an annual item and is affected by market interest rates each year, not only by rates in the year when the loan was made. This argument is valid from the government's perspective as Saudi Arabia deposits funds largely on a short-term basis. On the other hand, from the borrower's perspective, if the alternative is a long-term loan and at a fixed interest rate, then the subsidy should be based on the initial interest rate. Second, this method results in large yearly variations in the amount of subsidy.

These shortcomings suggest a second method for the subsidy calculation to estimate the foregone income to the government. The subsidy on a loan is calculated in year 1 as the differential in interest rates multiplied by the principal. In year 2, the subsidy is the differential in interest rates in year 2 multiplied by the accumulated principal, and so on in later years. By excluding the annuity aspect of interest foregone, this calculation *underestimates* the size of subsidy. This second method is reported in the tables as the annual capital subsidy.

Size of Subsidies

Before briefly discussing the overall estimates of the size of the various subsidies, it may be useful to repeat several points of caution. First, our major purpose is to present a more comprehensive perspective on subsidies rather than to question government figures. Second, these figures are estimates and, in a few cases, assumptions have been made as described in the footnotes to the tables (see Appendix III). Third, these numbers do not include all subsidies. Subsidies omitted are fuels used by the oil sector, some infrastructure (especially Jubail and Yanbu), education, health and other social services, water pumping and those for water (excluding desalination), and agricultural price supports except for wheat. But the omission of these subsidies is also due to the difficulties of quantifying meaningful figures. In the case of water and because of its importance, a brief qualitative discussion is called for.

Table VI.7. Nonrenewable Water Resources

Principle Aquifer	*Proven Reserves (Million cubic meters)*
Wasia/Biyadh	89,000
Wajid	69,000
Um Er Radhuma	65,600
Minjur/Dhurma	63,000
Saq	49,000
Tabuk	5,600
Dammam	5,000
Total	337,500

Note: Together with secondary aquifers, total proven nonrenewable groundwater reserves amount to approximately 500,000,000 cubic meters.
Source: Ministry of Planning (1985).

The only water subsidy included in this study has been that derived from desalination, which accounts for only 5 percent of total water consumption in 1985. But what of the rest of the water consumed? The Ministry of Planning's estimates for water consumption and sources of supply are given in Table VI.2 and their estimates of nonrenewable sources are in Table VI.7.

Several facts should be noted. Agricultural demand for water has quadrupled in five years and accounted for 84 percent of total consumption in 1985. Nonrenewable sources of groundwater accounted for 73 percent of the supply. Agriculture uses this water at zero cost. Given the subsidization of fuels and cheap loans, depth of pumping is of little importance to the individual company or farmer. But what is the cost of this water to society? There is clearly a cost because the major source of water in Saudi Arabia is finite.

Unfortunately, it is very difficult to quantify the implicit subsidy in water consumption because of the many unknowns. The quantity of water in nonreplenishable sources is debatable; the government figures are subject to debate, given the rapid drop in reservoir levels. There are reasons to believe that water is seeping into the Gulf, but at an unknown rate. Underground water varies in quality. Some of the water is fit for drinking, whereas some is not even directly useable in agriculture. All of these depend on the locality of the reservoir. At one extreme, one could argue that the opportunity cost of water is the cost of desalinated water. At another extreme, one could argue that the opportunity cost is zero because the water is seeping into the Gulf. The truth may be somewhere between these two extremes. On the other hand, the Ministry of Agriculture and Water maintains that the cost of treating most of the water from underground aquifers for portable use is higher than the cost of desalinated water.[1] As a result, it would be incorrect to assign an opportunity cost of desalinated water to the water used in agriculture because this water would not be used for anything else.

Tables containing the subsidy calculations are in Appendix III; in these tables only in individual sectoral subsidies that could be quantified are calculated. The aggregate tables for subsidies (Tables VI.8-10)—aggregate operating, capital, and total—and the ratio of total subsidies to GDP, oil revenues, government expenditures, and population are given in Tables VI.11-14.

In Table VI.10, the relative subsidies for each sector can be seen in the last column, the aggregate for the years 1975-1984 is calculated as US$93.4 billion and US$17.6 billion in 1984 alone; and at the bottom of each column the total annual subsidies are indicated. First, the aggregate numbers are large, both in absolute size and relative to what the government reports as annual subsidies (see Table VI.6). The annual size of subsidies has ranged from a low of US$1.1 billion in 1975, to a high of US$19.7 billion in 1982. The government's figure for budgetary subsidies for 1984 amounted to US$2.98 billion. Second, in all years, except 1975, fuel subsidies are the largest component, on an average representing roughly one third of the total. The true meaning or opportunity cost of this subsidy has been questioned by some people in Saudi Arabia on the basis that the opportunity cost of a barrel of oil in Saudi Arabia is less than the world price. But since oil is a tradable good, its opportunity cost should be the price on the international market; that is, the price that the government could have received if it had exported the marginal barrel instead of allocating it for domestic use.

And over time, if the market is in equilibrium, natural resource economics would indicate that the expected increase in the net price of oil is equal to the social rate of discount. It should, however, be noted that we have excluded one important source of oil subsidy—namely, crude oil subsidies to refineries—from our calculation.

A glance at Tables VI.11-14 reveal the relative importance of the size of subsidy expenditures to various indicators. Subsidies, as a percentage of GDP, have varied from a low of 2.4 in 1975, to a high of 39.6 in 1982. As a percentage of government expenditures from a low of 4.7 percent, to a high of 79.3 percent. And on a per capita basis, subsidies have gone from a low of $136 in 1975, to a high of $1,734 in 1982; these per capita figures are based on official population statistics, an overestimate.

As has been mentioned several times, these estimates of the size of subsidies are on the low side both because of the partial coverage and because of the method for calculating capital subsidies. But given these times of low oil revenues, it may be useful to ask what was the size of allocations from the 1984 budget for subsidies. Such an estimate can be derived by taking all operating subsidies minus fuel subsidies (these being foregone revenues)

Table VI.8. Noncapital (Operating) Government Subsidies (In US$ Millions)[a]

	1975	1976	1977	1978	1979	1980	1981	1982	1983	1984	Total
Agriculture	51[b]	52	68	105	130	212	354	576	825	1,425	3,797
Fuel	191	313	421	662	1,420	3,771	5,615	6,784	7,669	6,642	33,488
Electricity	47	77	144	269	470	598	772	1,081	1,026	1,161	5,646
Water Desal	137	103	104	110	108	109	1,179	1,172	1,152	1,126	5,299
Saudia	7	32	48	47	70	95	253	118	0	0	670
Food	411	170	200	241	431	902	1,464	1,303	458	727	6,307
Total	844	746	984	1,434	2,628	5,689	9,638	11,033	11,130	11,081	55,208

Notes: a. The following exchange rates were used in this and in the following subsidy tables: 1975:SR/US$3.530; 1976: SR/US$3.530; 1977: SR/US$3.505; 1978: SR/US$3.315; 1979: SR/US$3.365; 1980: SR/US$3.325; 1981: SR/US$3.415; 1982: SR/US$3.435; 1983: SR/US$3.495; 1984: SR/US$3.575.

b. Figure for agriculture 1975 includes US$13.1 million from 1974.

Table VI.9. Capital Government Subsidies
(In US$ Millions)

	1975	*1976*	*1977*	*1978*	*1979*	*1980*	*1981*	*1982*	*1983*	*1984*	*Total*
Agriculture	13	20	26	42	91	215	362	632	641	522	2,564
Industry	35	52	77	103	182	289	381	531	471	361	2,482
Water	29	33	36	50	87	338	629	1,244	1,393	1,279	5,119
Housing	66	243	325	468	900	1,481	1,959	2,725	2,525	2,041	12,733
PIF	72	140	214	310	517	896	1,334	2,002	1,792	1,353	8,631
Electricity	41	61	100	227	465	822	1,109	1,522	1,365	1,000	6,712
Total	256	549	778	1,201	2,243	4,041	5,775	8,656	8,186	6,557	38,241

Table VI.10. Total Government Subsidies: US$ Millions

	1975	*1976*	*1977*	*1978*	*1979*	*1980*	*1981*	*1982*	*1983*	*1984*	*Total*
Agriculture	64	71	94	147	221	427	716	1,207	1,466	1,947	6,361
Industry[a]	35	52	77	103	182	289	381	531	471	361	2,482
Water	166	136	140	160	195	447	1,808	2,416	2,545	2,405	10,418
Electricity	88	138	245	496	934	1,420	1,882	2,603	2,391	2,161	12,358
Housing[b]	66	243	325	468	900	1,481	1,959	2,725	2,525	2,041	12,733
PIF[a]	72	140	214	310	517	896	1,334	2,002	1,792	1,353	8,631
Food[b]	411	170	200	241	431	902	1,464	1,303	458	727	6,307
Saudia[b]	7	32	48	47	70	95	253	118	0	0	670
Fuel[b]	191	313	421	662	1,420	3,771	5,615	6.784	7,669	6,642	33,488
Total	1,100	1,295	1,762	2,635	4,871	9,730	15,412	19,689	19,317	17,638	93,448

Notes: a. Only capital subsidy.
b. Only operating subsidy.

Table VI.11. Total Government Subsidies: Percentage of GDP

	1975	*1976*	*1977*	*1978*	*1979*	*1980*	*1981*	*1982*	*1983*	*1984*
Agriculture	0.1	0.1	0.1	0.2	0.2	0.3	0.5	1.0	1.4	2.1
Industry[a]	0.1	0.1	0.2	0.2	0.4	0.6	0.8	1.1	1.0	0.8
Water	0.4	0.3	0.3	0.3	0.4	0.9	3.8	5.0	5.4	5.2
Electricity	0.2	0.3	0.5	1.0	1.9	2.9	3.9	5.4	5.1	4.7
Housing[a]	0.1	0.5	0.7	0.9	1.8	3.0	4.1	5.7	5.4	4.4
PIF[a]	0.2	0.3	0.5	0.6	1.1	1.8	2.8	4.2	3.8	2.9
Food[b]	0.9	0.4	0.4	0.5	0.9	1.8	3.0	2.7	1.0	1.6
Saudia[b]	—	0.1	0.1	0.1	0.1	0.2	0.5	0.2	—	—
Fuel[b]	2.4	2.7	3.7	5.2	9.7	19.1	31.0	39.6	39.3	36.1
Total	2.4	2.7	3.7	5.2	9.7	19.1	31.0	39.6	39.3	36.1

Notes: a. Only capital subsidy.
b. Only operating subsidy.

Table VI.12. Total Government Subsidies: Percentage of Oil Revenues

	1975	*1976*	*1977*	*1978*	*1979*	*1980*	*1981*	*1982*	*1983*	*1984*
Agriculture	0.2	0.2	0.3	0.4	0.5	0.5	0.7	1.7	4.0	6.3
Industry[a]	0.1	0.2	0.3	0.4	0.7	1.1	1.4	2.0	1.8	1.4
Water	0.6	0.5	0.5	0.6	0.7	1.6	6.8	9.2	9.8	9.5
Electricity	0.3	0.5	0.9	1.8	3.5	5.2	7.1	9.9	9.3	8.6
Housing[a]	0.3	0.9	1.3	1.7	3.4	5.5	7.4	10.4	9.8	8.1
PIF[a]	0.3	0.5	0.8	1.1	1.9	3.3	5.0	7.6	6.9	5.4
Food[b]	1.6	0.7	0.8	0.9	1.6	3.3	5.5	5.0	1.8	2.9
Saudia[b]	—	0.1	0.2	0.2	0.3	0.4	1.0	0.4	—	—
Fuel[b]	0.7	1.2	1.6	2.4	5.3	13.9	21.2	25.8	29.7	26.3
Total	4.3	5.0	6.7	9.6	17.8	34.8	56.3	72.0	73.0	68.4

Notes: a. Only capital subsidy.
b. Only operating subsidy.

Table VI.13. Total Government Subsidies: Percentage of Government Expenditures

	1975	*1976*	*1977*	*1978*	*1979*	*1980*	*1981*	*1982*	*1983*	*1984*
Agriculture	0.3	0.2	0.2	0.3	0.4	0.6	0.9	1.7	2.3	3.2
Industry[a]	0.2	0.2	0.3	0.4	0.8	1.2	1.6	2.2	2.0	1.6
Water	0.7	0.6	0.6	0.6	0.8	1.8	7.5	10.1	10.9	10.5
Electricity	0.4	0.6	1.0	2.0	3.8	5.8	7.9	10.9	10.2	9.4
Housing[a]	0.3	1.0	1.4	1.9	3.7	6.0	8.2	11.4	10.8	8.9
PIF[a]	0.3	0.6	0.9	1.3	2.1	3.6	5.6	8.4	7.7	5.9
Food[b]	1.8	0.7	0.9	1.0	1.8	3.7	6.1	5.5	2.0	3.2
Saudia[b]	—	0.1	0.2	0.2	0.3	0.4	1.1	0.5	—	—
Fuel[b]	0.8	1.3	1.8	2.7	5.8	15.3	23.4	28.5	32.8	29.0
Total	4.7	5.5	7.4	10.4	19.5	38.4	62.2	79.3	78.6	71.8

Notes: a. Only capital subsidy.
b. Only operating subsidy.

Table VI.14. Total Government Subsidies Per Capita (US$)

	1975	*1976*	*1977*	*1978*	*1979*	*1980*	*1981*	*1982*	*1983*	*1984*
Agriculture	8	9	11	16	24	44	70	113	132	170
Industry[a]	5	6	9	12	19	29	37	50	42	32
Water	32	17	16	18	21	46	177	227	230	210
Electricity	12	17	29	56	100	145	184	244	216	189
Housing[a]	9	30	38	52	96	151	191	256	228	178
PIF[a]	9	17	25	35	55	91	130	188	162	118
Food[b]	54	21	24	27	46	92	143	122	41	64
Saudia[b]	1	4	6	5	8	10	25	11	0	0
Fuel[b]	25	39	50	74	152	385	549	636	692	580
Total	136	152	197	279	496	949	1,437	1,734	1,610	1,370

Notes: a. Only capital subsidy.
b. Only operating subsidy.

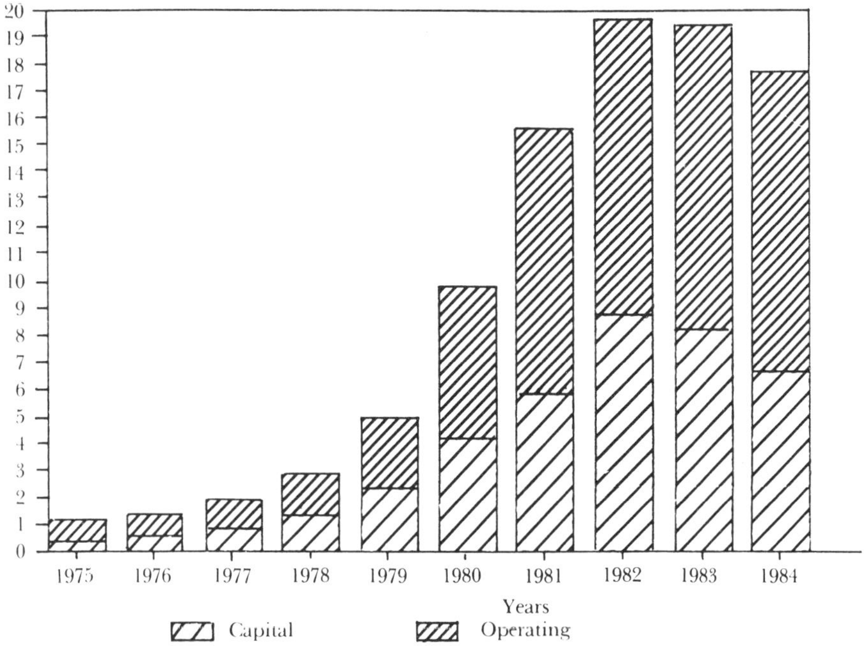

Figure VI.1. Saudi Arabian Government Subsidies (In US$Billions)

plus capital allocations for that year alone. The resulting figure is somewhat in excess of US$11.8 billion, or 45 percent of oil revenues in 1984; and these partial subsidy allocations in one year plus military expenditures represented roughly 80 percent of oil revenues; if this subsidy figure is further reduced to include only consumption-oriented subsidies (see p. 116) it represents about 31 percent of oil revenues and when combined with military expenditures, they account for 65 percent of oil revenues. All of this indicates a huge budgetary drain, even on an annual cash basis.

In the first instance, these numbers are large because subsidies are many and large. But they have become larger relative to GDP, government expenditures, and especially relative to oil revenues, *because* oil revenues have declined so dramatically in recent years. Of course, this increase is a direct result of the nature of the Saudi economy that is so heavily based on the depletion of oil and dependent on the vagaries of the international oil market. It is precisely this situation, the dramatic impact of a downturn in oil market on the domestic economy, which should be avoided through appropriate policy and planning. Has Saudi Arabia used subsidies in large part to compensate for the depletion of oil? If not, then future generations are subsidizing the present generation of Saudis.

IMPACT AND EVALUATION OF SUBSIDIES

In the previous section, the significance of government subsidies, in absolute size and relative to a variety of indicators, such as oil income, GDP, budget allocation, and population, has been established. But what did the government and people of Saudi Arabia receive for these exceptionally large subsidies? A complete answer to this question would alone be the content of an entire book. For our purpose, some general comments are called for, followed by a more detailed evaluation of one or two of the subsidies in question.

As a rule, the government had certain targets or objectives in the implementation of each subsidy program. The first question in each case is whether the objectives were appropriate. Second: Were the specific programs designed to achieve the objectives in an optimal manner? Both of these questions deserve a few general comments.

Were the objectives of the subsidy programs appropriate? First of all, it is difficult to disassociate appropriateness of an objective from its cost. Clearly, it may be desirable for social reasons, to have farms producing wheat in Saudi Arabia. But this may be a desirable goal if it can be achieved at an overall subsidy level that amounts to say, 200 percent of the world price of wheat, but it may not be desirable if the cost is 2,000 percent. Second, in assessing the appropriateness of any policy objective in a resource-depleting economy such as Saudi Arabia's, the nature of the economy must clearly be kept in focus. In this regard, the question is whether the expenditure on the subsidy results in a sufficiently high rate of return, in the form of future non-oil income, to compensate for the depletion of oil. In other words, government expenditures, or subsidies, should be motivated in large part by long-run economic reasons, as opposed to short-term social expediency. Clearly, some of the subsidies, such as food and housing, may yield no future income, but may be implemented for purely social, as opposed to economic, reasons. However, if *all* of the government expenditures, originating from oil, were to be targeted toward nonproductive ends, then the long-run outlook for the Saudi economy would be dismal.

In Table VI.15, a rough, general, and judgmental classification of the subsidies by their objective is given, with an average share of the categories in total subsidies. The share of electricity and water (desalinated) used by households is classified as social; as they are directly consumed by houeholds; food subsidies are classified as social for similar reasons.

Table VI.15. Classification of Subsidies by Overall Objective (Percentage of Total Subsidies for 1975-1984)

Classification Subsidies	*Largely Social Objectives with Little Impact on Development of Competitive Industries*	*Mixture of Objectives*	*Largely Productive Objectives*
Electricity	7.4	0.1	3.2
Water	12.2	—	—
Fuels	—	29.6	—
Agriculture	5.5	—	—
Food subsidies	6.6	—	—
Saudia (operating)	—	0.7	—
REDF	18.6	—	—
PIF	—	—	12.5
SIDF	—	—	3.7
Total	50.3	30.3	19.4

Housing subsidies are classified as social because housing does not directly result in productive industries. Agricultural subsidies are classfied as social because the size of these subsidies have been multiples (e.g., the case of wheat) of the world price; but more correctly, a part of this has been clearly productive. It should be noted that these were the objectives and not necessarily the end results.

Were the subsidies designed in the most efficient way to achieve their intended goals? As a general rule, economic efficiency requires that subsidies be applied directly at the source. Thus, if production increases are called for, general production subsidies should be given. Indirect input subsidies, in the form of cheap electricity, to stimulate production result in distortionary effects as they artificially promote the inefficient (not reflecting opportunity cost) use of electricity. With this in mind, it is evident that in Saudi Arabia most of the production subsidies have not been targeted at the source. In agriculture, if the goal was to increase output, capital, energy, and water subsidies have been clearly distortionary. In industry, if the goal was to increase output, capital, electricity, energy, and water subsidies have been distortionary. In both cases, general production subsidies should be given. Indirect input subsidies, in the form of cheap electricity, to stimulate production result in distortionary effects as they artificially promote the inefficient (not reflecting opportunity cost) use of electricity. In electricity generation and water, if the goal was to provide cheap electricity and water, capital and fuel subsidies have been distortionary; instead, capital and fuels

TELEPHONE RENEWAL POLICY
543 - 7368

Before dialing **TELEPHONE RENEWAL NUMBER (543 - 7368),** please have pen and paper ready to write down the code word for the day.

YOUR CALL WILL RENEW ALL ITEMS CHECKED OUT TO YOU THAT QUALIFY FOR PHONE RENEWAL.

WRITE DOWN VERIFICATION CODE:

* The recording will supply a special code word for the day
* SAVE for verification of your phone renewal

RECORDED MESSAGE WILL ASK FOR:

* Name and ASU ID number
* Daytime telephone number

NEW DUE DATE:

* Telephone renewal will not inform you of your new due date
* You are responsible for knowing the current length of your loan period
* Stop by or call the Circulation Desk at (543-8520) 48 hours or more after renewing materials to verify your phone renewal and obtain your new due date

PHONE RENEWALS WILL BE DENIED FOR THE FOLLOWING REASONS:

* If materials were checked out with special permission
* If materials were obtained through Interlibrary Loan
* If materials are being recalled by another patron
* If materials are from special departments (e.g., Microforms, Reserve)
* If borrower has delinquent account, expired ID, or otherwise currently suspended borrowing privileges

ALL CURRENT LOAN POLICIES APPLY TO PHONE RENEWALS

ASU WEST CAMPUS LIBRARY

should have been priced at their respective opportunity costs and then the charges or fees should have been subsidized. In the case of housing and food, if the goal was to have houses and cheap food for citizens, then the method of subsidy is efficient; but if the goal was to distribute income, then this could have been done more efficiently by direct transfers, with the choice of expenditure pattern left to the consumer.

As has been mentioned earlier, it should be noted that subsidies are the most efficient method (as opposed to tariffs) to protect infant industries, industries in which a country enjoys a long-run comparative advantage. But subsidies, if justified on these grounds, should be targeted toward the specific industries where long-run comparative advantage is identified, and they should be targeted at the source, as opposed to an input such as capital, which would introduce distortionary effects. In the case of subsidies in Saudi Arabia, these two criteria have not been adhered to. Industrial subsidies have not generally been given as the source, but have been afforded to the major inputs, such as capital, fuels, electricity, and water.

In most developing countries, tariffs, as opposed to subsidies, are used to promote infant industries. Although this is a less efficient method than subsidies, it is justified because of financial constraints. In Saudi Arabia, financial constraints have been less important and thus subsidies, as opposed to commercial policy (tariffs), should have been used for infant industries. This has been largely the case as tariffs have, up to recent years (see Chapter XII), played a relatively minor role in Saudi Arabia.

Agricultural and water subsidies are two cases that deserve more detailed discussion. The goal or policy objective of agricultural subsidies are basically threefold:

- food security
- employment of Saudis in agriculture and related social objectives
- development of agriculture

Since the Arab oil embargo of 1973-1974, Saudi Arabia has felt that food security is important because food exports to Saudi Arabia could be cut off if any country wanted to change its oil policy. Unfortunately, the objective is somewhat questionable and its implementation has been inefficient. In today's world economy, embargoes of anything, let alone food, have been shown to be ineffective; cases such as the export of high-tech and oil service equipment from the United States to the Soviet Union, can be cited. In the case of food, embargoes are unlikely to work because so many countries produce most items and producing countries have excess supplies of most food items, for now and in the foreseeable future. But more importantly, Saudi Arabia, after making enormous expenditures on agriculture, is not much closer to food security. The ratio of domestic production to consumption is up in most cases; over the period 1973-1984, this ratio for broiler chickens has increased from 41.5 percent to 45 percent; for eggs, from 54.8 percent to 100.4 percent; for meat, from 17.9 percent to 36.7 percent; for milk, from 36 percent to 50 percent; and for wheat, Saudi Arabia has become the net exporter (SAMA, 1988). However, self-sufficiency has declined in some other areas. For instance, although Saudi Arabia is now more than self-sufficient in wheat, its imports of other cereals have increased; although it produces more wheat, the seeds are imported; although it produces more chicken, its imports of "pure-bred" chickens and feed are up. A more cost-effective and viable avenue to achieve food security would have been to expand the storage of all essential food items. But the overriding consideration was social.

In the social goals-related agriculture, the performance has not been much better. In 1975, employment in agriculture totaled 695,000, or 40 percent of the total, and declined to 224,000 in 1983, or 5.9 percent of the total employment (Ministry of Planning, 1984 and 1985). The decline in employment may have resulted from increased efficiency, but clearly, agricultural employment was not increased. Moreover, casual observation would lead to the conclusion that in the large company farms and in the large private farms, a substantial proportion of the employees are foreigners as foreign know-how is a necessity. Additionally, the major beneficiaries of the wheat subsidies and other agricultural subsidies have not been the small farmers, but a few large companies and private landowners. Nearly all of the growth in output has come from these large, modern, capital-intensive farms. The Saudi Arabian Monetary Agency reports that in 1984, the Kingdom produced 1.3 million tons of wheat, and 200 millon chickens. But a single farm grew over 100,000 tons of wheat and a single poultry operation raised 75 million chickens. Similarly, the Saudi Arabian Agricultural Bank reports that in 1983, 263 projects, that is, 0.67 percent of the number of loans granted, received 31.3 percent of the total value of loans. Farmers in the traditional sector are not served by the bank to the same extent as are large commercial farmers. A survey of Jizan has shown that only 5 percent of the farmers had benefited from SAAB loans.

The government has not fostered its social goals through its land distribution program. Under the Public Land Distribution Ordinance of 1388 (1968), plots of 5 to 10 hectares were to be given to individuals to farm; land grants of up to 400 hectares to companies and organizations, and as large as 4,000 hectares for special projects were also allowed. However, the maximum limit on size of distributed land was clearly exceeded, and a few companies and projects received disproportionate shares as can be seen in Table VI.16. Clearly, it is not so much the land that is the subsidy, but all that goes with it; namely, the access to the other agricultural subsidies.

Table VI.16. Plots of Land Distributed Among Individuals, Projects, and Companies (To mid-1985)

Beneficiary	*Number*	*Percent*	*Area (hectares)*	*Percent*
Individuals	41,018	95	241,628	36
Projects	2,151	5	261,793	39
Companies	10	—	164,934	25
Total	43,179	100	668,355	100

Source: SAMA (1987, 103).

The other goal of agricultural subsidies was simply to develop Saudi agriculture. The minister of agriculture has said that after surveying the resources of the Kingdom—land, water, and climate—it was determined that Saudi Arabia could establish a small, efficient agricultural sector that would be competitive. The land was there. The water was available in underground acquifers. And most importantly, the Ministry's calculations reportedly show that most of this water would not be used for anything else but for agriculture, because the cost of desalinated water is lower than the cost of treating underground water.

Although one may question the methods of achieving these goals, as well as the goals themselves, it should be noted, that at least the size of agricultural subsidies are not seen as all cost by the Ministry of Agriculture. It has been pointed out to the authors that the government was acutely aware of the fact that the magnitude of the subsidies resulted in abnormally high rates of return in agriculture. The Ministry of Agriculture's studies maintain that the cost (excluding water and land) of producing a ton of wheat on the most efficient farms is around $200 per ton. The lion's share of wheat and other related subsidies were not, therefore, costs to the society at large because they were in fact, income transfers, in the form of large profits, to stimulate future agricultural investments.

Although wheat input, and capital subsidies are substantial, the most important subsidized input may have been water. This was discussed earlier and the figures need no further elaboration. But the unfortunate aspect of the water subsidy is that it was not necessary. First, the input subsidies could have been targeted only toward water-conserving equipment, as opposed to giving implicit incentives for water-wasting equipment, such as central pivot systems. And second, cheap loans for drilling wells should have reflected the opportunity of the cost of water to society at large. In the case of industrial and household users of water, the question is: What economic purpose is served by selling water, at least desalinated water, below its opportunity cost?

But again the most unfortunate aspect of the subsidy in agriculture and water has been the preponderance of indirect subsidies at the source. Namely, in the case of agriculture, capital subsidies have introduced the distortionary effect of excessive employment of capital-intensive equipment to the extent that capital has been priced below its opportunity cost; water subsidies have encouraged the excessive consumption of water in agriculture; and fuel subsidies have encouraged artificially energy-intensive methods (largely in the form of pumping water from deep acquifers) to the extent that energy pricing has not reflected opportunity costs. All of these distortionary effects in agriculture could have been avoided through direct production subsidies.

SUMMARY

The critical issue is not the exact size of subsidies, but their effects and implications for the future. Clearly, the quantified subsidies for water pumping, education, health, infrastructure, and the like, and the fact that the method used for the calculation of capital subsidies results in underestimation because the annuity component is omitted.

To assess their general implication, one has to keep in mind the oil-based nature of the Saudi economy. In other countries that do not rely so heavily on a depletable resource for income, subsidies are ultimately financed from renewable sources of output in the form of taxes. As a result, a social subsidy in the United States does not carry the same implications. But in Saudi Arabia, where in the long run, other sources of income must be established to compensate for oil depletion, the conclusion is different. If oil income is depleted to finance subsidies that do not result in competitive industries, then Saudi Arabia faces a grim economic future when all of its oil is depleted. Put differently, Saudi Arabia is making an intergenerational choice on the economic benefits every time it spends a riyal of oil income. If it spends it all on nonproductive subsidies, then the decision is to rob future generations in favor of the present; and if Saudi Arabia employs subsidies in a distortionary manner, then losses are incurred by present and future generations.

The task of assessing in detail which expenditures and subsidies are consistent with the long-term comparative advantage of the Saudi economy is beyond the scope of this book. But some general conclusions can be made. Subsidies to promote industrial production have not been targeted toward specific sectors, but have been made generally available. The major subsidies have not been afforded at the source (general production), but have instead been provided in the form of subsidized inputs that have had distortionary effects. The magnitude of these distortions and the resulting economic cost may be quite different from the size of subsidies; this magnitude has not itself been calculated. The majority of subsidies have been directed toward social-consumption goals as opposed to productive ends. Given Saudi Arabia's relative strong financial position, appropriately targeted subsidies, as opposed to tariffs, are the preferred policy to promote infant industries.

In the case of industrial subsidies, the question is whether the resulting industries that have developed, will be competitive in the long run, and on the world market without subsidies. The answer to this question requires a case-by-case analysis. A partial answer might be gauged from an examination of the non-oil exports of Saudi Arabia relative to the accumulated industrial incentives afforded by the government. This is at best, a partial answer, as some industries may be import substituting and/or the subsidies could be fruitful in the more distant future. In 1984, Saudi Arabia's total exports were US$37 billion (SR 1.4 billion); of this US$36.4 billion (SR127.8 billion) was classified as fuels and lubricants; of the remaining US$0.6billion (SR2.1 billion), US$0.4 billion (SR1.4 billion) was classified as refined materials (i.e., petrochemicals) (Ministry of Finance and National Economy, 1984). In 1987, non-oil exports constituted roughly 10 percent of the total; the two single largest components of these were wheat and petrochemicals. A casual conclusion indicates that most of the subsidies have done little to promote a viable non-oil sector to compensate for oil depletion; or at least, very little export diversification away from oil has been achieved thus far.

Saudi Arabia has used subsidies largely as a means of distributing oil wealth. These programs have at least resulted in increased consumption even if they are given with income distribution or productive objectives in mind. For example, subsidies for electricity generation translate into cheaper rates for electricity usage, in turn resulting in higher electricity consumption. The consumption has been in some instances plainly wasteful, such as leaving air-conditioning on while on vacation. Similar stories can be told in the case of water and fuels. In the case of subsidies afforded to nontraded good sectors such as housing, there will be no impact on future exports. Also, the subsidies are not targeted appropriately; they are not largely at the source and thus introduce distortionary effects in production and in consumption.

In retrospect, subsidies were initiated in the early 1970s to distribute oil wealth. But in time, given rising oil revenues during the 1970s, subsidies proliferated in every direction; with insufficient attention given to their productive impact. Moreover, all the while a strong domestic constituency has been established for the maintenance of most subsidies, making policy reversals more difficult. Since 1981, with declining oil revenues, it has become clear that the government cannot afford to maintain existing levels of subsidies, to finance large military outlays, development projects, foreign assistance, and other ongoing expenditures. There is clearly an important role for subsidies in the Saudi economy, but a comprehensive evaluation is called for to curtail and eliminate many subsidy programs, to retarget other subsidies more efficiently, and toward more productive objectives with a focus on sectors with a long-run comparative advantage. The government has recognized some of these deficiencies of subsidies as conveyed in the Fourth Development Plan and has already reduced some key subsidies, like the one on premium gasoline (the price was doubled in November 1987). But the subsidies that are more socially difficult to reduce, such as electricity, are likely to be more painful and drawn out. The question is, therefore, whether the government will reverse these policies at a sufficient pace.

NOTE

1. This information was discussed in private conversations with Hossein Askari.

Chapter VII

Domestic Policies to Promote Growth to Compensate for Oil Depletion: Private Sector Development and Primary Industries

PRIVATE SECTOR DEVELOPMENT

Introduction

Economic activity in Saudi Arabia is dominated by the production and export of oil. In addition to the direct impact on national income, changes in oil production and prices (terms of trade), play a central role in indirectly determining government expenditures and the pace of economic growth in the non-oil sector. Government expenditures stimulate domestic demand, thus encouraging domestic investment activity in the non-oil sector. Given the small size of the domestic productive base, most of the domestic demand has been met through increased imports, by both the public as well as the private sector. Higher imports have in themselves created increased domestic value added through trade, transportation, financial services, and in the case of capital goods, installation. Much of the induced domestic investment over the past ten years has been in the provision of nontraded inputs to the services and construction sectors.

Growth in the private sector, therefore, has in the past, been largely dependent on—and oriented toward—the government sector. With the inevitable decrease in government activity, due to the completion of infrastructural projects and the downturn in the oil market, the private sector has been adversely affected.

Private Sector Size

The size of the private sector (in current prices) is small, though growing (in large part due to declining oil output) (see Table IX.1). In 1981-1982, oil accounted for 64.7 percent, and non-oil 35.3 percent of GDP; of the non-oil component, the government accounted for 44.2 percent, and the private sector for 55.8 percent. In 1987, oil accounted for 26.4 percent, and non-oil 73.6 percent of GDP; of the non-oil component, the government accounted for 39.2 percent, and the private sector for 60.8 percent. Thus, the private sector accounted for only 19.7 percent of the total economy in 1981-1982 and 44.7 percent.

The growth in the non-oil sector of the economy has been largely determined by responses to rising demand for nontraded goods and services, especially for the nongovernment services and construction sectors. These two sectors have accounted for a gradually expanding share of total non-oil GDP. However, most recently, their relative importance has changed. While the share of construction activity fell, that of nongovernmental services rose. The relatively more rapid growth of the services sector reflects the changes in the economy as infrastructural development has been largely completed and housing requirements have been met. Despite steady expansion in the producing sectors, including agriculture, manufacturing, electricity, gas, and water, their share in the total non-oil output has actually fallen (see Table VII.1). Overall, the producing sector grew only at a real average annual rate of 0.7 percent between 1980 and 1985, largely due to the decline in construction activity. Excluding construction, this rate is over 10 times as high, or at 8.5 percent per year. The service sector, however, grew at a real annual rate of 4.5 percent per year.

Given the dominant role played by government spending through substantial transfer payments and investment, the pattern of aggregate domestic expenditure is principally determined by budgetary developments. This pattern, however, could be reversed since all major government projects have been largely completed.

To encourage and expand the role of the private sector, and to—at least—limit its decline in the face of reduced government projects, the government is searching for ways to expand the private sector's contribution to the economy. Indeed, the implementation of one of the stated objectives of the Fourth Development Plan (Ministry of Planning, 1985) "To continue with real structural changes in the Kingdom's economy to produce a diversified economic base with due emphasis on industry and agriculture", will depend on private sector initiatives.

The Dilemma of the Private Sector

Throughout this book, different facets of the private sector in Saudi Arabia have been discussed. At this juncture, it may be useful to examine some of

Table VII.1. Sectoral Shares of Non-Oil GDP[a]
(Based on Constant 1979-1980 Prices)
(In Percent)

	1979-1980		*1984-1985*		*1989-1990*	
Producing Sectors						
Agriculture	3.5		4.1		4.8	
Other Mining	1.0		1.1		1.1	
Other Manufacturing	4.8		7.3		10.4	
Petrochemicals	—		—		2.6	
Utilities	0.2		0.5		0.5	
Construction	32.3		23.5		17.7	
Subtotal	41.8		36.5		37.1	
Service Sectors						
Trade	13.4		15.8		15.5	
Transport	11.8		13.0		14.3	
Real Estate	8.2		7.1		6.2	
Finance	3.4		5.0		6.6	
Other Services	3.9		4.5		4.6	
Government	17.5		18.1		15.7	
Subtotal	58.2		63.5		62.9	
Total Non-Oil Sectors	100.0	(34.8)	100.0	(60.2)	100.0	(57.1)
		(65.2)		(39.8)		(42.9)
(Gross Domestic Product)		(100.0)		(100.0)		(100.0)

Note: a. Figures in brackets relate to Gross Domestic Product.
Source: Ministry of Planning (1985).

the critical issues facing the private sector—agriculture, and manufacturing and services.

Agriculture. Saudi Arabia is clearly committed to promoting the development of its agricultural sector.[1] The Ministry of Agriculture and Water believed that, after a careful assessment of domestic resources, the potential for a medium-sized and efficient agricultural sector in Saudi Arabia was indicated. This potential was further reinforced by social considerations, such as the opportunities of agricultural employment for Saudis and food security (see Chapter VI for an evaluation of these policies). Generous and varied input subsidies were afforded to this sector to stimulate production and to give farmers substantial profits to finance further development in agriculture. The phenomenal increases in production (see Chapter I) in certain areas, such as wheat, cannot be denied. But what are some of the current and future probems facing this sector of the economy?

The government's agricultural input subsidies have been clearly distortionary (see Chapter VI). The major effect has been to induce excessive consumption of water and distorted employment of cheap capital inputs. The Ministry of Agriculture appreciates these difficulties and intends to move to provide production subsidies and to abolish input subsidies. In the meantime, the Ministry is trying to subsidize inputs to the extent that it can reduce distortionary incentives, such as water-saving irrigation techniques and more appropriate implements. This will be at best, a slow process and will be met by a great deal of resistance on the part of farmers. But the wisdom and economic rationale of correcting the impact of one input subsidy by granting another input subsidy, is questionable; efficiency requires the elimination of input subsidies, not cross-subsidization.

The government production subsidy for wheat resulted in production exceeding domestic consumption. At first this was relieved by storage. Since then the purchase price of wheat was reduced from roughly US$1,000 (SR 3,500) to US$350 (SR 2,000) per ton. Still production was deemed as excessive. Then acreage quotas were enforced. This led to increasing yields. Finally, the government has placed strict production quotas on the large farms. For the future, the Ministry intends to reduce wheat subsidies further and to replace it with smaller production subsidies for other crops, to achieve a more diversified agricultural sector. The Ministry feels that the total cost (excluding only water and land subsidies) of wheat production on the efficient farms is now less than US$200 per ton. If this is indeed the case, then significant strides have been made in Saudi agriculture.

For the future, the Ministry is clearly assuming that Saudi agriculture has matured substantially; that the substantial profits of the past, resulting from generous subsidies, will be reinvested in the future diversification of agriculture but with reduced government subsidies; and that water from underground acquifiers will continue to be available at reasonable depths. If in fact, the level of efficiency as envisaged by the Ministry has been achieved, then water may be the only bottleneck. But if not, the private sector may be more reluctant to invest in other areas of agricultural production, knowing full well that government generosity will not be as high as in the past and that it will be reduced as output increases. Furthermore, the agriculture sector has been somewhat "spoiled" and its expectation may exceed future government generosity.

Manufacturing and Services. The nonagriculture sector has also received generous government assistance. The manufacturing sector in Saudi Arabia is still insignificant, and has not matured sufficiently to compete in regional, much less world, markets.

The problems facing the manufacturing and services sectors are numerous.[2] First, the government, in the name of free enterprise, has given little direction to the private sector. It has been left to the private sector to determine Saudi Arabia's areas of long-run comparative advantage, but without knowledge of long-run government policies. From the government's perspective, SIDF checks to ensure that private sector projects are profitable and are in accord with long-term comparative advantage. The results of this policy are questionable.[3] Second, and largely as a result of the absence of a planned industrialization policy, there are too many companies that receive government financing (SIDF) for the production of a given product; that is, too many companies given the size of the Saudi or even GCC markets. For instance, there are already (in 1988) three companies making refrigerators, with three more companies on the way. The government feels that this enhances competition and will, in time, result in competitive exports. The private sector, on the other hand, feels that one company would be sufficient and with appropriate government incentives, could capture economies of scale and maybe compete in regional and international markets.

Third, there are a variety of uncertainties facing the private sector that are claimed to be the most disruptive for progress—these are the financial environment, untimely government payments, and an absence of stated long-run policies on certain key subsidies. The banks by and large, stopped commercial lending activities because of the inability to recover their loans (see Chapter X). Thus, bank financing is unavailable at a time when it is critically needed. Some businesses allege that government payments on contracts have been delayed, resulting in slow payment to subcontractors, and in turn to employees. This alleged policy has caused serious bankruptcies and has had a very detrimental trickle-down effect on the rest of the economy. In the last three months of 1987, however, the government made a serious effort to speed up payments to contractors. The absence of stated long-run policies on the price of key inputs, such as fuels, electricity, and water, introduces great uncertainty into business investment decisions.

There appears to be a major schism between the government and the private sector. The government feels that it has given the private sector infrastructure and subsidies, and it is now up to it to produce. The rumblings in the private sector are seen as nothing more than businessmen trying to get more. While the private sector, truly appreciating the government's provision of infrastructure, believes that more direction and certainty are required before they can reach its potential.

Privatization in Saudi Arabia

In order to enable private sector growth and expansion, the government has already provided a wide array of incentives such as infrastructure and concessionary loans through SIDF. An additional avenue to encourage private sector participation is the privatization of public enterprises through the sale of government equity.

The government of Saudi Arabia has studied, and already begun, the process of privatizing, publicly-held companies. The major entity already partially privatized is SABIC. The public has acquired, through stock purchases, 30 percent of SABIC's equity capital. In addition, the Saudi Arabian Public Transport Company (SAPTCO) and the electricity companies are now partially privatized. Foreign-owned banks have also been "saudized." The complete privatization of SABIC and other government projects is under study.

The sale of government entities to the public, however, has done little to stimulate private sector activity. Its main impact has been to open up avenues for the participation of private sector capital. In the case of Saudi Arabia, privatization of some government-owned enterprises has been coupled with guaranteed dividends that only places additional burdens on the government. In the case of SABIC, it is still run by the same management, the only difference being that the private sector owns some shares. As a matter of fact, partial privatization coupled with guaranteed dividends, may only hamper the course of complete privatization as it provides little incentive for the current management to improve operations. Clearly, the government should develop plans that will, in the short-run, increase the participation of the private sector, and in the long-run, induce added private sector contribution.

There is little doubt that one of the overriding concerns of the government with privatization, is to find new avenues for fostering private sector activities. With the precipitous decline in construction activity and related services, the government is faced with having to fill the gap and to find ways to employ idle capital and labor. In addition to selling off government enterprises, contracting of government services to private sector firms is one way of satisfying that objective. Through this process government activity is essentially transferred to the private sector. But this policy may achieve little if government employment does not decline, while government services are transferred to the private sector. Thus, it may only result in underemployment in the government sector and give only the appearance of a more viable private sector.[4] Already many maintenance contracts for physical infrastructure have been contracted out and the government is investigating other areas for contracting services. The problem with contracting out these services is that it may not necessarily lead to improved efficiency, especially as there may not be adequately qualified local contractors to perform these functions. The dearth of qualified competition for such contracts reduces the likelihood that the firm, receiving a certain contract, prices it competitively. If foreign firms are asked to bid on these contracts, this certainly would defeat the intention of generating work for local companies. The government, therefore, faces a difficult situation to generate work for private local firms since there are no assurances that it can do so effectively and efficiently. The government has, therefore, insisted on a minimum percent of subcontracting to domestic firms.

As far as the sale of public enterprises is concerned, it was demonstrated in Chapter VI, that operations of the majority of public enterprises in the Kingdom are subsidized. If the government expects to reduce the role of the public sector by turning over some of the public enterprises, without having to continually subsidize operations, the operations of these enterprises should be completely restructured; otherwise, the government will have to sell its assets at a substantial discount, in addition to providing guarantees for the profitability of these ventures.

DEVELOPMENT OF PRIMARY INDUSTRIES

The development of primary industries has been based on the idea of exploiting Saudi Arabia's comparative advantage in hydrocarbon resources. To this end, SABIC has made substantial investments in developing a primary petrochemical industry.[5] It has also invested in steel mills, fertilizer factories, and a plastics factory. A detailed breakdown of SABIC industries is provided in Table VII.2. SABIC has invested approximately US$11 billion in capital on its "first generation" industrial projects and plans to spend an additional US$4.4 billion on "second generation" projects, which will include training, research and development, and establishment of a number of fertilizer, mineral, plastic, and petrochemical complexes with a total capacity of about 3.7 million tons for producing 20 downstream products (SABIC, 1986, 9 and 31). The investment on projects is expected to be broken down as follows: 50 percent on petrochemicals; 20 percent on minerals; 22 percent on plastics and rubber; 5 percent on fertilizers; and 3 percent on training, research, and development (Ministry of Planning, 1985, 209-210).

Saudi Arabia decided for two reasons, to organize investment in primary industry in the form of government enterprises. First, the financial commitment toward the development of these industries was too large a burden for private companies to shoulder, and second, since these industries are intrinsically linked to the oil sector, the objectives of private firms may at times interfere with national oil policies (Johany et al., 1986, 119).

Another feature of SABIC's investment policy is the joint venture approach toward project implementation. As can be seen in Table VII.2, almost all of SABIC's projects are implemented in conjunction with a foreign partner, which ostensibly, is supposed to benefit SABIC in three areas as Johany et al. (1986) elaborate:

- To provide incentives to the foreign partner to ensure ongoing viability of a project;
- To provide the local firm with the foreign partner's established worldwide marketing network
- To provide ongoing technical and managerial skills to the joint-venture.

Table VII.2. SABIC Industries and Affiliates

Industry Type	Project & Location	Partner	Feedstock	Products	Annual Capacity 1,000 ton	Start-up
Mineral	1. Saudi Iron & Steel Co. (HADEED) Al-Jubail	SABIC DEG W. Germany	Natural Gas Scrap Iron Iron Ore Limestone	Steel Rods and Bars	800	1983
	2. Jeddah Steel Rolling Mill Co. (SULB) Jeddah	SABIC KORF W. Germany	Steel Billets	Steel Rods and Bars	140	1962 (Expanded 1979)
Fertilizer	1. Saudi Arabian Fertilizer Co. (SAFCO) Al-Jubail	SABIC: 41$ Employees: 10% Public: 49%	Methane	Urea Sulphuric Acid Melamine	330 100 20	1970 1970 1st quarter 1985
	2. Al-Jubail Fertilizer Co. (SAMAD) Al-Jubail	SABIC: 50% TAIWAN Fert.: 50%	Methane	Urea	500	1983
	3. National Chemical Fertilizer Co. (IBN AL-BAYTAR)	SABIC: 50% SAFCO: 50%	Methane	Ammonia	500	1988
Petrochemical	1. Saudi Methanol Co. (AR-RAZI) Al-Jubail	SABIC: 50% Mitsubishi Gas Co.: 50%	Methane	Chemical Grade Methanol	600	1983
	2. National Methanol Co. (IBN SINA) Al-Jubail	SABIC: 50% Celanese & Texas Eastern: 50%	Methane	Chemical Grade Methanol	700	1984

	3.	Saudi Petrochemical Co. (SADAF) Al-Jubail	SABIC: 50% Pecten (Shell): 50%	Ethane Salt Benzene	Ethylene Ethylene Dichloride Crude Industr. Ethanol Styrene Caustic Soda	656 454 281 295 377	End 1984 Early 1985
	4.	Al-Jubail Petrochemical Co. (KEMY) Al-Jubail	SABIC: 50% EXXON: 50%	Ethylene Polyethylene	L.Low Density	270	End 1984
	5.	Saudi Yanbu PetrochemicalCo. (YANPET) Yanbu	SABIC: 50% MOBIL: 50%	Ethane	Ethylene Ethylene Glycol L.L. Density Polyethylene High Density Polyethylene	455 220 205 91	End 1984 1st Quarter 1985
	6.	Arabian Petrochemical Co. (PETROKEMYA) Al-Jubail	SABIC: 100%	Ethane Syrene	Ethylene Polystyrene Butene-1	500 100 50	2nd Quarter 1985 1988
	7.	Eastern Petrochemical Co. (SHARQ) Al-Jubail	SABIC: 50% Mitsubishi Gas: 50%	Ethylene	L.Low Density Polyethylene Ethylene Glycol	130 300	3rd Quarter 1985
Supporting	1.	National Industrial Gases Co. (GAS)	SABIC: 70% Saudi Partners: 30%	AIR	Nitrogen Oxygen	146 438	1984 1st Quarter 1985

(continued)

Table VII.2. (continued)

Industry Type	Project & Location	Partner	Feedstock	Products	Annual Capacity 1,000 ton	Start-up
Intermediate	1. National Plastic Co. (IBN HAYYAN) Al-Jubail	SABIC: 85% Lucky Goldstar: 15%	Ethylene Ethylene Dichloride	Vinyl Chloride Monomer Polyvinyl Chloride	330 200	1st Quarter 1986
	2. Saudi European Petrochemical Co. (IBN ZAHR) Al-Jubail	SABIC: 70% GRICHEM: 10% NESTE OY: 10%	Methanol Butane	MTBE	500	1988
Sabic & Gulf Joint Ventures	1. Bahrain Aluminum Smelter (ALBA)	SABIC: 20%	Alumina	Extruder Barrels Aluminum Blocks	170	1971
	2. Gulf Aluminum Rolling Mill Co. (GARMCO) Bahrain	SABIC: 20%	Aluminum	Aluminum Sheets and Laminates	40	1985
	3. Gulf Petrochemical Industries Co. (GPIC) Bahrain	SABIC: 33%	Methane	Ammonia Methanol	330 330	1985

Marketing Companies

1. SABIC Marketing Ltd.
As a wholly-owned affiliate of SABIC, SABIC Marketing Ltd. is charged with the task of selling SABIC's products as well as other industrial-related output.
2. SABIC Marketing Services Ltd.
Also an affiliate of SABIC Marketing Services Ltd., apart from rendering a variety of marketing services such as shipment, transportation and insurance, the company also provides customers with technical services.
3. Bahraini-Saudi Aluminum Marketing Company (BALCO).
This company, in whose capital SABIC subscribes for 25 percent, was established to market the Saudi/Bahraini share of ALBA's production.

Source: SABIC (1986).

The projects are expected to benefit from a cheap (subsidized) source of gas, which is harnessed by the Master Gas System,[6] both as feedstock and as a source of fuel. Unfortunately, because most of this gas is associated gas, the vagaries of the international oil market have played havoc with providing gas in a reliable manner. Indeed, proposed enterprises in and around the industrial cities are advised to have the capability to use both gas and fuel oil as source of energy since the continuous supply of gas cannot be guaranteed. Conversely, if the continuous supply of gas is critical for the survival of a certain industry, it may even reduce the government's ability to manipulate its oil policy.

There are two major issues regarding SABIC's projects that have been subject to controversy: Does the comparative advantage argument indeed hold, and was the choice and timing of these investments appropriate?

Calculating the cost per unit of output for SABIC's projects is difficult. There are numerous assumptions to be taken into consideration as feedstock and energy requirements may be cheaper in SABIC's projects, yet in the final analysis it is the transportation from Saudi Arabia to the markets that has the largest impact on the profitability of the venture (Fesharaki and Isaac, 1983, 118-130; Fesharaki and Yamaguchi, 1984). The true profitability of these projects is therefore highly inconclusive. It has been also argued that the product areas of the chosen industries were in depressed export markets, where demand was expected to be low for some time. On the other hand, others argued that if SABIC can weather the storm until markets improved, it would position itself advantageously for taking up market share of plants and capacity that have been reduced in other parts of the world (Fesharaki and Isaac, 1983, 118-130; Fesharaki and Yamaguchi, 1984; see also Turner 1979), as a result of the glut in world markets. Such an improvement in the petrochemicals market in fact started in 1987. And, in 1988, SABIC recorded large profits.

For most of the recently introduced joint ventures it may still be too early to judge their true long-run profitability, although many doubts have already been expressed (*Petroleum Economist,* 1984, 407-409). The assumption is that the foreign joint venture partner must have had an interest in ensuring the profitability of these ventures. While this may certainly be the case, one cannot overlook the fact that the real capital commitment of the foreign partners is usually below 10 percent, with the difference accounted for by intangibles, such as the sale of the joint venture the right to use patents, and the transfer of technology fees. Afterward, the foreign partners usually include hefty management and training fees, so that unless one is able to closely analyze operational data, it seems that the foreign partner may not have as much at stake in the long-term viability of a venture as it may at first appear. The real test of the foreign partner's commitment will be tested in a market characterized by large worldwide excess capacity.

Another inducement for the participation of foreign companies was a Saudi offer to provide large firms with a guaranteed allocation of oil at official prices for becoming a joint venture partner. The size of the allocation would be in proportion to the size of their investments. At the time some of these agreements were being entered into, the "security of supply" of oil was foremost on the minds of the joint-venture partners and, therefore, even if the projects did not become profitable, it was considered an appropriate price for guaranteed oil supplies. Naturally, this situation has changed and the security of supply is no longer as important an issue. Some of these companies have consequently requested a revision of their agreement.

Nevertheless, the investments have been made and plants are in operation. Now SABIC needs to carefully evaluate its options in furthering its expertise in the operations of these plants and to strive for actively marketing its products. The firm whose output is not likely to interfere with national oil policy should be sold to the private sector, if they have any chance of being profitable.

In conclusion, the heavy investment by Saudi Arabia in primary industries, largely petrochemicals, was motivated by economic diversification from oil and comparative advantage. The success of this policy has been questioned and its effective profitability and contribution to Saudi Arabia's economic development must await the passage of time. But given the booming markets of 1987 and 1988, SABIC appears to be highly profitable. For the future, as indigenous feedstock availability continues to decline in industrial countries, increasing input costs, SABIC's relative profitability may be further enhanced.

NOTES

1. We have greatly benefitted from discussions with H.E. Dr. Abdul-Rahman Al-Sheikh, Minister of Agriculture and Water.
2. Some of these also apply to agriculture.
3. It is alleged that several of the SIDF-approved projects were abandoned before they opened for business, but after most of the investment had been made. Others have argued that SIDF functions more like a bureaucracy than a profit-oriented lending agency, insisting on across-the-board reduction in requests, without fully comprehending the business and technology.
4. There are already an abundance of reports on underemployment in government agencies. For example, see *Middle East Economic Digest* (1985, 27).
5. SABIC was formed in 1976 as a separate entity, entrusted with the development of Saudi Arabia's primary industry.
6. US$0.5 per million BTU, compared to the international price of US$2.00 per million BTU.

Chapter VIII

Domestic Policies to Promote Growth to Compensate for Oil Depletion: Commercial and Exchange Rate Policies

COMMERCIAL POLICIES

Background

Commercial policy in Saudi Arabia has been quite liberal in comparison to the majority of developing countries. In 1988, however, tariffs were increased substantially for revenue reasons (see Chapter XI). Import licenses are not required. Foreign exchange for ımports is freely available. Export proceeds are free of exchange controls. And except for the prohibition of reexports of certain goods that receive government subsidies, exports are free of restrictions. Goods originating in the GCC are exempt from tariffs provded that 40 percent or more of the value added in the GCC, and that at least 51 percent of the ownership of the firm that produces the commodity is owned by GCC countries or citizens. Until the end of 1987, nearly half of the import from non-GCC countries (except Israel and South Africa where a total prohibition exists) were duty free, about 45 percent were subject to a minimum ad valorem tariff of 7 percent; and roughly 7-8 percent of the imports were subject to tariffs of 10 or 20 percent. These higher tariffs had been imposed in 1984 as an amendment to the custom tariff schedule (see Table VIII.1); but were again increased in 1988. In principle, these duties are imposed for a maximum period of up to 5 years in cases where local manufacturers are able to meet approximately 70 percent of the domestic demand. However, difficulties in ascertaining actual demand have meant that this criterion has not been applied uniformly. Domestic value added is also taken into consideration in determining the suitability of tariff

Table VIII.1. Tariff Schedule for Tariffs of 10 and 20 Percent (1984)

Item	*Tariff*
Tahina (sesame paste)	20
Candy (without chocolate)	20
Chocolate	20
Chocolate Candy	20
Other Foods (except powder)	
with Chocolate Pasta Products	20
Biscuits	10
Peanut Butter	20
Mineral and Ordinary Water	20
Common Salt	20
Quartz, other than Raw	20
Lubrication Oils	20
Plastic Bottles, Covers	—
Ashtrays	30
Plastic Rosaries	20
PVC Pipes and Tubes	20
Sponge Rubber Plates and Sheets	20
Wood Moldings	20
Wood Picture Frames	20
Wood Barrels	20
Wooden Household Utensils	20
Wooden Travel Boxes	20
Wooden Signs	20
Toothpicks, Clothes Hangers	20
Wooden Scales	20
Other Wooden Articles	20
Toilet Paper	20
Paper Boxes, Bags, etc.	20
Paper Files and Dossiers	20
Paper Table Covers and Towels	20
Paper Diapers and Sanitary Napkins	20
Woolen Cloaks	20
Animal Hair Cloaks	20
Prayer Rugs of Synthetic Fiber	20
Prayer Rugs Made of Cotton	20
Twine & Rope, Plaited	10
Woven Arab Cloaks of Wool	20
Scarves, Veils of Synthetic Fiber	20
Scarves, Veils of Cotton	20
Aluminum Angles and Shapes	20
Aluminum Tubes and Pipes	20
Aluminum Cans, Boxes, etc.	20
Aluminum Sanitary Ware, etc.	20
Zinc Cans & Boxes	20
Safes, Armored Boxes	20
File Cabinets and Metal Drawers	20

(continued)

Table VIII.1. (continued)

Item	Tariff
Desert Coolers	20
Dry Batteries with 1.5 Volt Capacity, for Portable Equipment	20 (US$70 per kg. min.)
Electric Water Heaters	20
Vehicle Bodies (including cabs) for Cars, Trucks and Road Tractors	20
Vehicles Not Mechanically Propelled (e.g. Wheelbarrows, Min. SR 15 Each)	20
Chairs and Seats of any Material	20
Other Furniture (except medical) of any Material	20
Mattresses, Bedding, etc.	20
Antique Furniture and Parts	20

protection. Goods subject to protective duties encompass a wide range, including agricultural products such as eggs and poultry, and intermediate industrial goods such as electric cables, suplhuric acid, lubricating oil, and batteries.

Until 1988, given that a relatively small number of items were subject to protective duties and to the relatively low rates, tariffs played only a limited role in protecting domestic manufacturing. Nonetheless, given that the domestic value added in most of the protected activities is quite small, effective protection afforded by these tariff duties have been much higher. More important than tariffs had been the preference given to the procurement of domestically produced goods and services by contractors working on public sector projects. Priority is also given by government agencies and by other public sector enterprises to domestic producers and suppliers in the procurement of goods and services. The list of commodities subject to procurement requirements includes transport equipment, electrical appliances, construction materials, agricultural goods (e.g., dairy products, poultry, and eggs), as well as transportation, and advertising and publishing services. In addition, foreign contractors working on public sector projects are required to subcontract at least 30 percent of the project to wholly-owned Saudi companies.

Assessment of Commercial Policy

Most developing countries use commercial policies (tariffs) in order to protect and stimulate industries in which they hopefully enjoy a long-term comparative advantage. While tariffs are a less efficient method than direct production subsidies (as opposed to input subsidies, which are also distortionary) to achieve their intended goal, tariffs are justified on the basis of financial constraints.

In Saudi Arabia, where a similar financial constraint as in other developing countries has not existed in recent years, and where subsidies are already indiscriminately in use, appropriate subsidies, as opposed to tariffs, should be employed. Focused and direct production subsidies should be the rule, as opposed to tariffs and input subsidies. Unfortunately, tariffs are being increasingly employed. Given recent budgetary constraints, tariffs provide a seemingly painless avenue to increase government revenues. These tariff decisions are, moreover, made on an *ad hoc* basis when companies cannot compete with foreign products, whether this is covered by unfair foreign trade practice or not. An example of this method is the tariff afforded in 1985 to the Saudi Cable Company. The company argued, with little or no sophisticated analysis, that Far Eastern firms were dumping in the Saudi market, and as a result the government, after lengthy deliberations, granted Saudi Cable a tariff of 20 percent.

Saudi Arabia should undertake a comprehensive assessment of its industrial subsidy structure to develop an environment appropriate for domestic industrialization and development. Currently, Saudi Arabia, along with the rest of the GCC, are negotiating with the United States, the European Commission (EEC), and Japan, to develop bilateral trade agreements. Bilateral arrangements, outside of the GATT, are not the way to proceed as Saudi Arabia (and the GCC) has not assessed in an integrated fashion its own tariff and subsidy policies. First, bilateral arrangements are suboptimal and they may have to be reversed when a comprehensive assessment is undertaken. Second, without a comprehensive subsidy policy in place, it is difficult to know what Saudi Arabia (and the GCC) can offer the United States, the EEC, or Japan. Clearly a rational subsidy policy must first be put in place.

The government does not have in place the institutional structure to assess unfair trade practices. Although companies have direct access to subsidized credit, there is no institution that is able to grant export financing of any kind. The newly-created Export Promotion Council (1986), with support from the Ministry of Commerce, is studying the various options for export financing. It is hoped that some appropriate scheme will be adoped in 1988. Export financing is an important component of export competitiveness and is an integral facet of the export policy of most OECD countries and newly industrializing countries (NICs). During 1987, Saudi Arabia has started to explore the potential of tying its aid as a mechanism to promote exports. This is a widely practiced policy by most OECD countries with diversified economies. But, in the case of Saudi Arabia, it is doubtful that the existing industrial and agricultural base can support such a policy, the one major exception being petrochemicals. If Saudi petrochemicals ever face prohibitive tariffs in major markets, tying its aid to petrochemicals could become an effective policy.

In conclusion, the general thrust of reliance on subsidies, as opposed to tariffs, has been the appropriate approach for Saudi Arabia to use in order to develop infant industries. However, subsidies should be better focused and afforded in the form of production subsidies. The development of appropriate institutional infrastructure and export financing could be also helpful as the industrial base develops further. Unfortunately, the tariff increases of 1988 (see Chapter XI) are unlikely to be helpful.

EXCHANGE RATE POLICIES

Background

In 1981, Saudi Arabia effectively readopted the policy of *de facto* pegging to the dollar. This change in policy was due to the substantive appreciation of the dollar vis-à-vis the other major currencies. By mid-1983, the Saudi riyal had deviated from its par value to the SDR by more than 7.25 percent. And, in the face of an appreciating dollar, the riyal was subjected to several devaluations, vis-à-vis the dollar. However, the formal exchange rate policy has still been an SDR peg with a band of 7.25 percent, although the actual exchange rate has in recent years been substantially outside of this band.

In Table VIII.2, the exchange rate of the riyal to the SDR, US dollar, pound, mark, franc, and yen, are given for the period 1973-1984. Several observations should be made:

1. Beginning in 1982 (actually during 1981), the riyal exchange rate exceeded the 7.25 percent band to the SDR. This divergence became quite large as the dollar appreciated, vis-à-vis other currencies during the period 1981-1984.
2. The riyal appreciated vis-à-vis the dollar during 1971-1980, but then depreciated for the remainder of the period; and, in 1984, it had depreciated to the point where it showed some depreciation relative to 1973.
3. Relative to the mark and the yen, the riyal depreciated substantially up to 1979 (mark) and 1980 (yen), but then appreciated during the period 1981-1984.
4. Relative to the pound and the franc, the riyal appreciated dramatically during the period 1981-1984.
5. Over the entire period 1973-1984 (i.e., relative to the 1973 base), the riyal appreciated vis-à-vis the SDR (18.2 percent), the pound (49.9 percent), the mark (13.5 percent), the franc (102.3 percent), and depreciated vis-à-vis the dollar (0.7 percent) and the yen (10.9 percent).

Table VIII.2. Exchange Rate: Saudi Riyal

	1973	*1974*	*1975*	*1976*	*1977*	*1978*	*1979*	*1980*	*1981*	*1982*	*1983*	*1984*
Riyals Per Currency												
SDR	4.2825	4.3464	4.1324	4.1013	4.2576	4.3187	4.4328	4.2407	3.9749	3.7892	3.6591	3.5043
Relative to 1973 base[ab]	—	(1.5)	3.5	4.2	0.6	(0.8)	(3.5)	1.0	7.2	11.5	14.6	18.2
Year-to-year change[b]	—	(1.5)	4.9	0.8	(3.8)	(1.4)	(2.6)	4.3	6.3	4.7	3.4	4.2
U.S. Dollar	3.5500	3.5500	3.5300	3.5300	3.5050	3.3150	3.3650	3.3250	3.4150	3.4250	3.4950	3.5750
Relative to 1973 base[ab]	—	—	0.6	0.6	1.3	6.6	5.2	6.3	3.8	3.2	1.5	(0.7)
Year-to-year change[b]	—	—	0.66	—	0.7	5.4	(1.5)	1.2	(2.7)	(0.6)	(1.7)	(2.3)
U.K. Pound	8.2474	88.3372	7.1430	6.0095	6.6805	6.7444	7.4838	7.9301	6.5158	5.5458	5.0698	4.1334
Relative to 1973 base[ab]	—	(1.1)	13.4	27.1	19.0	18.2	9.3	3.8	21.0	32.8	38.5	49.9
Year-to-year change[b]	—	(1.1)	14.3	15.9	(11.2)	(1.0)	(11.0)	(6.0)	17.8	14.9	8.6	18.5
German DMark	1.3134	1.4733	1.3461	1.4942	1.6651	1.8135	1.9434	1.6973	1.5145	1.4454	1.2831	1.1356
Relative to 1973 base[ab]	—	(12.2)	(2.5)	(1.38)	(26.8)	(38.1)	(48.0)	(29.2)	(15.3)	(10.1)	2.3	13.5
Year-to-year change[b]	—	(12.2)	8.6	(11.0)	(11.4)	(8.9)	(7.2)	12.7	10.8	(4.6)	11.2	11.5
Currency Per Riyal												
French Franc	1.3263	1.2520	1.2707	1.4079	1.3424	1.2609	1.1947	1.3582	1.6832	1.9578	2.3884	2.6831
Relative to 1973 base[ab]	—	(5.6)	(4.2)	6.2	1.2	(4.9)	(9.9)	2.4	26.9	47.6	80.1	102.3
Year-to-year change[b]	—	(5.6)	1.5	10.8	(4.7)	(6.1)	(5.3)	13.7	23.9	16.3	22.0	12.3
Japanese Yen	78.8732	84.7746	86.4448	82.9462	68.4736	58.7029	71.2333	61.0526	64.3924	68.4134	66.4378	70.2378
Relative to 1973 base[ab]	—	7.5	9.6	5.2	(13.2)	(25.6)	(9.7)	(22.6)	(18.4)	(13.3)	(15.8)	(10.9)
Year-to-year change[b]	—	7.5	2.0	(4.0)	(17.4)	(14.3)	21.3	(14.3)	5.5	6.2	(2.9)	5.7

Notes: a. Figures are given as Riyal appreciation or depreciation. Figures denoting depreciation are given in parentheses.
b. Figures are in percent.

Source: IMF (1985).

The Role of Real Exchange Rates

The role of real exchange rates is to allocate resources between production intended for the domestic market and for exports. In an economy such as Saudi Arabia's, with a dominant export sector, this function of exchange rate is made all the more difficult. When oil export revenues expand, due to either a price or quantity increase, government income increases. To the extent that the government does not invest this extra revenue abroad, domestic government expenditure increases the price of nontraded goods relative to traded goods, that is, an increase in the real exchange rate (the price of nontraded to traded goods). The appreciation of the real exchange rate in turn stimulates nontraded goods production to the detriment of tradeables (non-oil). The appreciation also shifts factors of production into nontradeables, resulting in higher wages and raising inflationary pressures. An appreciating real exchange rate, with a fixed nominal exchange rate, implies higher domestic inflation. A primary policy to combat higher inflation is to allow or manipulate an appreciation in the nominal exchange rate; a secondary policy, which is not as effective (as it is already quite liberal) in Saudi Arabia, is to reduce import constraints.

The major export (around 90-98 percent of total export earnings) of Saudi Arabia has been crude oil and refined products. The price for these products are set in the world market in dollar terms. On the side of imports, there has been little domestic production that could compete with imports. As a result, Saudi Arabia's exchange rate policy, in view of Saudi policy makers, has very little do do with either export earnings or domestic production. This view is, however, rather myopic. In order to develop non-oil exports and import substitutes, an appropriate macropolicy is indispensable.

Up to 1984, Saudi Arabia's oil export policy was determined by the need to ensure an adequate supply to meet world demand, as opposed to only fulfilling domestic resource requirements. The external surpluses were basically involuntary and, given their size, short-run adjustment could not be realized either through expansionary financial policies, or through an appreciation of domestic currency.

In view of the government, supply bottlenecks and limited domestic absorptive capacity was not conducive to an excessive use of expansionary policies. Saudi Arabia's economy is characterized by an absolute advantage in the production and export of oil, and by an almost total dependence on imports for goods and services. The non-oil sector has largely consisted of either public sector operations or nontraded services, which have not been sensitive to exchange rate movements. Since revenues originated almost entirely in the external sector and where denominated in foreign exchange, the expenditure policy and the associated investment strategy was not dependent upon the choice of the exchange rate, but on the availability of foreign exchange. The accumulation of reserves and foreign investments were evaluated in terms of foreign exchange rather than local currency units, and were again independent of exchange rate policy.

Consequently, Saudi Arabia chose a policy mix that combined financial policies consistent with a rapid expansion of domestic economy without excessive inflation, and reserve accumulation abroad. In essence, government policy ascribed only a supportive role to the exchange rate policy and differentials between domestic and external cost structures were equalized, mainly through subsidies. Exchange rate stability, vis-à-vis the U.S. dollar and among GCC countries, along with, and the containment of, inflation were given priority. This policy has discouraged the development of non-oil exports and import substitutes.

The government's exchange rate policy has not been explicitly focused on the problems of the non-oil export (private) sector. In an oil economy, rapidly increasing government expenditures tend to result in rapid price increases of nontradables and in turn, in an appreciation of real exchange rates. To the extent that real exchange rate appreciation occurs, it reduces the incentive for export production and diverts production activity toward nontradables. This negative effect can be reduced if the government accumulates assets abroad in the face of rising revenues, liberalizes imports (deflecting demand to imports), if it subsidizes nontradables or if it subsidizes exports.

In Table VIII.3, the nominal effective (weighted by imports) exchange rate index and the real effective index are shown for Saudi Arabia. Clearly, after the first oil boom in 1973-1974, real exchange rates appreciated dramatically; this was largely due to increased government expenditures that resulted in a rapid increase in nontradable goods prices and bottlenecks to increased imports. During the second oil boom of 1979-1981, there was a substantial increase in nominal exchange rates, due to the increase in the value of the dollar, but the increase in real rates was moderated. The moderation in real rates was due to the expansion of numerous domestic subsidies, reduced bottlenecks to imports, and a more measured increase in government expenditures. Thus, the real effective exchange rate fluctuated in a narrow range from the second oil boom up to mid-1985. But from mid-1985, the riyal depreciated in real effective terms, due to the depreciation of the dollar and declining nontradable prices in Saudi Arabia. This recent decline in the real effective exchange rate (and the real rate) is a step in the right direction to promote diversification and increased private sector participation in the export sector.

Table VIII.3. Nominal and Real Effective Exchange Rate Indices[a]

Year	*Nominal Effective Exchange Rates*	*Real Effective Exchange Rates*
1972	85	96
1973	90	104
1974	98	128
1975	100	132
1976	104	130
1977	107	128
1978	102	125
1979	98	111
1980	99	105
1981	102	99
1982	110	100
1983	125	102
1984	129	102
1985	140	107
1986	110	80
1987	95	67
1988	90	62

Note: a. Index reported is for beginning of each year and the average for 1980 is equal to 100. Note that in the absence of changes in commercial policy, the direction of movement of the Real Effective Rate and the Real Rate are the same.

The Impact of Exchange Rate Policies

Imports. Oil revenues in Saudi Arabia peaked at $101,813 million in 1981; government expenditures peaked in 1981-1982, and have declined since then. GDP (in purchasers' values) peaked in 1981-1982, and has declined since that time (SAMA, 1984). In Saudi Arabia, where such a large proportion of consumption and investment goods is imported, one would expect that imports would have also declined if the decline in income was seen as permanent, as opposed to transitory.

GDP declined from US$154,39 million in 1981-1982, to US$109,026 in 1983-1984, for a decline of 29 percent in two years. Total imports, however, increased from US$35,087 million in 1987, to US$38,691 million in 1983, and stood at US$33,925 in 1984 (see Table VIII.4). The major reason for the observed direction of imports was the strong nominal appreciation of the dollar, and thus the appreciation of the riyal to the currencies of major trading partners (see Table VIII.2). The riyal appreciated by roughly 17 percent vis-à-vis the SDR over the period 1980-1984; and given that the SDR includes the dollar, the appreciation was even more pronounced vis-à-vis other currencies.

Imports declined noticeably in 1984. Beginning in 1985, imports started to decline precipitously, both in terms of Saudi riyals as well as U.S. dollars.

Table VIII.4. Saudi Arabian Imports from Major Partners: Value (CIF) and Shares (SR Millions)

	1971	*1972*	*1973*	*1974*	*1975*	*1976*	*1977*	*1978*	*1979*	*1980*	*1981*	*1982*	*1983*	*1984*	*1985 (1st half)*
U.S.	615.1	916.7	1407.0	1735.3	2538.4	5738.6	9621.3	14433.5	16270.1	20086.1	25566.8	29193.3	36734.5	20655.2	6969.5
%	32.6	31.2	31.2	30.6	27.8	30.1	28.6	26.9	25.9	25.8	27.0	25.9	24.5	22.0	20.5
U.K.	327.7	345.0	466.1	491.6	1147.0	1814.6	3182.0	5093.0	5841.0	6504.0	7407.0	9166.0	8376.0	6898.0	2700.1
%	17.4	11.7	10.4	8.7	12.6	9.5	9.5	9.5	9.3	8.4	7.8	8.1	7.7	7.3	8.0
France	78.6	107.5	156.3	180.0	332.0	821.0	1728.0	2668.0	3753.7	5439.6	6843.0	7451.0	7232.0	9252.5	2162.7
%	4.2	3.7	3.5	3.2	3.6	4.3	5.1	5.0	6.0	7.0	7.2	6.6	6.6	9.8	6.4
Germany	289.0	293.8	457.5	612.0	1017.0	2538.0	4320.0	7467.0	9023.6	9112.0	11395.0	15310.0	13471.0	9860.6	3721.9
%	15.3	10.0	10.2	10.8	11.1	13.3	12.8	13.9	14.4	11.7	12.0	13.6	12.4	10.5	11.0
Italy	161.0	190.6	197.5	280.4	578.5	1503.8	3167.7	4945.1	6047.2	7345.8	8009.8	8463.3	10224.8	8594.5	3971.0
%	8.5	6.5	4.4	4.9	6.3	7.9	9.4	9.2	9.6	9.5	8.4	7.5	9.4	9.1	11.7
Japan	414.2	675.7	1132.6	1616.4	2267.4	3731.2	5981.0	10659.4	13020.5	17992.2	21825.0	26658.4	26366.9	23568.3	8289.6
%	22.0	23.0	25.2	28.5	24.8	19.6	17.8	19.9	20.7	23.1	23.0	23.7	24.2	25.0	24.5
S. Korea	—	7.7	22.6	33.0	81.0	218.0	665.0	11.5	1598.3	2408.3	3451.0	3744.6	3883.5	3579.3	1395.7
%	0.0	0.3	0.5	0.6	0.9	1.1	2.0	2.1	2.5	3.1	3.6	3.3	3.6	3.8	4.1
Taiwan	—	62.7	99.0	109.7	188.7	319.7	783.1	1576.8	1990.1	2237.7	2677.5	2910.9	3245.4	3235.6	1244.0
$	0.0	2.1	2.2	1.9	2.1	1.7	2.3	2.9	3.2	2.9	2.8	21.6	3.0	3.4	3.7
Netherlands	—	198.0	256.3	403.2	429.8	1135.1	2277.7	3011.0	2503.5	3176.7	3150.7	3484.4	3524.7	3165.4	1182.6
%	0.0	6.7	5.7	7.1	4.7	6.0	6.8	5.6	4.0	4.1	3.3	3.1	3.2	3.4	3.5

Switzerland	—	48.7	100.0	118.0	419.4	1093.7	1510.4	1951.8	1510.6	1740.9	2301.4	2751.5	3169.4	2379.3	1111.5
%	0.0	1.7	2.2	2.1	4.6	5.7	4.5	3.6	2.4	2.2	2.4	2.4	2.9	2.5	3.3
Australia	—	84.6	181.2	82.8	95.3	115.6	299.0	488.8	873.2	1224.2	1679.2	2551.9	1528.1	2127.9	898.7
%	0.0	2.9	4.0	1.5	1.0	0.6	0.9	0.9	1.4	1.6	1.8	2.3	1.4	2.3	2.7
Canada	—	8.1	24.9	16.5	34.9	36.3	129.7	239.3	429.1	455.9	556.9	930.0	1166.6	776.2	166.7
%	0.0	0.3	0.6	0.3	0.4	0.2	0.4	0.4	0.7	0.6	0.6	0.8	1.1	0.8	0.5
Total Major Partners	1885.6	2939.1	4501.0	5768.9	9129.4	19065.6	33664.9	53638.7	62860.9	77723.4	94863.3	112615.3	108922.9	94092.8	33812.0
%	100.0	100.0	100.0	100.0	100.0	100.0	100.0	100.0	100.0	100.0	100.0	100.0	100.0	100.0	100.0
Total World	3667.5	4708.3	7197.0	10149.0	14823.0	30690.7	51662.0	69177.7	82223.2	100349.6	119297.7	139335.1	135417.2	118736.7	43622.4
Major Partners: % of World	51.4	62.4	62.5	56.0	61.6	62.1	65.2	77.5	76.5	77.5	79.5	80.8	80.4	79.2	77.5

Sources: SAMA (1974, 1977, 1980, 1983, 1985).

This is to be expected, given the rapid depreciation of the dollar starting in February 1985. The decline in imports, besides being affected by depreciation of the dollar, has been also impacted by the continuing decline in GNP and disposable income. Thus, imports did not decline substantially after 1981, but begining in 1985, the depreciating riyal and declining income reinforced each other to produce dramatically lower imports.

The impact of exchange rate policy is also partially born out by the changing pattern of imports (see Table VIII.4). *A priori,* one would expect a decline in the share of trade with the United States over the period 1981-1984, and an increase in the shares of the other major partners. The data confirm a drop in the U.S. share from 27 to 22 percent, and an increase in the shares of France, Italy, and Japan; there is, however, a decrease in the share of the United Kingdom and Germany.

The effective pegging of the riyal to the dollar has tended to artifically distort the direction of trade. This has resulted in trade and trade shares changing more with nondollar countries, as opposed to a peg to a trade weighted basket.

Import Prices. Given the nominal appreciation of the dollar over the period 1981-1984, one would expect a dampening effect on import prices. In Table VIII.5, a weighted index of import prices is given. This index is calculated by taking the riyal prices of imports from each of Saudi Arabia's major trading partners and weighing it by the share of Saudi Arabia's imports from that country. As can be seen from Table VIII.4, import prices—while increasing from 1974 to 1980—have declined in every year beginning in 1980-1981 to 1984-1985. The drop in the index has been from 1.034 in 1980-1981, to 0.9708 in 1984-1985. This decline in import prices has, however, also occurred during a period of weak commodity prices; as a result, only a part of the decline in import prices can be attributed to exchange rate policies.

Inflation. Exchange rate policy has been an important tool for insulating the economy from imported inflation, and thus reducing overall inflationary pressures. Thus, beginning in mid-1980, the exchange rate policy had a strong dampening effect on domestic inflation. However, it should be noted that the major tool for fighting inflation has been government expenditure policy. In Table VIII.6, two measures of inflation are given. The first is the consumer price index. The second is the GDP deflator; derived as a ratio of GDP valued at current market prices to GDP value at constant market prices. The deflator provides a broader measure of price changes than do consumer or wholesale price indices, since it covers the domestic economy as a whole. A casual comparison of inflation to exchange rate movements confirms a relationship. More appropriately, one should establish a relationship between effective exchange rates and import price index (in foreign currency).

Table VIII.5. Price Index: Imports of Goods and Services

1974-1975	*1975-1976*	*1976-1977*	*1977-1978*	*1978-1979*	*1979-1980*	*1980-1981*	*1981-1982*	*1982-1983*	*1983-1984*	*1984-1985*
0.6239	0.6584	0.6952	0.7718	0.8554	0.9485	1.0304	1.0275	1.0000	0.9854	0.9708

Source: Saudi Arabian Government Sources.

Table VIII.6. Domestic Indices

	1973	*1974*	*1975*	*1976*	*1977*	*1978*	*1979*	*1980*	*1981*	*1982*	*1983*	*1984*
Consumer Prices (1980 = 100)	40.2	48.8	65.6	86.4	96.2	94.7	96.4	100.0	102.7	103.8	104.8	103.7
GDP Deflator (1980 = 100)	18.9	40.2	56.3	61.1	66.1	68.1	70.9	100.0	125.0	124.0	109.9	100.1

Source: IMF (1985).

GCC Exchange Rates. The pegging of the riyal to the dollar also resulted in relatively stable exchange rates within the GCC. Given that all the currencies of GCC countries, except Kuwait, were pegged to the dollar, this resulted in stable cross-rates for five of the six GCC countries.

Up to the mid-1970s, most GCC countries maintained their currencies in more or less fixed relationship with the U.S. dollar. However, the depreciation of the U.S. dollar in the second half of the 1970s made it difficult to protect against imported inflation without a shift in the pegging arrangement. Therefore, four countries (Bahrain, Qatar, Saudi Arabia, and the United Arab Emirates) shifted to an SDR peg with margins of 2.25 percent, while Kuwait established its rate in terms of an undisclosed basket of currencies. Only the Omani Rial continued to be explicitly tied to the U.S. dollar. Despite a switch in the pegging arrangement, GCC countries attempted to maintain as stable a rate as possible with the U.S. dollar, without changing the parity rate with the SDR.

Beginning in the late 1970s, the SDR peg was found to present difficulties as the wide fluctuations in the value of the U.S. dollar did not permit the maintenance of a stable rate in terms of the U.S. dollar, while leaving the SDR parity unchanged. The four countries concerned, responded to this by widening the margins from 2.25 to 7.25 percent. With the U.S. dollar's appreciation after 1980, the wider margins themselves have been substantially exceeded as Bahrain, Qatar, and the United Arab Emirates along with Oman have maintained constant exchange rates of their currencies against the U.S. dollar, while Saudi Arabia has permitted only small changes in the U.S. dollar exchange rate of the riyal.

Even though, in the recent past, the stability of exchange rates in the GCC region have been promoted by a *de facto* peg to the U.S. dollar, its continuation has been disruptive as the U.S. dollar undergoes cyclical changes. The adverse effects of this instability might outweigh the benefits deriving from the resultant intraregional exchange rate stability and may force member countries to make unilateral changes in exchange rates, thus disrupting intraregional exchange rate stability. Moreover, the rapid depreciation of the U.S. dollar will make it difficult to contain inflationary impulses originating abroad.

It would be more conducive to the domestic financial and economic stability of GCC member countries to shift to a multicurrency peg such as the SDR. This would facilitate the maintenance of stable intraregional exchange rates without allowing excessive fluctuations in exchange rates with non-GCC currencies.

Impact on Households and Government. On the one hand, exchange policy afforded the household sector with a substantial subsidy over the period 1980-1981—1984. On the other hand, this implicit subsidy has since been continually reduced with the depreciation of the dollar beginning in 1985. The impact in the reduction of this subsidy is being compounded at a time when nominal incomes are being reduced, due to government expenditure policies. In turn, the exchange rate subsidy, due to its impact on real incomes, resulted in increased imports (from what they would have been); and the depreciation of the dollar-riyal since 1985, and the resulting negative effect on real incomes, and reduced nominal incomes have combined to produce a dramatic downturn in imports. Imports in the first half of 1985 were about 26 percent lower than comparable 1984 figures, also accounting for a drop in government expenditures.

The impact of exchange rate policy on the business sector has been threefold. First, during the period 1980-1981—1984, because of the appreciation of the dollar, the demand for imports were higher than they would have been. This was a clear benefit to the business sector, given that a substantial component of Saudi Arabian business activities is associated with import trade, and that the provision of services has also a large import component (i.e., labor and foreign travel).

Second, the appreciation of the real exchange rate up to mid-1985 (the appreciating dollar) has hurt domestic business activity by reducing exports and by reducing the attractiveness of domestic production, both for the domestic market and for exports.

Third, the appreciating dollar contributed to a larger presence of foreign labor. Because most foreign labor is ultimately interested in its savings in foreign currency, the higher value of the riyal resulted in the increased attractiveness of employment in Saudi Arabia, and because of higher savings in terms of foreign exchange to foreign workers. In sum, Saudi businesses hired their foreign labor at effectively subsidized wages.

It would appear that the period of the appreciating dollar-riyal induced increased economic activity. On the one hand, an appreciation, because it induces higher imports and reduced exports, dampens domestic economic activity. On the other hand, increases in real incomes caused by an appreciation, results in increased expenditures and economic activity. Normally, the former tends to outweigh the latter. In Saudi Arabia, where oil exports are, by and large, unaffected by exchange rates, where there is little domestic production to compete with foreign competition, and where trade (imports) and foreign labor are an important component of the domestic economy, the appreciation of the riyal probably resulted in increased domestic economic activity.

Because oil revenues, the major source of government revenues, are denominated in dollars, the dollar value of export receipts-government revenues are largely unaffected by the exchange rate policy. However, there have been some nominal revenue losses in riyal terms as a result of pegging to the dollar when the dollar was appreciating. This loss in government riyal revenues has to be, however, qualified. First, the exchange rate policy as just mentioned; afforded the private sector (household and business) with an implicit subsidy. Thus, the value of this implicit subsidy should be subtracted from the impact of exchange rate policy on government riyal revenues. Second, exchange rate policy was neutral with respect to government expenditures on imports, a substantial component of all government expenditures. Because of these complications, it is difficult to calculate the size of this effect.

SUMMARY

Saudi Arabia's *de facto* exchange rate policy of nominal pegging to the dollar, during a period of an appreciating dollar, has been largely motivated by the desire to insulate the domestic economy from imported inflation, to provide an implicit subsidy to consumers and importers, and to maintain stable nominal rates with most GCC countries. But there has been less government focus on real exchange rates.

There have been costs to this policy. Real exchange rates have not been allowed to play their normal allocative role. For the entire period from 1974 to 1985, the riyal exchange rate based on any indicator, such as relative wage rates and salaries (relative to other countries), was greatly overvalued. This has discouraged non-oil exports, contributing to only a minimal degree of diversification of the domestic economy. To be successful, Saudi Arabia needs domestic diversification and the production of the non-oil exports. The problems of an overvalued real exchange rate can be ameliorated through a higher level of investments abroad, appropriately focused production (not input) subsidies, and appropriate macropolicies. The real effective depreciation of the riyal since 1985 is a helpful development. A more market-oriented real exchange rate that makes exporting a profitable activity, would be almost essential for the development of a viable and diversified exports sector. Additionally, pegging to the dollar has placed increasing pressure on financial policies and has rendered a fixed rate to the dollar more burdensome in the adjustment process.

Chapter IX

Budgetary Policy and Institutional Considerations

ECONOMIC PLANNING AND BUDGETARY PROCESS

Saudi Arabia's basic approach to economic development has been to provide infrastructure and input subsidies, as opposed to direct and focused stimulus to development. In such a setting and given that oil revenues directly accrue to the government, the composition and size of government expenditures, through fiscal linkages, have been the key factors in determining the terms of trade, the level and composition of investment, and consumption. Thus, the budget has been the critical factor in determining the development growth and diversification of the Saudi economy. Development planning, although receiving some attention, is of less practical importance.

Development Planning

Development planning started in Saudi Arabia in 1970-1971. Three Five-Year Development Plans (1970-1971—1974-1975, 1975-1976—1979-1980, 1980-1981—1984-1985) have been completed, and currently Saudi Arabia is in the middle of its fourth Five-Year Development Plan (1985-1986—1989-1990).

The first two development plans emphasized the expansion of large physical infrastructure projects. The basis for this policy was to expand the absorptive capacity of the economy after the substantial increases in oil revenues in 1971, especially in 1974, and to reduce barriers to the development of a healthy private sector. In the Third Plan, the major economic thrust was primarily to develop what was considered to be Saudi Arabia's comparative advantage: namely, the implementation of capital-intensive hydrocarbon-based indsutries, export refineries, and petrochemicals. A secondary goal, more for social as opposed to purely economic reasons, was the development and expansion of agriculture; the basis for this program was not that Saudi Arabia enjoyed a comparative advantage in wheat cultivation, but that food security, Saudi agricultural employment, and farm ownership were important social goals. But of equal importance as economic goals was the government emphasis on education and social services.

The Fourth Plan stresses health, education, and other social services. At the same time, the plan envisages the promotion of more balanced regional growth, an expansion in the role of the private sector, and diversification of the economy away from oil toward smaller industrial projects and agriculture. And, given the reduced level of oil income at the initiation of the Fourth Plan, the government has voiced increased concern for efficiency and basic economic criteria in project and program selection and implementation; the rationalization of subsidies has been singled out for special attention (Ministry of Planning, 1985, 140-141).

What has been the actual achievements of these plans? Tables IX.1-IX.3 give a concise picture of the major developments. From Table IX.1, it is clear that the GDP grew dramatically in nominal terms up to 1981-1982 and declined somewhat thereafter as a result of a big drop in oil GDP. In real terms, the increase in GDP was still substantial. But, at least by 1984-1985, because of the drop in oil activity, the growth of non-oil GDP had been even more impressive than that of oil. But, even if earlier years are taken as the end point, the performance of the non-oil sector, including the private sector, was quite substantial. The figures contained in Table IX.2 reveal that the major investment component of this growth was construction. The information in Table IX.3 indicates why the private sector has grown so rapidly. Electricity, water, and agriculture, all heavily subsidized, contributed over 20 percent of the private sector's share in 1984-1985; transport, storage, and communication—again heavily subsidized—contributed another 18 percent; trade, hotels, and restaurants contributed nearly 34 percent; but manufacturing (excluding refining) contributed only 10.8 percent.

In sum, the contribution of the non-oil private sector has been largely directly due to trade, and indirectly to subsidies. Government subsidies and other expenditures have in effect encouraged these sectors, as opposed to manufacturing. Manufacturing contribution to the total GDP was only 5.8 percent in 1984-1985 and 10.8 percent of the private sector GDP. These results are not surprising, given the almost indiscriminate availability of subsidies and the absence of focus to encourage specific infant industries.

Table IX.1. Gross Domestic Product By Sector[a] (In Millions Riyals)

	Year Before First Plan (1969-70)	*Last Year First Plan (1974-75)*	*Last Year Second Plan (1979-80)*	*Third Plan (1980-81)*	*(1981-82)*	*(1982-83)*	*(1983-84)*[b]	*(1984)*	*Fourth Plan (1985)*	*(1986)*[b]	*(1987)*[c]
At Current Prices											
GDP	17,152	139,224	383,589	517,994	522,176	411,797	367,622	347,424	310,031	267,846	272,041
Oil Sector	9,566	111,101	252,705	360,741	337,884	206,360	157,989	132,555	96,958	67,461	71,702
Non-Oil Sector	7,586	28,123	130,884	157,253	184,292	205,437	209,633	214,869	213,073	200,385	200,339
Private	5,328	18,252	74,559	88,520	102,874	117,445	126,078	129,998	130,981	123,686	121,767
Government	2,258	9,871	56,325	68,733	81,418	87,992	83,555	84,871	82,092	76,699	78,572
At Constant 1969-1970 Prices											
GDP	17,152	31,539	49,053	52,971	53,886	48,030	47,679	46,842	44,936	47,511	46,481
Oil Sector	9,566	18,903	23,869	24,653	22,383	14,309	13,052	11,453	9,286	13,032	11,746
Non-Oil Sector	7,586	12,636	25,184	28,318	31,503	33,721	34,627	35,389	35,650	34,479	34,736
Private	5,328	8,439	16,876	21,280	23,619	24,804	24,684	26,699	26,993	26,041	26,256
Government	2,258	4,197	8,308	9,454	10,223	10,102	9,823	8,690	8,657	8,438	8,480
Implicit Deflators[d]											
GDP	100	441	782	978	984	874	771	742	690	564	585
Oil Sector	100	588	1,059	1,463	1,545	1,500	1,210	1,157	1,044	518	610
Non-Oil Sector	100	223	520	555	585	609	605	607	598	581	577

Notes: a. The approximate exchange rates for these years (SR per US$) were 4.5, 3.7, 3.4, 3.3, 3.4, 3.4, and 3.5, respectively. GDP and components are measured at producer's value and exclude import.

b. Revised estimates.

c. Preliminary estimates.

d. 1969-1970 = 100.

Source: SAMA (1985 and 1988).

Table IX.2. Gross Fixed Investment[a]
By Type of Capital Goods

	Year Before First Plan		*Last Year of First Plan*		*Last Year of Second Plan*		*Third Plan*									
	(1969-1970)		*(1974-1975)*		*(1979-1980)*		*(1980-1981)*		*(1981-1982)*		*(1982-1983)*		*(1983-1984)*		*(1984-1985)*	
	Amt.[b]	*Share*	*Amt.*	*Share*	*Amt.*	*Share*	*Amt.*	*Share*	*Amt.*	*Share*	*Amt.*	*Share*	*Amt.*	*Share*	*Amt.*	*Share*
Construction	1,969	75.8	13,222	74.7	77,805	80.2	81,470	76.6	92,227	75.4	87,070	75.4	82,482	74.9	71,646	74.1
Transport Equipment	309	11.9	2,253	12.7	6,997	7.2	7,449	7.0	7,988	6.5	8,599	7.4	9,063	8.2	8,153	8.4
Machinery and Equipment	319	12.3	2,021	11.4	11,601	11.9	16,059	15.1	20,003	16.4	19,716	17.1	18,474	16.8	16,797	71.4
Others	—	—	203	1.2	666	0.7	1,398	1.3	2,097	1.7	69	0.1	76	0.1	50	0.1
Total Gross Fixed Investment	2,597	100.0	17,699	100.0	97,069	100.0	106,376	100.0	122,315	100.0	115,454	100.0	110,095	100.0	96,646	100.0

Notes: a. The approximate exchange rates for the referenced years (SR per US$) were 4.5, 3.7, 3.4, 3.3, 3.4, 3.4, and 3.5, respectively.
b. Amounts are in millions Riyals.
Source: SAMA (1985).

Table IX.3. Non-Oil GDP[a] By Major Economic Activities (At Constant 1969-1970 Prices) (In Millions Riyals)

	1983-1984	*1984-1985*
Electricity, Gas and Water	1,855	2,042
Agriculture, Forestry and Fishing	2,172	2,216
Manufacturing (excluding Refining)	2,599	2,645
Construction	5,394	4,899
Transport, Storage, and Communication	4,441	4,403
Wholesale, Retail Trade, Restaurants, and Hotels	8,362	8,299
Total	24,823	24,503

Note: a. The approximate exchange rate (SR per US$) was 3.5.
Source: SAMA (1985).

Historically, economic planning in Saudi Arabia has basically involved the exposition of a set of general goals that appeals to top government officials. These goals are in turn translated into a few large projects, such as the industrial cities of Jubail and Yanbu, refineries, petrochemical complexes, hospitals, and universities. Large projects are easier to formulate and implement, given the limited expertise and experience in planning. The Ministry of Planning's role in the overall process is limited. The Ministry, about a year or two before the plan, requests information from government agencies regarding their plans, projects, and the like. Then, the Ministry of Planning essentially compiles a document containing, as its framework, the major goals expressed by the government, and integrates the plans of individual government agencies; and gives a macroeconomic outlook, given expected government revenues and the plans of government agencies. But the Ministry of Planning does not do detailed sectoral planning, does little assessment, does not have much influence in the implementation of policies, and has little budgetary input—although actual expenditures during the Third Plan were 95.2 percent of planned expenditures, actual sectoral expenditures diverged significantly from the plan (Ministry of Planning, 1985).

Up to the end of 1986, neither the Ministry of Planning, nor any other government agency, had undertaken a comprehensive analysis and assessment of tariffs, subsidies, exchange rates, export financing, and the like. Economic planning toward the private sector, even in an indicative sense, has been scarce. The government's view has been that the infrastructure is in place, that there are a variety of subsidies, and that now it is up to the private sector to do the rest. But, unfortunately, the government has not assessed the comprehensive requirements of the private sector. Economic planning has been primarily concerned with the dissemination of overall goals and with the packaging of a vision to go with the plans of numerous government agencies.

Another important consideration in the area of economic planning, is the absence of general directions or guidelines for private sector investments. There is little government indication of Saudi Arabia's long-term comparative advantage. The underlying philosophy of this approach is Saudi Arabia's commitment to a free enterprise system. The Ministry of Commerce believes that there is an important "check" in the system in the form of SIDF. Namely, SIDF loan review process is a safeguard against unprofitable investments. The ramifications of this approach has already been discussed in Chapter VII.

In short, economic planning in Saudi Arabia has been passive and not forward-looking.

Budgetary Process

Although economic planning has had a relatively minor impact on economic development in Saudi Arabia, the budget has been all important. The size and detailed allocation of the budget is not determined by the economic plan; but instead is heavily influenced by sociopolitical considerations.

Historically, government spending in Saudi Arabia has determined resource allocation, the level of investment, and the growth of non-oil GDP. The budget is a key factor in determining domestic liquidity. The budget includes the financial operations of the government (including defense) and transfers to finance operations of many public sector agencies (The Royal Commission for Jubail and Yanbu; universities; schools; utilities; ports; municipalities; the Grain Silos and Flour Mills Organization; the Saudi Fund for Development; and the five specialized credit institutions of PIF, SIDF, REDF, SCB and SAAB).

In recent years, before budget figures were even seriously suggested, the Ministry of Finance had asked the IMF to carry out a prebudget study. This exercise is based on a simple aggregated macromodel, with little detail on the structure of the economy. The results of the exercise are used to project the impact of various budget scenarios on variables such as the growth rate of non-oil GDP and prices. At the next stage, the budget is a political exercise as in most countries; its size is determined by the size of revenues and by sociopolitical considerations, and its allocation by the pet programs or projects of the hierarchy and important ministers. Historically, in determining the size of the budget, the government forecasts oil revenues; foreign investment income; and fees, duties, and taxes. It also estimates the size of the expenditures based on request by the various ministries and agencies. If the ministry and agency requests are significantly less than projected revenues, then the size of the budget is largely determined by these requests. If, however, requests are of the same size or exceed projected revenues, a great deal of "horsetrading" occurs between the Ministry of Finance and individual ministries and agencies to reduce expenditures. In this process, military and essential social expenditures receive priority. And if minimum acceptable expenditures still exceed projected revenues, then the size of the deficit, to be financed from the drawdown of foreign assets, has to be sanctioned at the highest level of government. But clearly what is missing from this overall process is a deliberate allocation to foreign investments to promote diversifications.

The military has received on an average, 35-40 percent of the total budgetary expenditures in 1986, nearly equalling the total oil revenues (see Chapter III): agriculture has been a favorite of several important individuals; and, in part, becasue of the spread of Islamic fundamentalism, the expansion and construction of new mosques have received special attention. But the most important consideration in the allocation decision has been short-run social and political considerations, as opposed to economic productivity and the need to compensate for the depletion of oil. In addition, the distribution of subsidies throughout sectors of the economy has led to the creation of important constituencies. Consequently, budgetary flexibility in reducing or abolishing subsidies is hampered.

Government revenues and expenditures for recent years are shown in Table IX.4. As can be seen, a small share of government spending has been targeted directly toward productive areas. Defense, municipal service subsidies, and public administration have accounted for roughly 57 percent of budgetary allocations. Of the remaining 43 percent (much of which consists of subsidies, see Chapter VI) of expenditures, very little has gone to directly productive industries. In essence, expenditures have been targeted toward laying an expensive "basis" for *future* development—infrastructure; an educational system more concerned with quantity, as opposed to quality, cheap capital, and showcase health centers. But, unfortunately, unless the government adopts a *comprehensive* long-term economic progam, the private sector will not be able to take advantage of this expensive base that the government has so lavishly made available. It is expensive both in its original cost, and in its ongoing maintenance (accounting for about 14 percent of actual budgetary expenditures in 1985-1986).

The rapid reduction in government expenditures, in the face of falling revenues is rather unique. In the case of Saudi Arabia, this has been achieved for several reasons. First, the government has had to take a generally tough poisition as oil revenues were not projected to increase substantially over the medium term. Second, most of the large showcase projects had been already complete. Third, the government has reduced some subsidies (most importantly for wheat production and for the doubling of premium gasoline

Table IX.4. Budget Allocations By Sector[a]
(In Millions Riyals)

	1982-1983	*1983-1984*	*1984-1985*	*1985-1986*	*1987*	*1988*
Total Revenue	246,182	230,186	216,363	181,498	169,995	143,300
Oil Revenue	186,006	145,123	103,880	63,822	65,277[c]	68,935[c]
Other Receipt (transfers from the petroleum sector)	—	—	15,120	23,853		
Other Revenues	60,176	61,296	52,510	43,823	52,018	36,365
From General Reserves	—	23,767	41,853	50,000	52,700	8,000
From Treasury Bonds						30,000
Expenditure	244,912	230,186	216,363	181,498	169,995	143,300
Human Resource Development	25,951	25,714	26,430	24,328	25,720	21,721
Transport and Communications	30,641	24,633	20,159	12,477	11,954	10,194
Economic Resource Development	17,614	15,802	16,132	12,966	8,499	6,509
Health and Social Development	13,025	14,504	14,449	12,731	9,034	9,837
Infrastructure Development	12,533	11,055	7,082	5,584	4,300	3,127
Municipal Services	15,385	11,406	11,120	8,681	4,100	7,699
Defense and Security	66,508	63,805	67,912	60,462	64,752	50,800
Public Administration and Other Government Spending	46,252	42,419	40,348	35,805	31,266	25,022
Government Lending Institutions[b]	17,003	20,848	12,731	8,464	10,370	6,822

Notes: a. The exchange rates (SR per US$) for the referenced years were 3.4, 3.5, 3.55, and 3.65, respectively.
b. Includes local subsidies.
c. Includes transfers from the petroleum sector.

Source: SAMA (1985).

prices), government salaries, and general waste; these measures were somewhat easier to implement in Saudi Arabia than in other developing countries because of their higher standard of living and wealth, and because of the existence of a great deal of "fat," or waste, in the budget.

In retrospect, budgetary decisions and allocations have not been targeted to promote specific private sector industries. Subsidy expenditures have important implications for today's economic conditions in Saudi Arabia. Had these expenditures not been made, Saudi Arabia would have much higher foreign revenues today, or if they had been made on the basis of economic criteria and efficiency, Saudi Arabia's economy would be more diversified today, more productive, and much more able to cope with a downturn in oil revenues.

INSTITUTIONAL CONSIDERATIONS

The Kingdom's financial structure is a prominent institutional consideration for its economic progress.

Background

Saudi Arabia's financial structure is deeply rooted in Islamic principles. SAMA is Saudi Arabia's equivalent to a central bank and has the role of striking a balance between employing modern monetary principles and traditional concepts. SAMA's functions include:

- issuance of currency
- bank regulation (reserve requirements and normal regulatory controls, which are rarely used)
- depository for the government and its agencies
- management of external assets (under the ultimate control of the Ministry of Finance)

In addition to these functions SAMA deposits interest-free government funds with selected banks to help them with liquidity and financial problems. The SAMA also holds regular meetings with commercial banks to assess their financial conditions and to "advise" them.[1]

In addition, Saudi Arabia has commercial banks, specialized credit institutions, and non-bank financial institutions (which include money changers).

There are 11 commercial banks in Saudi Arabia; another Al-Rajhi, has been recently incorporated. The two largest banks, the National Commercial Bank and Riyadh Bank, have over 50 percent of total bank assets, are entirely

Saudi-owned with SAMA owning over 50 percent of Riyadh Bank. Most of the other banks have foreign ownership of differing percentages. The commercial banks perform normal banking functions and also act as stockbrokers.

There are five specialized credit institutions, most of which were established in the early 1970s. These institutions are financed by government appropriations and allocate government funds interest-free, or at a low service charge, to the private sector and to certain public sector entities. By effectively taking over the medium- and long-term component of the market, the specialized credit institutions have limited commercial bank operations primarily to the short-term end of the market. The REDF was established in 1974 to provide finance to the private sector for the construction of housing for both personal and commercial use. The SIDF, also established in 1974, provides credit and assists the private sector in the establishment and expansion of industries. It also disbursed funds to finance electric utility projects on behalf of the Ministry of Industry and Electricity under the Electric Lending Program, which ended in 1983-1984. The PIF, set up in 1971, finances (through loans and equity participation) larger industrial and commercial projects undertaken by the public sector both directly and jointly with the private sector. A significant part of the financing for Petromin's and SABIC's projects have been provided by the PIF. SAAB, which was established in 1965, extends credit with maturities ranging from 6 months to 25 years, aimed at encouraging the development of the agricultural sector. In addition, it disburses part of the direct budgetary subsidies from the government to the agricultural sector. The Saudi Credit Bank was established in 1973 and grants small-scale loans for up to five years for specified purposes.

The nonbank financial institutions encompass a wide range of financial institutions, including investment and insurance companies and money changers. The money changers have played an important role in the economy. Until 1981, they took deposits and made loans in addition to normal exchange activities, without being subject to SAMA regulations. Since then, their activities have been restricted because SAMA had little control over their activities while they represented a significant component of the domestic money supply; the largest of the money changers, Al-Rajhi, has become a commercial bank. No new licenses have been issued and the money changers were required, within three years, to cease accepting deposits and engaging in other banking activities. Their activities are now limited to the purchase and sale of foreign currencies and travelers' checks, the purchase of bank drafts, and the transfer of remittances. Their operations are subject to SAMA inspection.

Financial Reforms

The role of a sound financial system is to provide a competitive return to attract and allocate resources efficiently, to activities having the highest expected return. At the same time, some regulation is required within the banking system to prevent undue risk taking, which could in turn, reduce the public's confidence in banks as financial intermediaries. To attain these results, several ingredients are necessary: a central monetary authority to provide sound supervision of banks, and a healthy and competitive banking sector regulated only by laws that facilitate the development of an efficient financial system and encourage bank participation in local financing.

Unfortunately, in Saudi Arabia many of the required ingredients for a healthy financial sector, which could in turn contribute to economic growth, are still not in place.

First, SAMA's charter is not fixed, and thus it uses *ad hoc* measures and coercive actions on banks. SAMA does no allow the commercial banks to form their own association, and banks can only meet under SAMA's auspices. Although many central banks restrict the products offered by their banks, SAMA's restrictions are more significant, resulting in no bearer instruments or other financial innovations. SAMA does not act as a lender of last resort, yet it deposits interest free funds on an *ad hoc* basis with selected commercial banks. SAMA does not allow banks to take positions in any stocks; instead, banks have to match both sides of any transaction before they can be transacted. SAMA's impact on influencing economic activity is, therefore, reduced through the nature of its monetary tools (Abdeen and Shook, 1984, 56). All of these have resulted in a less than efficient financial system.

Second, besides SAMA's regulations, commercial banks, are faced with other major obstacles. The government is the source of major savings in the economy and it bypasses the traditional intermediary function of banking institutions. Concessionary loans made through specialized government institutions have deprived banks from the normal medium- and long-term business that is an integral component of commercial bank operations in most countries (Abdeen and Shook, 1984, 56). Even in the absence of the specialized government lending institutions, it is questionable whether local banks would lend to many of the projects that have highly uncertain outcomes and that rely on concessionary financing. It is difficult for banks to obtain the normal credit information that is available in most countries. As a result, many of the loans are largely made on faith and on the "good name" of the borrower.

Third and most importantly, the religious courts in Saudi Arabia, Sharia, have, up to now, largely closed the door on the recovery of bank loans. In the cases where loans have carried interest, that is, nearly on all loans, banks trying to recover their loans have had to pay back all past interest payments (because of the religious prohibition on interest), which in some cases have amounted to more than the principal. For similar reasons, it has also been difficult for banks to seize collateral in case of default.

In the heydays of the 1970s, businessmen were making high returns and paid their debts. But now that many businesses are not as successful as in the past, they are unwilling to use some of their prior earnings to meet interest and principal payments. Instead, they are hiding under the protection of Sharia courts to retain their previous gains. Only a few well-established merchant families have continued to meet their obligations. As a result, the commercial banks have, by and large, stopped making domestic business loans.

As a result, SAMA has taken some steps to ameliorate certain problems: (a) it has strengthened the role of its arbitration board to deal more forcefully with Islamic court rulings regarding repayments of interest; and (b) it is enforcing the practice of banks reporting their nonperforming loans to it. The most promising development has been the establishment of the three-man committee through SAMA to review cases that banks bring before this body. The committee is composed of people with knowledge of the Saudi economy, but with no ties to the banks. The few cases brought to the committee, as of the end of 1987, were noncontroversial, and the rulings have been favorably received by the banks. But in no case did the debtor later appeal to the Sharia courts. Thus, it is still too early to determine what kind of authority the committee will have and the role that it will play in inducing the banks to play a positive role. But the mere fact that such a committee was established, is a credit to the authorities in perceiving the dimension of the problem at hand.

Besides the area of banking, Saudi Arabia also has institutional deficiencies in investment banking, stock dealing, and brokerage services. Investment banking is prohibited. There are no market makers in Saudi stocks. There are no stockbrokers. Instead, banks act as stockbrokers to the extent that they match buyers and sellers, that is, they cannot take a position. The reluctance of the authorities to allow these and other innovations, such as new instruments, stems from their basic conservatism, their desire to protect investors, and from the speculation that occurred in Kuwait at the Soukh-El-Mannakh. However, the average citizen is paying a price for the absence of such financial services. To invest, they rely on foreign brokers who come to Saudi Arabia and entice them, but they know little of the foreigners' reputation. The average Saudi would prefer the government to license and regulate a few entities, as opposed to prohibiting such services altogether.

In summary, the financial structure of the Saudi economy has been, and continues to be, a negative factor in the development process. Domestic savers prefer to deposit their savings abroad where they can earn a competitive rate, have a choice of instruments, and attain anonymity. Banks are not lending domestically at a time when their involved participation would be particularly beneficial for increased domestic economic activity. A recent bright spot has been that the external assets of the private sector are being repatriated. In short, the financial structure currently in place does not promote the development and growth of the private sector as it has reduced the participation of commercial banks. In order to encourage the development of a full-fledged banking industry, SAMA has to implement a comprehensive set of rules and regulations that introduce an element of certainty into the financial sector. But given the political and social structure of Saudi Arabia, it would be naive to expect changes overnight. The establishment of the three-man committee through SAMA is a positive step. However, it seems that other changes, such as investment banking, brokerage services, and innovations in financial investments, will be very slow in coming. At the end of 1987, the only one of these that was under consideration was the possibility of allowing banks to take a position in stocks. But it is an important area that requires serious consideration for the further development of the Saudi economy.

NOTE

1. For a comprehensive discussion of the Saudi financial system, see Abdeen and Shook (1984).

Chapter X

Educational and Social Considerations

EDUCATION

Background

An essential component for effective development of an economy is a skilled and literate workforce. The government of Saudi Arabia has put in place an ambitious effort to educate its people. The new campus of King Saud University on the outskirts of Riyadh, which cost US$4 billion to construct, stands as a symbol of the government's financial commitment to education.

Over a period of only 15 years, the number of schools has risen over fourfold from 3,100 in 1969, to over 14,000 in 1983 (see Table X.1). The number of teachers, as a percentage of the total student body (excluding students abroad) was nearly 6 percent in 1983, up from 4 percent at the beginning of the First Development Plan. Albeit, the ratio of Saudi teachers declined from over 70 percent to less than 15 percent as the Saudi student body rose from 1970-1983. Traditionally, women have had a higher profile in teacher training and most recently, this situation at institutions of higher education has also shown significant improvement. In 1983, nearly 25 percent of university students were women, up from practically zero only a decade earlier.[1]

In order to provide technical and vocational training, schools and training centers have been established to fill demands in this area. In the Fourth Plan, US$1.8 billion has been allocated to the General Organization for Technical Education and Vocational Training (GOTEVT).

Students have been given ample incentives to pursue higher education. In addition to the spectacular facilities and free tuition, they are provided with free board, an 80 percent subsidy on food, 75 percent subsidy on books, free airline tickets home, and US$300 a month in spending money.

Table X.1. Development in Education (Males and Females)

	1969-1970	Male (%)	1974-1975	Male (%)	1979-1980	Male (%)	1982-1983	Male (%)
Number of Schools	3,107	85	5,634	74	11,070	71	13,426	63
Number of Teachers (full-time)	23,118	79	43,777	72	78,309	64	104,524	60
Number of Students (thousands)								
Preschool	4	75	14	57	24	58	39	38
Elementary Education	397	70	634	65	862	62	1,070	60
Intermediate Education	61	92	137	72	245	67	301	64
Secondary Education	16	88	42	76	93	69	131	61
Higher Education[a]	7	100	19	84	48	73	75	67
Training Abroad	2	100	5	80	10	90	20	95
Teacher Training	11	36	15	73	22	45	18	61
Technical Training	1	100	3	100	7	85	11	91
Adult Education	43	100	100	75	142	73	141	60
Other	5	100	14	93	9	89	30	100
Total	547	75	983	68	1,463	65	1,836	62

Note: a. Ministry of Education.
Source: In the case of higher education, faculties are counted as schools.

According to the Fourth Development Plan (Ministry of Planning, 1985, 52), Saudi Arabia needs to grapple with the following educational issues:

- low operational efficiency, following from high rates of both repetition and dropout;
- questionable effectiveness, as evidenced by output that is not in full harmony with national manpower needs;
- staffing patterns that are generous and continue to be heavily dependent on non-Saudi personnel.

In Table X.2, two of these issues can be examined. Of the estimated 43,400 male students enrolled in 1984-1985, only 30 percent are studying technical- and science-oriented subjects. The ratio is even lower for women (25 percent).

Table X.2. Estimated Enrollment and Graduate Production By Broad Field of Study for Saudi Undergraduates (1984-1985)

	Percentages		*8-year Change Rates*	
Fields of Study[a]	*Enrollment*	*Graduates*	*Enrollment*	*Graduates*
Males				
Religious Studies	12.3	12.4	1.5	1.1
Arts and Humanities	22.1	22.1	2.8	2.1
Education	11.5	15.9	5.7	0.7
Social Sciences	23.9	21.4	7.8	9.3
Natural Sciences	5.7	4.0	2.6	-1.2
Engineering	15.0	13.9	6.0	4.6
Medicine	6.1	5.1	9.1	6.4
Agriculture	3.4	5.2	7.2	6.6
Total	100.0	100.0	5.9	4.7
Estimated Number	43,400	3,992		
Females				
Religious Studies	7.1	6.6	1.1	1.0
Arts and Humanities	44.6	41.5	6.5	5.9
Education	21.6	32.8	5.3	4.9
Social Sciences	11.0	7.1	7.3	13.7
Natural Sciences	6.3	7.8	7.3	3.8
Medicine	8.4	3.5	5.9	3.0
Agriculture	1.0	0.7	8.5	17.6
Total	100.0	100.0	6.5	6.5
Estimated Number	22,900	2,330		

Notes: a. Sciences include economics, commerce, general studies, and home economics. Engineering includes a preparatory year at UPM. Medicine includes allied fields (dentistry, pharmacy, nursing, and veterinary medicine).

Source: Ministry of Planning (1985).

Table X.3. Additional Manpower Requirements (By Occupation) and Projected Saudi New Entrants to the Labor Force (By Level of Education) (1984-1985—1989-1990)

Projected Total Job Openings (1984-1985—1989-1990)		*Projected Total Saudi New Entrants to the Labor Force*				*Repatriation of Non-Saudi Workers*
Occupation Group	*Total Job Openings*	*Highest Level of Education*	*Males*	*Females*	*Total*	
	(000)		(000)	(000)	(000)	(000)
Professional, Technical, Administrative, and Managerial Workers	4.3	University & College Graduates	40.7	14.1	54.8	
Subtotal	4.3		40.7	14.1	54.8	50.5
Office Workers	6.5	Incomplete Postsecondary Education	34.4	4.6	39.0	
Manual Workers (skilled/semiskilled)	26.3	Secondary & Intermediate School Graduates	20.1	7.9	28.0	
		Technical & Vocational Training Programs	100.2	1.0	101.2	
		Incomplete Secondary or Intermediate Education	87.7	12.0	99.7	
Subtotal	32.8		242.4	25.5	267.9	235.1
Unskilled Workers	-143.1	Elementary School Graduates & Dropouts	42.0	2.0	44.0	
		New Entrants from the Households	120.1	7.4	127.5	
Subtotal	-143.1		162.1	9.4	171.5	314.6
Total	-106.0		445.2	49.0	494.2	600.2

Source: Ministry of Planning (1985).

The same holds true for graduates. The social sciences account for the highest number of enrolled students. This enrollment pattern does not match the prescribed national goal of technological advance in the Kingdom and the highly technical skills for jobs that need to be filled by the repatriation of non-Saudi workers. The second problem lies in the rate at which Saudi students are completing their university education. Less than 10 percent of the undergraduate body was expected to graduate in 1984-1985, and based on past growth rates, this ratio is not only expected to improve, but may even deteriorate.

In Table X.3, a comprehensive projection of Saudi manpower needs and new entrants into the labor force are presented. The obvious solution to meeting new entrants' demand would be the "Saudiization" of existing jobs, especially with the cooperation of the private sector. There are two problems, however, which need to be addressed. It may be difficult to match new entrants' skills with that of the departing foreign labor force in the professional ranks, and to encourage Saudi nationals to fill some of the positions that are vacated by foreigners in the skilled and unskilled labor categories. While for the time being problems can be averted by relocating new participants in the labor force around the country, the government cannot hope to alleviate this situation simply by reducing foreign labor and by replacing them with Saudi nationals who may not be able, or willing, to fulfill the obligations of their jobs. According to the Fourth Plan, the government is aware of the impending crisis and plans to ease bottlenecks by restructuring its incentives so that students are encouraged to enter fields that will be in demand. But it is difficult to take the unpopular steps necessary for changing the existing incentive structure. Saudi Arabia should take Egypt's bloated bureaucracy as an example of how not to deal with underqualified graduates of schools, who were encouraged to go through the university system under the late Egyptian president Nasser's policy of free university education.

Educational progress has brought with it other mixed results. While it is true that education for its own sake may be useful, it may become very difficult to ignore its impact on Saudi women, and their attitudes toward the traditional restrictions put upon women by society. Currently, Saudi women are principally involved in teaching and some health-related activities that allow for strict separation between males and females at the workplace.

It is, therefore, apparent that while Saudi Arabia has encouraged education, this has not been done with adequate planning. As was demonstrated earlier, it will be more and more difficult to provide jobs for the 500,000 job entrants during 1985-1990. Over 60 percent of the new entrants are expected to be in the areas of skilled and professional workers where repatriation of foreign personnel will not solve the problem if the incoming workforce is not adequately prepared to fulfill their jobs. Instead of providing across-the-board incentives, the government should assess its expected manpower requirements relative to new contracts and support the development of skills and professions that will be needed.

PROVISION OF SOCIAL SERVICES

One avenue for distributing Saudi Arabia's oil wealth has been through the provision of health and social services to its population. The two primary vehicles for distributing Saudi Arabia's social services have been the provision of health care and a system of social assistance.

Provision of Health Services

Health care in Saudi Arabia, provided free of charge to its citizens, is delivered through hospitals and dispensaries of the Ministry of Health, as well as through specialized agencies such as the Ministry of Defense, the Ministry of Interior, The Red Crescent Society, The Specialist Hospitals, The Royal Commissions for Jubail and Yanbu, universities, and the private sector.

In Table X.4, some aspects of expansion in health care are presented. The ratio of hospital beds per 1,000 people has risen from 1.9 in 1980, to 2.2 in 1984-1985. Of the 26,410 hospital beds in the Kingdom, 13 percent were provided by the private sector. The number of physicians has grown as well, through the large influx of foreign medical personnel. The same holds true for nurses and health care technicians who are not expected to be replaced in the foreseeable future. The total enrollment of Saudi nationals in the fields of medical and allied health training was 4,342 in 1983-1984. Considering the relatively low graduation rates and the still unsatisfied demand for health services in the hinterlands, demand for foreign medical personnel will stay high.[2] In 1980, the ratio of Saudi medical manpower to the total medical manpower at the Ministry of Health hospitals was 13 percent. For physicians, this rate was as low as 7 percent (Ryan, 1984, ch. 2).

A balanced geographical distribution of primary health care provision is another important concern for the Kingdom. While statistically speaking, Saudi Arabia has made improvements in health care delivery, for instance, reducing the infant mortality rate from 148 in 1965, to 65 in 1984 (World Bank, 1986, 233),[3] there are still imbalances in the adequacy of delivering primary health care to the outlying regions of the country; this is the main reason for the relatively high national infant mortality rate in 1984; in the major cities this rate is similar to that of developed countries. On an

Table X.4. Health Facilities[a]

Year	Hospitals, Dispensaries, and Health Centers	Hospitals	Hospital Beds	Medical and Paramedical Personnel				
				Physicians	*Nursing Staff*	*Technical Assistants (including Pharmacists)*	*Other Technicians*	*Total*
1970	566	47	7,165	789	2,253	910	542	4,494
1975	693	62	9,250	2,275	4,721	1,737	1,186	9,919
1980	958	69	11,968	3,793	6,859	2,928	1,366	14,946
1983	1,170	78	16,990	5,635	10,702	4,520	1,640	22,497
1984-1985[b]	1,964	145	26,410	14,267	23,785	11,587	—	49,639

Note: a. The above statement does not cover facil ties offered by the private sector or government agencies, other than the Ministry of Health.
b. Includes all health facilities.

Source: Ministry of Health (1985).

anecdotal note, one can compare the lack of funding for a study on the provision of Red Crescent services to the hinterlands to building the King Faisal Specialist Hospital, which provides the latest in specialized health care. An argument could be made for prioritizing the delivery of adequate primary health care to all, before venturing into projects that only appear attractive, especially if the cost of treating a patient for services, such as open-heart surgery, may be less abroad.

In the Fourth Development Plan, the need for extending the coverage of primary health care has been reconfirmed (Ministry of Planning, 1985, 329). It is in the interest of Saudi Arabia to shift priorities from concentrating on showcase projects, to a more broad-based distribution of health services.

SOCIAL SERVICES

The government's program of providing social services is "designed to reduce existing social imbalances, to improve living standards and the quality of life of the population, to stimulate citizen participation in community development activities, and to provide remedial care and assistance for the disabled and the deprived" (Ministry of Planning, 1985, 338).

The government has implemented a variety of such measures, foremost of which is the provision of subsidies on various basic consumer commodities and housing, and loans that were made on highly concenssionary terms. These subsidies were discussed in Chapter VI. In addition, there are social security and comprehensive occupational insurance schemes that spread a safety net to benefit the disadvantaged.

In Table X.5, social security payments are broken down into relief assistance and regular assistance. By 1982-1983, total assistance amounted to $0.44 billion, of which 9 percent was paid out in relief assistance. This amount translates to $1,429 per family (or case) that has applied for assistance.

Social services payments have increased rapidly during the Third Plan. It seems as if, despite the drastic changes in the Kingdom brought about by its oil wealth, certain segments of the population were not able to partake in the new wealth. This can be attributed to many causes. It has been difficult to reach nomads and the rural poor until settlement policies took effect, and until access to remote areas was made possible. In addition, until recently, minorities in the eastern region did not receive the same attention when it came to social services. New attempts have recently been made to better serve outlying communities and to provide aid to minorities. For example, a hospital was dedicated by King Fahd in a largely Shiite-populated region of the eastern province in 1986.

Table X.5. Social Security

			All Assistance		
Year	*Regular Assistance Amount Received (Million Riyals)*	*Relief Assistance Amount Received (Million Riyals)*	*Amount Received (Million Riyals)*	*Number of Families or Cases (Thousand)*	*Amount Received per Family or Case (Riyals)*
1969-1970	39.4	2.3	41.7	64	652
1974-1975	349.0	8.5	357.5	140	2,554
1979-1980	960.1	118.7	1,078.8	271	3,981
1982-1983	1,402.0	138.0	1,540.0	309	4,984

Sources: Central Department of Statistics (1984); Ministry of Labour and Social Affairs (1984).

In the Fourth Plan, attention has been paid to these existing imbalances and there is a public recognition of the need for an improved expanded distribution of services to the outlying areas.

The issue at hand, however, is how policies have contributed to the economic growth and development of the kingdom. Many of the aforementioned policies have distributed some of the oil wealth and have been primarily directed toward social considerations, so as to raise the standard of living. But except for raising the level of consumption among those who were not able to share in the wealth, these policies have contributed little toward encouraging efficient economic production. In short, the general thrust of policies have been toward social goals, as opposed to direct, efficient, and long-run productive objectives. Government policies have attempted to create an appropriate environment (through subsidies and infrastructure) for development and growth, as opposed to directly stimulating appropriate industries. Such a policy, especially that of infrastructure and subsidies, will, by nature, require more time before a definitive evaluation of its effects can be made.

NOTES

1. In Saudi Arabia, male and female students are segregated starting with the first grade. Traditionally, female education had been afforded less emphasis.
2. In 1984, 73 percent of the Ministry of Health's hospital beds were located in Riyadh and Madinah, the western and eastern regions.
3. For the sake of comparison, the infant mortality rate for industrial market economies for the same periods is 24 and 9, respectively.

Chapter XI

Government Policy Initiatives of 1987-1988

INTRODUCTION

Since the late 1970s, the government of Saudi Arabia has publicly recognized the need to invest a large portion of current oil revenues to compensate for oil depletion and to diversify income away from oil. From 1974 to 1981, however, oil revenues far exceeded expenditures and as a result, only lip service was afforded to this all-important policy pursuit. Although large government expenditures were made on infrastructure and a variety of costly subsidies were given to industry and agriculture, very little diversification in the form of competitive industries and agriculture developed. From 1981 to 1987, oil revenues declined, and although expenditures were somewhat reduced, the government budgetary deficit resulted in a large drawdown of accumulated external assets.

In 1987, the projected short- and medium-term shortfalls in oil and other revenues, projected budget deficits well into the future and a level of useable external assets of about three to five years to finance deficits, prompted the government to look at alternative policy options. In December 1987, the government announced a series of policies that were designed to address these and other economic problems, which have been addressed in the previous chapters.

THE POLICY PACKAGE

The domestic policy initiatives of December 1987 were incorporated into the 1988 budget. The government's goal was to increase revenues, reduce expenditures and, in the process, to address some of the then existing policy shortcomings.

The government announced a variety of measures to increase revenues:

1. New taxes and service fees: The most important new service fee (tax) was a 5 percent levy on all real estate transactions. Additionally, an airport tax (approximately US$12 for each international trip), a road tax (approximately US$56) and some increased user fees (largely on telephone and telex usage) were proposed. After these measures were announced, most were repealed in January 1988, due to public pressure. The only new tax that was retained was the road tax and the only increases in fees were a modest surcharge in telephone and telex charges.
2. Import duties: Tariffs were raised to 12 percent for most items, with the prominent exception of some food products and medicines. A 20 percent tariff was imposed on several important items that compete with domestically-produced substitutes, such as steel and cement. The government's goal was to reduce imports, to save foreign exchange, and to protect domestic products from foreign competition.
3. Expatriate income tax: On January 1, 1988, the government announced an income tax on all foreign workers. The motive behind this initiative was threefold—to increase revenues, to reduce the level of foreign workforce in favor of Saudis, and to introduce the idea of an income tax through the "back-door." Expatriates were up in arms, but more importantly, Saudi businessmen were upset. Businessmen correctly perceived the measure as indirectly increasing their expatriate wage bill, because they would have to make up for the taxes if they were to retain their expatriate workers whose salaries had been already reduced and whom they needed. After intense lobbying with the King, the measure was rescinded four days later.
4. Government borrowing: Given the expected budget deficit in 1988 and probably for some years to come, the government announced a program to borrow in the domestic market. During 1988, SAMA was to issue bonds to finance a part of the deficit during 1988. These bonds had maturities of 1 to 5 years and carried a premium of 25 to 30 basis points over comparable U.S. treasury securities.

ASSESSMENT

The 1988 budget contained expenditure reductions of 12 percent over actual 1987 expenditures, and 17 percent over budgeted allocations for 1987 (for details see Chapters I and IX). In 1987, the budget deficit was US$17 billion, representing almost a 40 percent deficit in relation to actual expenditures of US$42.6 billion. The deficit was largely financed from drawing down on reserves; and over the previous four years total deficits exceeding US$60 billion have been financed in the same manner. The budget for 1988 and the policies it contained were supposed to reverse this trend. Unfortunately, these measures will do little to address the basic problems facing the Saudi economy.

The announced measures to increase revenues and to broaden the revenue base are, if anything, on balance detrimental in the long run. After rescinding the expatriate income tax and many user fees, what was basically left were new and higher tariffs and increased user fees for telephone and telex facilities. The tariff measures should add about $1 billion to 1988 revenues and in user fees about US $250 million. Tariffs are a seemingly painless way to enhance revenues, but they portend ominous signs for the future if they protect inefficient domestic industries. In the time, the protection of inefficient industries will reduce long-run productivity growth, and in turn, economic growth. Moreover, as has been argued throughout this text, focused subsidies at the source are always preferable to tariffs. The basic reason for this revenue measure was that other revenue-enhancing measures would have been initially unpopular because of domestic pressures. However, the government has, in the process, established another domestic constituency for tariffs, which will, over time, exert its own selfish interests to the detriment of the economy. In short, this is not an efficient way to develop competitive non-oil industries, but it is instead a measure, which is likely to be harmful in the long run.

Clearly, the major source of revenues for the government is a broad domestic income and/or sales tax. The government continues to be slow in recognizing the fact that this is the only viable long-run option at its disposal. Tariffs produce additional distortions and cannot provide the government with a broad revenue base. An income and/or sales tax system will require careful planning and a long lead time. The aborted expatriate tax demonstrated little appreciation of the economic and political complexities involved.

On the expenditure side, although most expenditures were cut from their 1987 levels (see Chapters I and IX), the government has again taken the "easy" approach. It has not made the big cuts that are potentially available in the big subsidies (see Chapter VI), most of which are either not in the budget or are not categorized under subsidies. Again, cuts in subsidies, such as electricity and water, are unpopular and thus the government has been apprehensive. Equally as important, the government did not change the implementation of subsidies. Subsidies continue to be distortionary; they are largely given in the form of input subsidies as opposed to production and income transfers (see Chapter VI).

The overall budgetary picture may be substantially worse than portrayed by the government. The projected oil revenue of US$18.4 billion for 1988 is on the high side, unless oil prices and/or oil exports increase from their current levels. In view of the unfavorable outlook for the oil market for the next four to five years, the medium-term budget picture could deteriorate further unless the government takes more drastic measures.

The bond financing scheme, though helpful in preserving SAMA's foreign assets, is not a solution to budgetary problems as it may delay required economic adjustments. During 1988, bond sales amounted to about SR42 billion. About 80 percent of these bonds were purchased by government agencies, 20 percent by commercial banks (largely substituted for purchases of other claims on SAMA), and none were purchased by the non-bank private sector. This program has been continued into 1989.

The necessary policy measures are clear. To improve budgetary outlook, expenditures (largely implicit and explicit subsidies) should be cut drastically, and revenues increased through a broad income and/or sales tax. At the same time, the method of implementing domestic subsidies should be changed to reduce inefficiencies and to promote the development of a competitive domestic non-oil sector. Delays in implementing such policy changes will render future choices even more difficult by reducing prospects for the domestic non-oil economy, further solidifying domestic interest groups and requiring even more drastic changes in policies.

Chapter XII

Summary: Lessons from the Past

INTRODUCTION

Our conclusion is that given the depletable basis of the Saudi Arabian economy, oil, the Kingdom should follow certain basic principles to promote economic development. First, although social considerations are important, Saudi Arabia should save and invest a large portion of its national product in productive investments to ensure alternative sources of output to compensate for oil depletion. Second, the government should promote export and income diversification. Third, the government would have added flexibility in the pursuit of these goals to the extent that it tends to maximize discounted oil revenues.

Saudi Arabia's many achievements have not come cheaply and, by and large, policies may not have compensated for oil depletion. Saudi Arabia has not relied on foreign investments as a major source of income diversification, but has instead adopted expensive domestic policies—largely socially-oriented subsidies and massive expenditures on infrastructure. Decision making in Saudi Arabia has not afforded sufficient importance to economic criteria and to the fact that oil is a nonrenewable resource. Additionally, many of these policies, such as subsidies, have not been efficiently formulated and will continue to burden Saudi Arabia and are practically difficult to terminate.

Why did these shortcomings in economic policy occur? First and foremost, policies in Saudi Arabia have been largely oriented toward social objectives, subsidies being an obvious case in point. Second, the dramatic decline in oil revenues was not foreseen by the Saudis, or by most oil analysts, and it was felt that ongoing revenues would be sufficient to finance ongoing expenditures. Third, given the traditional and tribal nature of Saudi society, noneconomical considerations are often afforded more attention than economic criteria and efficiency.

LESSONS FROM OTHER COUNTRIES

The general lessons that can be learned from successful developing countries indicates that good performance requires government commitment to a set of policies to increase the efficiency of resource allocation. The exact form may differ from country to country, but the core of the program is the same—timely removal of controls, increased private sector participation, and improvements in resource allocation.

Fischer (1987, 31-32) has noted the important lessons:

> Harberger (1984) has summarized lessons professionals have learned from studying and advising on economic policy in developing countries—and most apply also to developed countries. Here are his thirteen commandments:
>
> 1. Don't get too technical. Detailed long-term projections are rarely useful.
> 2. Keep budgets under adequate control. Absolute balance may be impossible, but there is not much room for deficits.
> 3. Keep inflationary pressures under control, which means also maintaining fiscal discipline.
> 4. Take advantage of international trade.
> 5. If tariffs are used, keep effective tariff rates reasonably uniform.
> 6. If tariffs become excessive, use export incentives.
> 7. Make tax systems as simple and neutral as possible.
> 8. Avoid excessive income tax rates.
> 9. Avoid excessive tax incentives.
> 10. Use price and wage controls sparingly if at all.
> 11. It is rare that quotas, licenses and quantitative restrictions are justified. They are inefficient and breed corruption.
> 12. Adopt a technical view of public enterprises. The right criterion is the efficient operation of the enterprise.
> 13. Keep the boundaries between public and private sector activities as sharp as possible.
>
> The missing, most important, commandment is:
> Don't let the exchange rate become overvalued.
>
> This impressive list is evidence not only of what should be done, but also of what ofen is done. The domestic distortions and problems that new policies have to cure were usually introduced within the same political economy of reform, except to note that the outcome of policy packages depends not only on the economics but also on the political equilibrium.
>
> There are two reasons for hope. One is that deep-rooted distortions are most likely to be eliminated at times of deep crisis. The other is that well-designed conditionality of outside lending can provide incentives for the adoption of better policies.

This list of recommendations are general and could apply to any country. In the case of Saudi Arabia, it would have to be applied in a modified form. The special characteristics of the Saudi economy that should be acknowledged in this context are the political and social setting, the heavy reliance on a nonrenewable resource, and the fact that until recently Saudi Arabia was not confronted by financial constraints that plague most developing countries.

The major distortions in Saudi Arabia that cannot be afforded are the size and method of the implementation of subsidies and the general inefficiency of government programs.[1] But Saudi Arabia has one major advantage. Namely, unlike most developing industries that embark on the road to economic liberalization invariably have to either reduce expenditures or to increase borrowing because of severe resource limitation, Saudi Arabia has oil and oil revenues with which to finance its development.

However, while oil gives relief to Saudi Arabia, it is a two-edged sword. If oil is not effectively employed now, with the depletion of oil, the economy has very little sustainable sources of output. In a nondepletable resource-based economy, there would still be a sustainable productive base. Also, given the fact that Saudi Arabia has not had to borrow, external financing has not provided an incentive for the adoption of more appropriate policies. While oil revenues were increasing, Saudi Arabia did not concern itself with economic efficiency, but now, given that oil revenues are unlikely to increase substantially and quickly, efficiency consideration should become more important. In fact, future growth in income will have to come in large measure from the non-oil sector; this will require increased economic efficiency. This underscores the fact that overproduction of oil reduces the importance of economic criteria for government expenditures, creating various distortions, which may inflict more harm than good on the economy; avoiding overproduction of oil will impose economic discipline, increase investment in the form of oil in the ground, and will be intergenerationally more equitable.

INDICATIONS FROM THE PAST

From the domestic development perspective, Saudi Arabia must always evaluate all proposed policies to determine if they adequately compensate for the depletion of oil and promote efficient (competitive on world markets) diversification of the economy. With this basic principle in mind, the government should reorient several key policies to ensure the future development of the Saudi economy.

1. Foreign Investment: Foreign investments can provide a very attractive channel for income diversification and for avoiding many of the problems associated with domestic expansionary policies, especially in surplus oil-exporting countries; resulting in waste and an overvalued real exchange rate that hamper the development of a viable non-oil sector. Saudi Arabia could have, in the past, usefully reduced domestic expenditures, increased its current account surplus, and invested the proceeds aggressively abroad as Kuwait has done. For the future, and as part of an overall development strategy, more aggressive foreign investment policies could be given serious consideration as a means of diversification.

2. Subsidies: Many subsidies, although socially desirable, have been, and continue to be, costly, while contributing little to efficient economic development in Saudi Arabia. Most indirect government subsidies (in the form of input subsidies) distort resource allocation. The government should set a timetable to reduce and potentially to eliminate some operating and capital subsidies, and to increase user charges to reflect opportunity costs. Industrial subsidies should be targeted to specific industries in which Saudi Arabia enjoys a comparative advantage but where some assistance is needed because of infant industry-type arguments.

To promote infant industries, subsidies are more efficient than tariffs. Given that Saudi Arabia is financially stronger than most developing countries, tariffs, though relatively insignificant in the context of the Saudi economy until 1988, should not become a major instrument of development. Additionally, subsidies are an appropriate policy to counteract the negative effects of a real exchange appreciation for domestic industries. In short, there is an important role for subsidies, both socially and productively, but not in the manner currently implemented in Saudi Arabia. All subsidies should be focused at the source and not given indirectly in the form of cheap inputs.

3. Infrastructure: The rapid achievement in the development of infrastructure in Saudi Arabia has been impressive. The government should now consolidate its gains through three policies; first, not to throw good money after bad money; second, not to be halala-wise and riyal-foolish; and third, to adopt an appropriate schedule of user fees. If a particular infrastructure is unlikely to be used in the foreseeable future, then it should be abandoned now, and not after sinking even more money into its maintenance. But, in the case of productive infrastructure, sound maintenance should be implemented as opposed to cutting corners that will, in the end, require quicker replacement and even larger expenditures. Additionally, in the case of another boom, the government should not repeat the rapid infrastructural development of the past. Instead, infrastructure should be developed in a more deliberate and thoughtful manner, with due consideration to basic needs in outlying areas, as requirements cannot be predicted into the distant future. Last, the future growth in demand for

infrastructural services will be too rapid and wasteful unless the government implements a schedule of user fees and charges that more adequately reflect opportunity costs.

4. Exchange Rates: Exchange rates should play a more important resource allocation function. The maintenance of relatively fixed and overvalued real exchange rates is economically counterproductive. Real exchange rates should encourage competitive non-oil exports. If this is not done, it is unlikely that substantial non-oil exports, competitive in the world marketplace, will develop in the foreseeable future. Moreover, the exchange rate system should be based on a basket of currencies, reflecting Saudi Arabia's trading pattern, in order to afford reasonable exchange rate stability; and real effective exchange rates should be the target of government policy. The real effective depreciation since 1985 is a welcomed development. The Saudi authorities are somewhat concerned about a unified exchange rate system within the GCC. But trade within the GCC is not large, and more importantly, the overall GCC exchange rate regime should be a competitive rate tied to a basket reflecting GCC trade weights.

5. Financial Reforms: A sound, stable, and competitive financial environment is an absolute requirement if domestic private savings are to be encouraged and banks are to participate in financing domestic development. The SAMA should allow banks to operate as modern institutions: to issue new instruments, to offer competitive rates and desired denominations, and to take positions in stocks. The SAMA should itself act as a lender of last resort. Additionally, the goverment should devise some way to circumvent religious courts (Sharia) in order to safeguard the ability of banks to collect their debts (interest and principal). These policies would result in the removal of economic and financial uncertainties currently facing the Saudi economy; in a healthy and competitive financial sector that could, in turn, finance a large component of Saudi Arabia's future economic development from increased repatriated private savings and the desire of banks to participate in industrial financing. More timely payment of bills by the government would be also helpful in reducing uncertainty; a policy change in this direction was instituted toward the end of 1987.

6. Economic Planning and Budgetary Allocations: Economic planning should become more forceful. It should become a forum for national debate and participation on the future course of the Saudi economy, to solicit the commitment of the private sector to participate in the future of the Saudi economy. To encourage the private sector, more direction to the private sector and a comprehensive set of economic policies is required. Budgetary allocations should follow the dictates of economic planning. In general, there is a requirement for expenditure-switching policies toward more productive ends, as opposed to projects with little or no direct economic output. Additionally, given budgetary dependence on oil revenues, it is time for Saudi

Arabia to think about implementing an income and/or sales tax system. Given that implementation of a successful income policy requires a long lead time, the government should start now in order to have a viable option in the foreseeable future. If the implementation of an income tax is seen as politically and administratively difficult, a sales tax system could be contemplated.

7. Oil Policy: Past Saudi oil policy may result in substantial losses in long-term oil revenues. By acting as a swing producer, Saudi Arabia allowed oil prices to go too high, relative to long-run equilibrium in the oil market, and thus encouraged new production of oil and non-oil sources. These developments have resulted in lower Saudi exports and thus reduced revenues. But even more importantly, these negative results will continue to adversely impact the oil market in the future as they are partially irreversible.

For the future, Saudi Arabia should more forcefully pursue a policy within OPEC to a price path that may result in long-run revenue maximization (admittedly this is a difficult policy to implement) and to produce at a level that supports such a price. The actual dollar price will also depend on the exchange rate of the dollar to other major currencies. It may be useful to initiate a currency bascket pricing of oil to avoid frequent price changes and fluctuations in the oil market. Additionally, once the appropriate price structure has been determined, Saudi Arabia may need to expand its production capacity; this will be a useful investment, as it increases Saudi Arabia's potential power in the oil market; in 1989, Saudi Arabia announced such a policy.

POLICY INITIATIVES OF 1987-1988

The government policy initiatives of December 1987 and January 1988 did little, if anything, to change the course of economic policy as outlined above. The expatriate income tax was narrow and ill-conceived; it was rescinded. The revenue measures did not include the all-important national income tax (or even sales taxes) and the most important user fees were left untouched. Most of the announced revenue measures were repealed because of public pressure, a predictable outcome. The largest revenue item, tariff increases, may not be beneficial to the future development of the Saudi economy. Inefficient industries are protected and could be protected in the future at ever-increasing rates, due to domestic pressures.

On the expenditure side, small cuts were made, but not in the all-important subsidies; a politically-sensitive issue. Even more important, the method of implementing subsidies, both for investment and consumption, were not addressed.

All in all, these well-publicized policy initiatives did little to change the course of economic policy in Saudi Arabia.

FINAL COMMENT

Substantial and rising oil revenues from 1974 to 1981 afforded Saudi Arabia with an unusual opportunity to develop a productive non-oil domestic economic base. Saudi Arabia's achievements in the areas of social services and infrastructure have been impressive. But the direction and impact of economic policies on the development of a viable non-oil sector to compensate for the depletion of oil are questionable, requiring the passage of more time for a definitive assessment. The government did not pay sufficient attention to foreign assets as a source of income diversification, but proceeded rapidly with domestic programs, with social goals as the major objectives. It did not, and has not yet, developed a competitive private sector. Instead, it adopted a series of short-term policies, such as socially-oriented subsidies, which were implemented inefficiently and have done less than might have been expected for economic development. At the same time, the necessary complementary ingredients for economic development, such as a financial environment and exchange rate policy, have not been fully developed with a unified objective in mind. In the context of the Fourth Development Plan, most of these shortcomings have been explicitly or implicitly recognized. The important issue now is how fast will the government implement the required changes in policy.

Finally, the important lesson is that in all countries economic resources are, by nature, scarce and should be used wisely. In Saudi Arabia this is even more poignant, as the lion's share of income and opportunities are derived from oil, a finite resource. The bright possibilities and opportunities, afforded by oil, should be pursued prudently to the benefit of all generations.

NOTE

1. Saudi Arabia, like most other developing countries, has also had an overvalued exchange rate, but the government feels that this is not a major problem as (1) export expansion and import-substitution possibilities are scarce, (2) an overvalued exchanged rate reduces inflation, and (3) given that Saudi Arabia has no external debt to service, the budgetary impact of exchange rate is not pronounced.

Appendix I

NET NATIONAL PRODUCT FOR AN EXHAUSTIBLE RESOURCE ECONOMY

Martin L. Weitzman
Department of Economics, M.I.T.

The extraordinary rise in the world price of oil and its unusual concentration in certain geographical regions, has given rise to an anomalous situation where for certain countries oil is, in fact, the overwhelming contributor to the national product. That the economic base of several important countries is almost entirely based on the extraction of an exhaustible natural resource, is a situation with little precedent in modern world history. This chapter is a theoretical inquiry into the proper way of thinking about how to calculate the national product for a country whose earnings come essentially from the extraction of a depletable natural resource.

At the outset, it should be noted that a careful treatment of extractive industries is nowhere to be found in the standard and voluminous literature on national income accounting. No doubt this reflects the fact that, until recently, extractive industries were a relatively small part of the economic activity in virtually all countries. In other words, the standard economic literature gives very little guidance on how to properly treat depletion as a component of the national product. For this reason it will be necessary to go back to first principles and develop our own imputation procedure for dealing with oil extraction.

The standard way of including mining-like activities in national product is to simply add the market value of the crude output extracted at the earliest stage of production. It does not take a great deal of thought to understand that this procedure has some peculiar ramifications. If Saudi Arabia increases oil production from 8-12 million barrels per day, the national product originating in oil production increases by half. As we shall see, this arbitrariness goes against some rather basic notions about what net national product ought to represent, and the fact that standard procedure gives the wrong answers.

To determine the contribution of oil extraction to net national product, we have to go back to the beginning and determine what it is that net national product is meant to represent. This is an old economic theme, about which a great many words have been written. Basically, the fundamental abstraction is to treat the nation as if it were a single individual. Then net national product is intended to measure the hypothetical individual's degree of well-being in some sense. There is no way that a single index number can compress all the information about the welfare of each member of a society. Thus, the Net National Product (NNP) cannot make a statement about income distribution. But it can be measure of the well-being of what might be called an "average" or "typical" member of the economic society.

Most theoretical work about the meaning of the NNP focuses on the static case where there is no capital to be accumulated or pools of exhaustible resources to be run down. There is extensive literature on the welfare interpretation of the NNP for a static economy. Much of this has to do with the issue of what it means to aggregate together different goods using their prices as weights. While the answers can be quite sophisticated, involving the theory of index numbers and revealed preference, for our purposes it is sufficient to note that if prices represent marginal rates of transformation, they are the appropriate weights for aggregation into what might be called total or aggregate consumption, and aggregate consumption at real prices is an appropriate welfare measure for the nation viewed as an artificial person.

Quite a different set of issues are involved in a dynamic world of capital investment, depreciation, and depletion of exhaustible resource pools. On this subject there is much more sparse literature. The usual welfare interpretation of index numbers can perhaps be used to combine apples and oranges using their prices as weights, but it falls short of telling us how to treat investment-like activities in a dynamic economy.

We start in an economy with reproducible capital, but no depletable resources. The most resonable and commonly accepted interpretation of net national product in such a dynamic economy is that it is the largest permanently maintainable amount of consumption. With reproducible capital, the reason we add net investment to consumption in standard national product accounting is that the resulting number represents what the economy could consume forever if it chose to devote all its resources to consumption and to stop growing. If all net investment were converted into hypothetical consumption, the economy could go on enjoying that hypothetical level of consumption forever because the capital stock base is neither increasing nor decreasing (since net investment is zero).

In other words, to figure out net national product we perform a kind of thought experiment. As if our aim were to enjoy a constant stream of

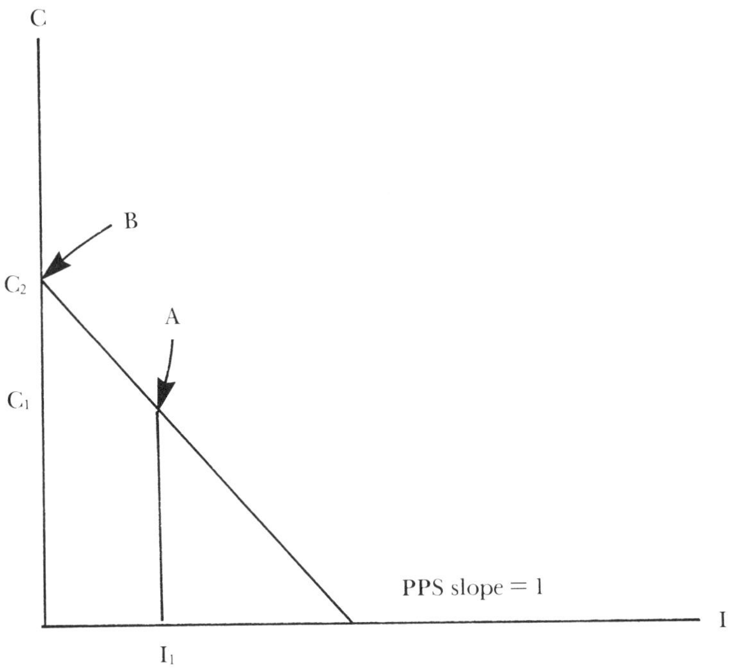

Figure AI.1. Geometric Representation of Net National Product

consumption, we ask: What is the largest possible value of steady consumption, given the resources of this economy? It is not necessary that the economy actually carry out this experiment. The NNP is what the maximum constant level of consumption *would* be, *if* that were the goal of the economy. With reproducible capital, the power of the community to consume at a constant level is measured by current consumption plus current net investment because the economy is neither growing nor shrinking if the capital base is intact and in that case it could enjoy a consumption level equal to what it now consumes plus the current net investment that could be transformed into additional consumption without altering the existing capital stock. Such reasoning is expressed here verbally because the basic ideas are not complicated, but a rigorous mathematical formulation can be put behind it.

Figure AI.1 shows the basic idea. The horizontal axis measures net investment, the vertical asix is consumption. Suppose for the sake of simplicity the production possibilities frontier between consumption and investment for this period is a straight line with a 1:1 rate of transformation.

(More advanced theory goes some way toward justifying this assumption, since a competitive economy behaves "as if" it were true.) Suppose we are located at point *A*, where the economy is consuming C_1 and investing I_1. What is the NNP? It is the largest permanently maintainable stream of consumption, which in this case is C_2. If the economy did zero net investing ($I_2 = 0$), its capital base would remain constant, and in principle it could consume at the rate C_2 forever.

Thus, we are inclined to call $C_2 = C_1 + I_1$ the net national product of the economy because it represents the largest permanently sustainable hypothetical level of consumption, even though the economy is actually consuming at the rate C_1.

So far, the discussion has been in terms of a dynamic economy that can accumulate capital, but without stocks of depletable natural resources. In turning to the main theme of this chapter, how to measure the NNP for an economy with a significant exhaustible resource base, we first have to recognize that we are breaking new ground. The standard literature simply does not deal explicitly with exhaustible natural resources. So we are forced to work out a theory of our own. The resulting theory is far from arbitrary, however. The basic principle is the same one that is widely accepted as a basis for national income accounting in a dynamic economy with capital accumulation—the NNP should measure the largest consumption level that is indefinitely sustainable. The principle remains the same; only its application to a different scenario is novel.

To develop the basic idea of the model, we abstract heroically. Since it is only the income originating in the extraction of the exhaustible natural resource that is in question (income originating in other sectors would be treated in the standard fashion of commonly accepted national income accounting procedure), we abstract to an economy whose *only* activity is the extraction of an exhaustible resource. To spare the repetitious use of a phrase, and because it is the primary example we have in mind, from now on we will identify the exhaustible natural resource as oil, although the theory is general enough to handle similar examples.

Suppose that the pool of oil is a known stock of size *S*, and, for the sake of simplicity, costs of extraction are negligible. We also suppose, initially, that the annual extraction rate, denoted *E*, has been fixed beforehand and cannot be altered. Of course the extraction rate is in fact a control variable, and later we will wish to examine its most economical value, for the time being we treat *E* as if it is a technologically determined constant. In this scenario, then, oil will be extracted for $T = S/E$ years, during which time, presumably, other capital stock has been created that can be used to build up a base for providing consumption income after time *T*.

In what follows everything will be expressed in *real* terms, that is, after taking account of the effects of a general inflationary rise in prices.

The future trajectory of world oil prices is a subject of much controversy. There are theories that derive the growth of real oil prices either as a consequence of competitive assumptions, or as a consequence of various other assumptions about the form of imperfect competition inherent in a cartel, and about very simple assumptions about the costs of oil extraction. Because there is no theoretical consensus, it seems that perhaps the most practical course is to postulate an exponential growth of oil price and then do sensitivity analysis on the assumed growth rate.

Thus, we presume the real price of world oil in ten years hence will be:

$$p(t) = p_o e^{gt} \tag{1}$$

where p_o is the price today, and g is the postulated growth in the real price of oil. Most observers believe that for purposes of determining long-run trends, g is rather modest, and in the long run the price of oil will outstrip the general price level by perhaps 1 or 2 percent per year on an average, maybe less.

We suppose that all revenues from the sale of oil are either consumed or saved. If saved, we assume that savings consists of acquisition of assets (real or monetary) paying a uniform *real* interest rate of r per annum. In the case of Saudi Arabia, the monetary authorities are pretty much restricted to buying high-grade bonds of stable governments. Even if direct investment is permitted, we assume it yields the same real return of r. This is not a far-fetched assumption for Kuwait or Saudi Arabia, where domestic investment projects have been pushed so far to the margin that their real rates of return are probably close to that earned on foreign bonds. The assumption allows for analytical convenience, and, if found to be too unrealistic, can be replaced by a more complicated set of assumptions.

The important point, I think, is that the investment opportunities facing a country like Saudi Arabia offer extremely low, or even negative real rates of return (after taking account of inflation). Even without accounting for a negative trend in the terms of trade, the real return on government bonds in the United States has been slightly negative over the last few decades, and also over the longer run. Corporate bonds yield rates of return slightly higher, but still net out to about zero real interest rate after the growth of inflation is factored out. Only common stock yields positive rates of return. What the future will bring, no one knows for sure, but it seems plausible to expect that the real rate of interest available on investment is quite low, perhaps at best in the neighborhood of 1 or 2 percent per annum, if investments are wisely managed.

By standard national income accounting practice, the oil-based economy would have a national product this year of

$$P_o E \tag{2}$$

since that is the income originating in the economy. But, as we have already noted, this is not really a meaningful or well-founded economic concept because no account is being taken of the run-down or depleted stock of oil.

Let us pose the question in the usual dynamic way. For our hypothetical oil-based economy, what is the largest permanently maintainable real stream of consumption? Call this fictitious annual real consumption stream Y, to stand for the true measure of net national product.

Let $K(t)$ be the real value of accumulated capital investments at time t, by assumption earning a real rate of r. Initially,

$$K(o) = o. \tag{3}$$

Our question is: What is the *largest* value of hypothetical real consumption Y, such that in each year $t \leq T$,

$$Y \leq p_o e^{gt} E + rK(t) - \dot{K}(t) \tag{4}$$

and for each year $t > T$,

$$Y \leq rK(t) - \dot{K}(t), \tag{5}$$

where

$$\dot{K}(t) = \frac{dk}{dt},$$

and

$$\lim_{t \to \infty} K(t) \geq 0 \tag{6}$$

(in the limit, a debtor position is not allowed).

The largest value of Y satisfying (4) – (6) will obviously satisfy (4) and (5) with full equality. This optimal value of Y, call it Y^*, will obey

$$\dot{K}(t) = o \tag{7}$$

at time $t \geq T$ (after the oil has run out, if $\dot{K} > O$, that is inefficient for max-min consumption; if $\dot{K} < O$, condition (5) will be violated). Thus,

$$Y^* = rK(T). \tag{8}$$

Substituting for $Y = Y^*$ from (8) into (4), we have

$$rK(T) = p_o e^{gt} E + rK(t) - \dot{K}(t), \tag{9}$$

which can be rearranged into

$$\dot{K}(t) = r[K(t)] + p_o e^{gt} E \tag{10}$$

for $O \leq t \leq T$.

The solution of the differential equation (10) with the initial condition (3) is

$$K(t) \;=\; \frac{Po\,E\,(1-e^{-(r-g)t}),}{r-g} \tag{11}$$

for $O \leq t \leq T$.

Thus, from (8) and (11),

$$Y^* \;=\; \frac{rPoE}{r-g}\;(1-e^{-(r-g)T}), \tag{12}$$

where

$$T \equiv S/E \tag{13}$$

Equation (12) is the fundamental result.

We have reduced the calcuation of the theoretical NNP to a relatively simple formula, expressed directly in terms of the underlying data of the problem. The formula (12) can be given an elementary economic interpretation. With a real interest rate r and an asset yielding $p_o E e^{gt}$ in year t, the perpetual consumption flow Y^* is possible where

$$Y^* \int_o^\infty e^{-rt} dt \;=\; \int_o^T \;(EPoe^{gt})e^{-rt} dt \tag{14}$$

Expression (14) of course reduces to (12).

One question of immediate interest is the relation of our theoretically justified NNP Y^* to the standard measure $P_o E$. Suppose, as a base case, that $r = g$. This is a case that is actually suggested by the theory of resource extraction and it is not a bad assumption, empirically. With $r = g$, (12) yields an indeterminate quotient of the form O/O. Applying l'Hospital's rule, we obtain

$$Y^* = rE\,PoT = rS\,Po \tag{15}$$

when $r = g$. Comparing (15) with (2), we have that the ratio of conventionally measured to the theoretically correct NNP is

$$\frac{PoE}{Y^*} = \frac{PoE}{rSPo} = \frac{1}{rT} \tag{16}$$

[using (13)].

Assuming $r = g = 1$ percent and $T = 40$,

$$\frac{PoE}{Y^*} = 2.5.$$

In other words, the conventionally measured NNP is 2½ times as large as the theoretically justified value. Of course, such conclusions depend crucially on assumptions about r and g. If $r = g = 2.5$ percent,

$$PoE = Y^*,$$

for example, the conventionally measured NNP is exactly equal to the theoretically justified value and could exceed it if $r = g > 2.5$ percent when $T = 40$.

In the general case,

$$\frac{PoE}{Y^*} = \frac{r}{r - g}\,(1 - e^{-(r-g)T}). \tag{17}$$

The formula (17) for the ratio of conventionally measured to the theoretically correct NNP is simple enough so that the interested reader can easily plug in values to derive numerical results for any specific case of interest. For empirical values of T around 40 years and values of r and g each equal to about 1 percent, one is left with the distinct impression that current measures of national product overvalue the "true" measure of the power to consume at a steady rate.

So far we have taken E, the annual extraction rate, as given. Suppose now that current reserves S are fixed, but E and hence $T = S/E$, may be freely varied. What is the optimal value of E? An equivalent way of stating this question is to ask what value of E maximizes the true NNP?

From (15), if $r = g$, any value of E maximizes Y^*. The reason is that if the discount rate just equals the growth rate of price, it doesn't matter how the oil is taken out of the ground—if we wait until later, the oil is worth more but this price effect is offset by a higher discounting factor that leaves the present discounted value exactly the same.

From (12), if $r > g$ an optimal policy pulls the oil out of the ground as quickly as possible. The opposite conclusion is true if $r < g$. If the growth in real oil prices will exceed the real rates of return on alternative assets, it is most economical to draw the oil out of the ground slowly to take advantage of future high prices.

Whatever the time duration T of oil extraction, an optimal savings policy will smooth consumption over time by accumulating capital during the oil-producing years in sufficient quantities to guarantee satisfactory consumption levels in the years $t > T$ after oil runs out. In other words, it can be very misleading to view the conventionally measured national product pE as an income stream, most of which is to be consumed. In industrialized economies whose economic base is primarily reproducible capital, it is reasonable to think in terms of consumption rats of 80 or 90 percent. But for an economy based on a depletable resource, it would be very foolish to think in terms of such high consumption rates as a percentage of conventionally measured national income. The resource base of such an economy is dwindling as the oil is extracted, and hence, the early years call for extra large investments to offset future deprivations.

These points can be illustrated by a suitably modified optimal growth model. Let $K(t)$ be the value of accumulated capital at time t, which earns a real annual rate of return r. Let L be the rate of pure time preference and $U(C)$ the cardinal utility of consuming C units of income. Assume the extraction rate is a fixed constant E. As before, real oil prices grow at a constant rate g.

The problem is to choose a consumption control $[C(t)]$ to maximize

$$\int_o^\infty U[C(t)]\, e^{-Lt} dt \qquad (18)$$

subject to

$$\dot{K}(t) = p_o e^{gt} E(t) + rK(t) - C(t) \qquad (19)$$

$$K(o) = K_o, \text{ given} \qquad (20)$$

$$E(t) = E, \text{ given for } O \leq t \leq T = S/E \qquad (21)$$

$$\text{E}(t) = o \text{ for } t > T$$

Without much loss of generality, and in order to obtain an explicit closed form solution, we assume $U(C)$ is a member of the constant elasticity of marginal utility family, or that

$$U'(C) = \frac{1}{C^a} \tag{22}$$

where the parameter a is minus the (constant) elasticity of marginal utility. Thus,

$$U'(C) = \begin{cases} \dfrac{1}{1-a} C^{1-a} & \text{for } a \neq 1 \\ \log c & \text{for } a = 1 \end{cases} \tag{23}$$

The paramenter a is a measure of the strength of diminishing returns in the utility of consumption. The problem is not meaningful except in the parameter range

$$r > L > (1-a)r.$$

The solution, using optimal control theory, can be described as follows. First of all, the problem can be simplified by a restructuring. Let

$$X_o = K(o) + \int_o^T P_o E e^{gt} e^{-rt} dt = K(o) + \frac{PoE(1 - e^{-(r-g)T})}{r-g} \tag{24}$$

In other words, $X(o)$ is the initial productive capital plus the capitalized present discounted value of the oil earnings. We can replace (19) – (21) by the simpler equivalent conditions

$$\dot{X}(t) = rX(t) - C \tag{25}$$

$$X(o) = X_o, \text{ given} \tag{26}$$

The original problem has been replaced by an equivalent one where the entire stock of oil has been "cashed in" for its equivalent present discounted value and we work this artificial imported capital stock X. Naturally,

$X(t) = K(t)$ for $t \geq T$. But for $t < T$, the imputed capital is

$$X(t) = K(t) + \int_t^T P_o E\, e^{gs} e^{-r(s-t)} ds \tag{27}$$

The problems (18), (25), and (26) are in simple enough form to enable us to solve them directly. The solution for C and X to grow forever at the same steady rate

$$Y = \frac{r - L}{a}, \tag{28}$$

where the "savings rate out of artificial capital," $(rX - C)/rX$ is

$$s = \frac{r - L}{ar} \tag{29}$$

Thus, in an optimal solution

$$C(t) = C(o)e^{Yt}, \tag{30}$$

where [from (29)]

$$C(o) = X(o) \frac{[L - (1 - a)r]}{a}, \tag{31}$$

or [using (24)]

$$C(o) = \left[K(o) + \frac{PoE(1 - e^{-(r-g)T})}{r - g} \right] \left(\frac{L - (1 - a)r}{a} \right) \tag{32}$$

While we could analyze the optimal consumption patterns (28), (30), and (32) as a function of the underlying paramenters, and of course the solution "makes sense," our major interest here is in the broad qualitative properties and in their implications for savings policy.

Optimal consumption grows smoothly and exponentially. And savings measured as the rate on "artificial capital" is constant. But, and this is the important point, optimal savings as *conventionally* measured, behaves quite differently. To keep consumption growing exponentially forever at rate g calls for very *high* conventional savings rates initially, which gradually come down to (29) just at the time $t = T$ when oil runs out. See, for example, Chakravarty (1962) or Weitzman (1971).

Initial national income as conventionally measured is, by (19) – (21),

$$P_oE + rK(o). \tag{33}$$

The conventionally measured optimal savings rate at the beginning is, therefore,

$$\hat{s} = 1 - \left(\frac{(1 - e^{-(r-g)T})}{r - g} \right) \left(\frac{L - (1 - a)r}{a} \right) \tag{35}$$

Suppose $r = g$ again as a base case. Using l'Hospital's rule, (35) becomes

$$\hat{s} = 1 - T\frac{(L - (1 - a)r)}{a}, \tag{36}$$

or, using (29) and rearranging

$$\hat{s} = 1 - rT(1 - s) \tag{37}$$

Suppose $r = g = 1$ percent, $T = 40$, $s = 20$ percent. If the *eventual* (when all the oil runs out) rate of savings out of capital is to be 20 percent, the conventionally measured savings rate now should be

$$s = 68 \text{ percent.}$$

The reader can work out other cases from (37), but the lesson from optimal growth theory seems to be clear. In order to achieve reasonable savings rates in the future, when oil is depleted, a country should start now (at least with the parameter values assumed here) saving at extremely high rates as conventionally measured by the fraction of investment to oil revenues. If the oil economy has a utility function consistent with eventually saving 20 percent (after oil has run out), the optimal policy is to now invest approximately 70 percent of the national product in productive capital.

A few final lessons are hidden more deeply in the mathematics. The low real rates of return that drive many of the extreme numerical conclusions are those available on safe government bonds. A more aggressive investment strategy, which would include a mixed portfolio, might earn higher rates on average, which would make the distortions between conventionally measured and ideally measured national product less striking.

We have not dealt with risk or uncertainty in these models, because it is so difficult to easily incorporate this feature. But almost surely, the presence of uncertainty would tend to argue against keeping so much invested in one particular type of asset (oil in the ground), and in favor of diversifying risk by extracting at higher rates than are appropriate for a risk free world and by spreading out the proceeds in a variety of different types of assets. If it is most profitable to pump oil out of the ground slowly in a risk free world, the diversification effect would argue in favor of pumping it out somewhat more rapidly in a risky world. Again there appears to be a case for a mixed investment portfolio.

NOTE

The views represent those of the author and not any individuals or institutions with whom he is affiliated.

SELECTED REFERENCES

Anderson, K.P. (1972) "Optimum Growth When the Stock of the Resource Is Finite and Depletable," *Journal of Economic Theory:* 256-267.

Chakravarty, S. (1962) "Optimal Savings with Finite Planning Horizon," *International Economic Review:* 338-355.

Cremer, J. and Weitzman, M.L. (1976) "OPEC and the Monopoly Price of World Oil," *European Economic Review* 8: 155-164.

Dasgupta, P.S. and Heal, G.M. (1979) *Economic Theory and Exhaustible Resources.* New York: Cambridge University Press.

Hotelling, H. (1931) "The Economics of Exhaustible Resources," *Journal of Political Economy:* 137-175.

Kuznets, S. (1941) *National Income and Its Composition, 1919-1938.* New York: National Bureau of Economic Research.

Samuelson, P.A. (1950) "Evaluation of Real National Income," *Oxford Economic Papers:* 1-29.

Samuelson, P.A. (1961) "The Evaluation of Social Income: Capital Formation and Wealth," in Lutz and Hague (eds.), *The Theory of Capital.* New York: St. Martin's Press.

Sen, A. (1979) "The Welfare Basis of Real Income Comparisons: A Survey," *Journal of Economic Literature* XVII (1): 1-45.

Solow, R.M. (1974) "Intergenerational Equity and Exhaustible Resources," *Review of Economic Studies Symposium,* Cambridge, MA, M.I.T. Working paper no. 103.

Solow, R.M. (1974) "The Economics of Resources or the Resources of Economics," *American Economic Review,* Papers and Proceedings: 1-15.

Solow, R.M. and Wan, F.Y. (1977) "Extraction Cost In the Theory of Exhaustible Resources," *Bell Journal of Economics* 1: 359-370.

Weitzman, M.L. (1971) "Shiftable versus Non-Shiftable Capital: A Synthesis," *Econometrica* 39: 511-529.

Weitzman, M.L. (1976) "On the Welfare Significance of National Product in a Dynamic Economy," *Quarterly Journal of Economics* 90: 156-162.

Appendix II

CORRESPONDENCE OF THE HIJRI TO THE GREGORIAN CALENDAR

The Hijri calendar follows the lunar year of 354 days with 11 leap years of 355 days in each cycle of 30 years. The first year of this calendar corresponds to 622 A.D. The starting dates in the Gregorian calendar for Hijri years used here are as follows:

Hijri Year	*Started On*	*Hijri Year*	*Started On*
1390	March 9, 1970	1397	December 22, 1976
1391	February 26, 1971	1398	December 11, 1977
1392	February 16, 1972	1399	December 1, 1978
1393	February 4, 1973	1400	November 20, 1979
1394	January 24, 1974	1401	November 9, 1980
1395	January 13, 1975	1402	October 28, 1981
1396	January 2, 1976	1403	October 18, 1982

The fiscal year in Saudi Arabia begins from the middle of one Hijri year to the middle of the next Hijri year. The fiscal year of 1389-1390, for instance, began from Rajab 1, 1389 to the last day of Jamad II and corresponds to Gregorian calendar dates of September 12, 1969 to September 1, 1970. The corresponding Gregorian calendar dates for some fiscal years are as follows:

Fiscal Year	*Started On*	*Fiscal Year*	*Started On*
1389-1390	September 12, 1969	1396-1397	June 28, 1976
1390-1391	September 2, 1970	1397-1398	June 17, 1977
1391-1392	August 22, 1971	1398-1399	June 6, 1978
1392-1393	August 10, 1972	1399-1400	May 27, 1979
1393-1394	July 30, 1973	1400-1401	May 15, 1980
1394-1395	July 20, 1974	1401-1402	May 4, 1981
1395-1396	July 10, 1975	1402-1403	April 24, 1982

The following comparisons can be used for quick approximate reference:

Hijri Year	*Gregorian Year*	*Fiscal Year*	*Gregorian Year*
1390	1970	1389-1390	1969-1970
1391	1971	1390-1391	1970-1971
1392	1972	1391-1392	1971-1972
1393	1973	1392-1393	1972-1973
1394	1974	1393-1394	1973-1974
1395	1975	1394-1395	1974-1975
1396	1976	1395-1396	1975-1976
1397	1977	1396-1397	1976-1977
1398	1978	1397-1398	1977-1978
1399	1979	1398-1399	1978-1979
1400	1980	1399-1400	1979-1980
1401	1981	1400-1401	1980-1981
1402	1982	1401-1402	1981-1982
1403	1983	1402-1403	1982-1983
1404	1984	1403-1404	1983-1984
1405	1985	1404-1405	1984-1985
1406	1986	1405-1406	1985-1986
1407	1987	1406-1407	1986-1987

Appendix III

TABLES FOR INDIVIDUAL AND OVERALL CALCULATED SUBSIDIES (IN SAUDI RIYALS)

Table AIII.1. Electricity Generation—Operating Subsidy

	1395	*1396*	*1397*	*1398*	*1399*	*1400*	*1401*	*1402*	*1403*	*1404*	*Total*
Average Government Subsidy per kwh Sold (SR)	.044	.051	.08	.106	.117	.114	.122	.139	.115	.113	—
Millions of kwh Sold	3,760	5,322	6,364	8,465	13,449	17,436	21,643	26,631	31,177	36,986	—
Government Operating Subsidy (SR Millions)	165.4	271.4	509.1	897.3	1,573.5	1,987.7	2,640.4	3,707.7	3,585.4	4,179.4	19,511.3

Source: Various government sources.

Table AIII.2. Electricity Generation—Capital Subsidy

	1395	*1396*	*1397*	*1398*	*1399*	*1400*	*1401*	*1402*	*1403*	*1404*	*Total*
SIDF											
Annual Loan Disbursement[a]	1,409	1,570	3,278	6,540	5,178	5,483	4,551	4,238	4,169	1,495.5	—
Average Eurodollar Rate (6 mos.)	10.84	7.75	6.12	6.37	9.20	12.15	14.03	16.72	13.60	9.93	—
Less: 0.5% Annual Charge	10.34	7.25	5.62	5.87	8.70	11.65	13.53	16.22	13.10	9.43	—
Implicit Capital Subsidy[a]	146	216	351	751	1,563	2,737	3,789	5,230	4,770	3,575	23,123

Note: a. Figures are given in SR Millions.
Source: SIDF (1403-1404 [1983-1984]).

Table AIII.3. Water Desalination Projects—Operating Subsidy

	1395	*1396*	*1397*	*1398*	*1399*	*1400*	*1401*	*1402*	*1403*	*1404*	*Total*
Volume of Annual Production[a]	71,723,230	53,801,730	53,801,730	53,801,730	53,801,730	596,478,620	596,478,620	596,478,620	596,478,620	596,478,620	—
Cost of Production (excluding capital)[a] (SR)	7.00	7.00	7.00	7.00	7.00	7.00	7.00	7.00	7.00	7.00	—
Charge[a] (SR)	.25	.25	.25	.25	.25	.25	.25	.25	.25	.25	—
Annual Operating Subsidy (SR Millions)	484.00	363.00	363.00	363.00	363.00	4,026.00	4,026.00	4,026.00	4,026.00	4,026.00	22,066.00

Note: a. Figures are calculated per cubic meter.
Source: The General Water Conversion Corporation.

Table AIII.4. Water Desalination Projects—Capital Subsidy[a b]

	1395	*1396*	*1397*	*1398*	*1399*	*1400*	*1401*	*1402*	*1403*	*1404*	*Total*
Capital Cost of Project Annually[c]	934.00	563.00	563.00	563.00	563.00	6,064.00	6,064.00	10,245.00	10,245.00	10,245.00	—
Eurodollar Rate (6 mos.)	10.84	7.75	5.12	6.37	9.20	12.15	14.03	16.72	13.60	9.93	—
Implicit Capital Subsidy[c]	101.00	116.00	125.00	167.00	293.00	1,124.00	2,149.00	4,273.00	4,869.00	4,573.00	17,791.00

Notes: a. All loans carry zero interest.

b. Figures for the capital cost of project annually represent the following:

1975 : 2,814/5 + 371 (1974)
1976-1979 : 2,814/5
1980-1981 : 30,320/5
1982-1984 : 30,320/5 + 12,544/3

c. Figures are given in SR Millions.

Source: The General Saline Water Conversion Corporation.

Table AIII.5. Fuels—Operating Subsidies

	1395	*1396*	*1397*	*1398*	*1399*	*1400*	*1401*	*1402*	*1403*	*1404*	*Total*
Total Annual Domestic Consumption (millions of barrels)[a]	42.80	57.80	69.30	93.80	149.60	190.00	225.40	248.90	281.60	301.30	—
Domestic Price (SR/barrel)[b]	21.38	21.38	21.38	21.38	21.38	21.38	21.38	21.38	21.38	21.38	—
World Price (SR/barrel)[c]	37.13	40.49	42.68	44.77	53.31	87.38	106.45	115.01	116.56	100.19	—
Difference in Price (SR/barrel)	15.75	19.11	21.30	23.39	31.93	66.00	85.07	93.63	95.18	78.81	—
Total Annual Subsidy on Production (SR Millions)	674.00	1,104.00	1,476.00	2,194.00	4,777.00	12,540.00	19,175.00	23,304.00	26,803.00	23,745.00	115,792.00

Notes: a. These figures exclude consumption by the oil industry.
b. The figures for the domestic price per barrel are estimates based on an average of the prices for the different kinds of products sold domestically.
c. World crude price for Saudi oil is used as the opportunity cost, instead of a price based on product prices.

Sources: SAMA (1395-1402 [1975-1982]); author's estimates (1402-1404 [1982-1984]).

Table AIII.6a. Agriculture—Operating Subsidies[a]

	1395[b]	*1396*	*1397*	*1398*	*1399*	*1400*	*1401*	*1402*	*1403*	*1404*	*Total*
Agricultural Inputs[c]	180.80	182.00	236.70	347.90	436.00	616.00	979.00	1,321.00	1,023.00	1,378.00	6,700.40
Wheat[c]	—	—	—	—	48.82	89.96	231.19	656.03	1,861.98	3,714.83	6,602.81
Total[c]	180.80	182.00	236.70	347.90	436.00	705.96	1,210.19	1,977.03	2,884.98	5,092.83	13,303.71

Notes: a. Wheat subsidies only started in 1399 (see Table AIII.6b for calculations).
b. 1395 figure includes SR 46.3 million for 1394 and SR 134.5 million for 1395.
c. Figures are given in SR Millions.
Source: SAAB.

Table AIII.6b. Agriculture—Wheat Subsidies

	CIF Price in Saudi Arabia	*Average Exchange Rate (SR)*	*Subsidy Per Million Ton (SR)*	*Total Subsidy*
1399	213.0	3.340	2,789	48.82
1400	228.5	3.345	2,736	89.96
1401	235.5	3.370	2,706	231.19
1402	219.5	3.475	2,737	656.03
1403	209.5	3.535	2,760	1,861.98
1404	205.5	3.610	2,758	3,714.83
1405	203.5	3.645	1,258	2,138.60

Note: Wheat prices were obtained from the United Nation's Food and Agricultural Organization (FAO) trade book for the years shown.
Source: SAAB.

Table AIII.7. Agriculture—Capital Subsidy[a]

	1395[b]	*1396*	*1397*	*1398*	*1399*	*1400*	*1401*	*1402*	*1403*	*1404*	*Total*
Short-term[c] New Loans Granted by SAAB	15.43	17.29	43.71	15.29	22.70	39.20	29.50	25.30	18.50	—	—
Medium-term[c] New Loans Granted by SAAB	399.50	472.60	542.00	693.80	1,106.00	2,491.60	2,903.40	4,140.80	3,495.80	—	—
Total New Loans Granted by SAAB	414.90	489.80	585.70	709.00	1,128.70	2,550.90	2,933.00	4,166.00	3,495.80	2,322.00	—
Average Eurodollar Rate (6 mos.)	10.84	7.75	6.12	6.37	9.20	12.15	14.03	16.72	13.60	9.93	—
Implicit Capital Subsidy	45.00	70.00	91.00	140.00	306.00	714.00	1,236.00	2,170.00	2,240.00	1,866.00	8,880.00

Notes: a. Figures are for fiscal years; all figures are in SR millions except Eurodollar Rate.
b. Loan figures for 1395 include 1394 amounts.
c. Short-term loans = 1 year; medium-term loans = 7 years.

Source: SAAB and SAMA Annual Reports (1978, 1982, 1986).

Table AIII.8. Food Subsidies

	1395[a]	1396	1397	1398	1399	1400	1401	1402	1403	1404	Total
Food (million SR)	1,450	600	700	800	1,450	3,000	5,000	4,476	1,600	2,600	21,676

Note: a. Figure for 1395 includes SR 750 million from 1394 and SR 700 million from 1395.

Table AIII.9. Housing—Capital Subsidy[a]

	1395	1396	1397	1398	1399	1400	1401	1402	1403	1404	Total
Actual Disbursement[b]	2,159.00	8,901.00	7,534.00	5,766.00	8,575.00	7,598.00	7,141.00	8,307.00	8,909.00	8,598.00	—
Average Eurodollar Rate (6 mos.)	10.84	7.75	6.12	6.37	9.20	12.15	14.07	16.72	13.60	9.93	—
Implicit Capital[b]	234.00	857.00	1,138.00	1,552.00	3,030.00	4,925.00	6,689.00	9,360.00	8,825.00	7,297.00	43,907.00

Notes: a. The loans carry zero interest.
b. Figures are given in SR Millions.
Source: Real Estate Development Fund (1395-1403 [1975-1982]); SAMA (1404 [1984]).

Table AIII.10. Saudi Arabian Airlines Corporation—Operating Subsidy

	1395	1396	1397	1398	1399	1400	1401	1402	1403[a]	1404[a]	Total
Operating Loss[b]	24	113	167	157	237	317	863	405	—	—	2,283

Notes: a. For 1403 and 1404, there was a profit of SR 75 million and SR 138 million, respectively.
b. Figures are given in SR Millions.
Source: Saudi Arabian Airlines Corporation (1984).

Table AIII.11. Capital Subsidy to Industry

	1395[a]	*1396*	*1397*	*1398*	*1399*	*1400*	*1401*	*1402*	*1403*	*1404*	*Total*
SIDF Industrial Loans[b]	1,178	1,151	2,091	987	1,339	1,259	1,425	2,663	1,223	939	—
Less: 2.5% Upfront Fee[b c]	1,149	1,219	2,038	962	1,305	1,227	1,379	1,621	1,192	915	—
Average Eurodollar Rate (6 mos.)	10.84	7.75	6.12	6.37	9.20	12.15	14.03	16.72	13.60	9.93	—
Implicit Capital Subsidy[b]	125	184	270	342	614	960	1,302	1,822	1,645	1,292	8,554

Notes: a. For 1395, loans equal SR 150 million from 1394, plus 1,028.
b. Figures are given in SR Millions.
c. For the calculation assumed, a 2.5% upfront fee and zero interest thereafter.
Source: SIDF (1404-1405 [1984-1985]).

Table AIII.12. Public Investment Fund (PIF) Capital Subsidy

	1395[a]	*1396*	*1397*	*1398*	*1399*	*1400*	*1401*	*1402*	*1403*	*1404*	*Total*
Loan Disbursements Less Repayments[b]	2,345	4,031	5,886	3,893	2,760	5,617	7,940	8,662	4,910	2,674	—
Average Eurodollar Rate (6 mos.)	10.84	7.75	6.12	6.37	9.20	12.15	14.07	16.72	13.60	9.93	—
Implicit Capital Subsidy[b]	254	494	750	1,029	1,740	2,981	4,556	6,878	6,262	4,838	29,782

Notes: a. The figure for loan disbursements less repayment for 1395 includes SR 263 million from 1393, SR 603 million from 1394 and SR 1,479 million from 1395.
b. Figures are given in SR Millions.

Source: Ministry of Finance and National Economy.

Table AIII.13. Noncapital (Operating) Government Subsidies[a]

	1395	*1396*	*1397*	*1398*	*1399*	*1400*	*1401*	*1402*	*1403*	*1404*	*Total*
Agriculture	181[b]	182	237	348	436	706	1,210	1,977	2,885	5,093	13,254
Fuel	674	1,104	1,476	2,194	4,777	12,540	19,175	23,304	26,803	23,745	115,792
Electricity	165	272	506	893	1,580	1,989	2,638	3,712	3,587	4,152	19,494
Water Desalination	484	363	363	363	363	363	4,026	4,026	4,026	4,026	18,403
Saudia	24	113	167	157	237	317	863	405	—	—	2,283
Food	1,450	600	700	800	1,450	3,000	5,000	4,476	1,600	2,600	21,676
Total	2,978	2,634	3,449	4,755	8,843	18,915	32,912	37,900	38,901	39,616	190,902

Notes: a. Figures are given in SR Millions.
b. Figure includes SR 46.3 million from 1394.

Table AIII.14. Capital Government Subsidies[a]

	1395	*1396*	*1397*	*1398*	*1399*	*1400*	*1401*	*1402*	*1403*	*1404*	*Total*
Agriculture	45	70	91	140	306	714	1,236	2,170	2,240	1,866	8,880
Industry	125	184	270	342	614	960	1,302	1,822	1,645	1,292	8,554
Water	101	116	126	167	293	1,124	2,149	4,273	4,869	4,573	17,791
Housing	234	857	1,138	1,552	3,030	4,925	6,689	9,360	8,825	7,297	43,907
PIF	254	494	750	1,029	1,740	2,981	4,556	6,878	6,262	4,838	29,782
Electricity	146	216	351	751	1,563	2,732	3,789	5,230	4,770	3,575	23,123
Total	905	1,937	2,727	3,981	7,547	13,436	19,720	29,733	28,611	23,440	132,036

Note: a. Figures are given in SR Millions.

Table AIII.15. Total Government Subsidies[a] (Capital and Operating)

	1395	*1396*	*1397*	*1398*	*1399*	*1400*	*1401*	*1402*	*1403*	*1404*	*Total*
Agriculture	226	252	328	488	742	1,420	2,447	4,147	5,125	6,959	22,134
Industry[b]	125	184	270	342	614	960	1,302	1,822	1,645	1,292	8,554
Water	585	479	489	530	656	1,487	6,175	8,299	8,895	8,599	36,194
Electricity	311	488	857	1,644	3,143	4,721	6,427	8,942	8,357	7,726	42,617
Housing[b]	234	857	1,138	1,552	3,030	4,925	6,689	9,360	8,825	7,297	43,907
PIF[b]	254	494	750	1,029	1,740	2,981	4,556	6,878	6,262	4,838	29,782
Food[c]	1,450	600	700	800	1,450	3,000	5,000	4,476	1,600	2,600	21,676
Saudia[c]	24	113	167	157	237	317	863	405	—	—	2,283
Fuel[c]	674	1,104	1,476	2,194	4,777	12,540	19,175	23,304	26,803	23,745	115,792
Total	3,882	4,571	6,175	8,736	16,390	32,351	52,632	67,633	67,512	63,056	322,939

Notes: a. Figures are given in SR Millions.
b. Only capital subsidy.
c. Only operating subsidy.

Appendix IV

GLOSSARY OF SAUDI ARABIAN INSTITUTIONS

Arab Bureau of Education for the Gulf States
Arab Investment Company SAA
Arab Petroleum Investment Corporation
Arab Satellite Communictions Corporation
Arabian American Oil Company

Central Department of Statistics
Civil Service Commission
Council of Ministers
Council of Saudi Arabian Chambers of Commerce and Industry
Credit Fund for Contractors

Department of Religious Research, IFTAA, Dawah and Guidance
Directorate General of Posts
Directorate of Agriculture and Water—Riyadh

General Directorate of Broadcasting Coverage
General Directorate of Education
General Electricity Corporation
General Investment Fund
General Organization for Social Insurance
General Petroleum and Mineral Organization
General Presidency for Girls' Education
General Presidency for Youth Welfare
Grain Silos and Flour Mills Organization
Grievance Board
Gulf Co-Operation Council
Gulf Postal Organization
Gulf Standards Organization
Gulf Television Council

Hassa Irrigation and Drainage Authority

Industrial Studies and Development Center
Institute of Public Administration
International Airports Projects
Islamic Development Bank

Ministry of Agriculture and Water
Ministry of Commerce
Ministry of Communications
Ministry of Defense and Aviation
Ministry of Education
Ministry of Finance and National Economy

Ministry of Foreign Affairs
Ministry of Health
Ministry of Higher Education
Ministry of Industry and Electricity
Ministry of Information
Ministry of Interior
Ministry of Justice
Ministry of Labor and Social Affairs
Ministry of Municipal and Rural Affairs
Ministry of Petroleum and Mineral Resources
Ministry of Pilgrimage and Endowments
Ministry of Planning
Ministry of Posts, Telegraphs and Communications
Ministry of Public Works and Housing

National Agricultural Development Company
National Commercial Bank
National Guard
National Shipping Company of Saudi Arabia

Pensions Directorate
Ports Authority
Presidency of Civil Aviation
Public Investment Fund
Public Morality Committee

Real Estate Development Fund
Riyadh Bank Limited
Royal Commission for Jubail and Yanbu

Saline Water Conversion Corporation
Saudi Arabian Agriculture Bank
Saudi Arabian Agriculture and Dairy Company
Saudi Arabian Airlines
Saudi Arabian Fertiliser Company
Saudi Arabian Monetary Agency
Saudi Arabian National Center for Science and Technology
Saudi Arabian Standards Organization
Saudi Basic Industries Corporation
Saudi Consolidated Electric Company
Saudi Consulting House
Saudi Credit Bank
Saudi Domestic Airports
Saudi Fisheries Company
Saudi Fund for Development
Saudi Industrial Development Fund
Saudi Press Agency
Saudi Public Transport Company
Saudi Railways Organization
Saudi Red Crescent Association
Saudi United Fertilisers Company

United Arab Shipping Company

Appendix V

GENERAL SOCIAL AND ECONOMIC DATA

The data in Appendix V are from IMF and World Bank sources, as indicated in the accompanying documentation. These data are not totally consistent with the data reported in the text, which are largely from Saudi government sources.

Data Sources

Many of the statistics assembled here come from agencies outside the World Bank. In some cases, preliminary statistics are obtained from another agency and revised by World Bank staff. For example, demographic statistics are received from the United Nations and updated with more recent information obtained by World Bank staff working within a particular country.

This appendix includes only a portion of those social indicators that are available from source agencies. Data on other indicators can be obtained from the organizations listed in Table AV.1, or from their recent publications. These volumes often are available at the reference desks of public libraries.

Table AV.1. Organizations and Publications

Organization	*Recent Publication*
Population, Demographic, and Housing Data	
United Nations Statistical Office Department of International Economic and Social Affairs, Publishing Division United Nations New York, NY 10017 USA	World Population Trends and Policies, Monitoring Report (1984) Statistical Yearbook (1982) Compendium of Human Settlements Statistics, 1983 Demographic Yearbook (1985)
Population Council One Dag Hammerskjold Plaza New York, NY 10017 USA	Population and Family Planning Programs (1985)
Health, Nutrition, and Food Supply Data	
World Health Organization (WHO) Director, Statistics Division 1211 Geneva 27, Switzerland	World Health Statistics Annual (various years)
Food and Agriculture Organization (FAO) Via delle Terme di Caracalla 00100 Rome, Italy	FAO Production Yearbook (1985)
Employment Data	
International Labour Office (ILO) Chief, Bureau of Statistics CH-1211Geneva 22, Switzerland	Yearbook of Labour Statistics (1984) Labour Force Estimates and Projections, 1950-2000 (1986)
Education Data	
United Nations Educational, Scientific and Cultural Organization (UNESCO) Director, Office of Statistics 7 Place de Fontenoy 75700 Paris, France	Statistical Yearbook (1986)
Social Indicators Analysis	
United Nations Research Institute for Social Development Palais des Nations 1211 Geneva 10, Switzerland	Measurement and Analysis of Socioeconomic Development (1986)

Table AV.2. Social Indicator Data Sheet (1987), Saudi Arabia

				Reference Groups (MRE)	
	1965	*1973*	*Most Recent Estimate*	*High-Income Oil Export*	*Industrial Market Economy*
Area					
Total land area (thousand sq. km.)	2,149.7	2,149.7	2,149.7	—	—
Agricultural (% of total)	39.9	40.0	40.1	—	—
GNP per Capita (current US$)	400	980	8,840[a]	11,366	11,920
Population and Vital Statistics					
Total population (thousand)	4,793	6,606	12,007	—	—
Urban population (% of total)	39	55	72	73	75
Population growth rate (%)					
Total		4.0	4.9	5.3	0.7
Urban		8.6	7.3	7.7	1.5
Life expectancy at birth (yrs.)	48	54	62	63	76
Population projections					
Population in 2000 (thousand)	—	—	20,215	—	—
Stationary population (thousand)	—	—	37,000	—	—
Population density per sq. km. of agricultural land	6	8	11	180	534
Population age structure (%)					
0-14 yrs.	44	45	44	43	21
15-64 yrs.	53	52	54	55	67
65 and above	3	3	3	2	12
Crude birth rate (per thousand)	48	47	42	41	13
Crude death rate (per thousand)	20	16	8	8	9

(continued on next page)

Table AV.2. (continued)

				Reference Groups (MRE)	
	1965	*1973*	*Most Recent Estimate*	*High-Income Oil Export*	*Industrial Market Economy*
Population and Vital Statistics (continued)					
Total fertility rate	7.3	7.3	7.1	6.9	1.8
Infant mortality rate (per thousand)	160	107	61	61	9
Child death rate (per thousand)	38	26	4	5	0
Family planning:					
Acceptors, annual (thousand)	—	—	—	—	—
Users (% of married women)	—	—	—	—	—
Food, Health and Nutrition					
Index of food production per capita (1979-1981 = 100)	—	146	212	91	102
Per capita supply of					
Calories (per day)	1,866	1,906	3,057	114	3,417
Proteins (grams per day)	47	50	87	89	92
Population per physician (thousand)	—	7.5	2.7	1.5	1.5
Population per nurse (thousand)	3.9	2.1	1.5	0.6	0.2
Population per hospital bed (thousand)	—	0.8	0.7	0.6	0.1
Access to safe water					
(% of population): Total	—	64	93	82	—
Urban	—	97	100	84	—
Rural	—	56	68	78	—

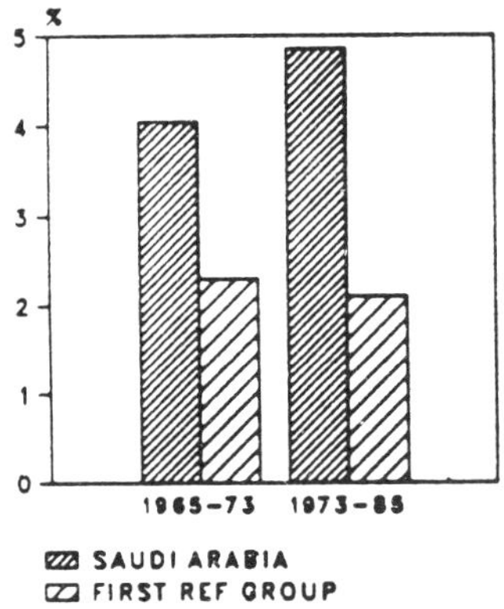

Figure AV.1. Population Growth

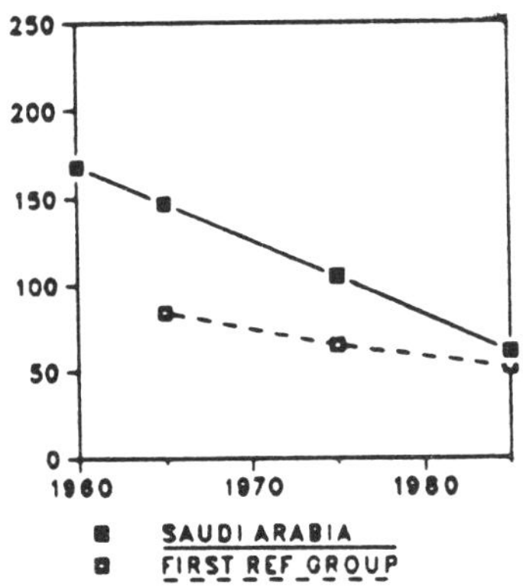

Figure AV.2. Infant Mortality

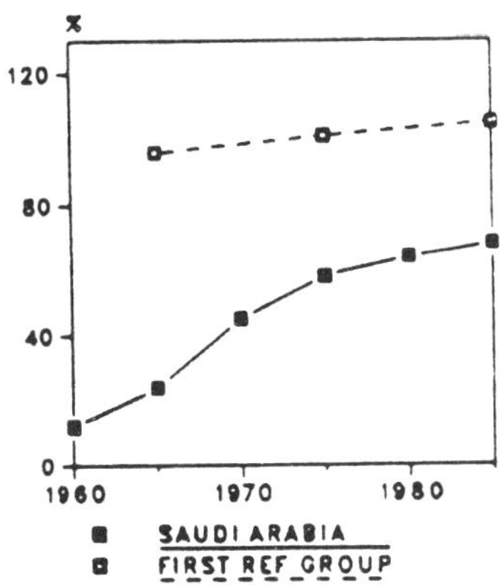

Figure AV.3. Primary School Enrollment

Table AV.3. Social Indicator Data Sheet (1987), Saudi Arabia

				Reference Groups (MRE)	
	1965	*1973*	*Most Recent Estimate*	*High-Income Oil Export*	*Industrial Market Economy*
Labor Force					
Total Labor Force (thousand):	1,333	1,861	3,540	—	—
Female (%)	4	6	7	4	37
Agriculture (%)	68	59	48	34	7
Industry (%)	11	13	14	21	35
Participation rate (%):					
Total	28	28	30	27	47
Male	52	51	51	47	60
Female	3	4	4	3	35
Age dependency ratio	0.9	0.9	0.9	0.8	0.5
Housing					
Average size of household:					
Total	NA	NA	NA	NA	NA
Urban	NA	NA	NA	NA	NA
Rural	NA	NA	NA	NA	NA
Percentage of dwellings with electricity:					
Total	NA	NA	NA	NA	NA
Urban	NA	NA	NA	NA	NA
Rural	NA	NA	NA	NA	NA
Education					
Enrollment rates:					
Primary: Total	24	58	68	60	102
Male	36	72	77	68	102
Female	11	43	58	52	101

Secondary: Total	4	22	38	35	90
Male	7	28	47	39	89
Female	1	15	29	31	91
Pupil-Teacher ratio:					
Primary	22	21	16	17	20
Secondary	15	14	14	12	14
Pupils reaching grade 6 (%)	NA	81	79	82	99
Income, Consumption, and Poverty					
Energy consumption per capita (kg. of oil equivalent)	1,759	3,259	3,653	3,863	4,883
Percentage of private income received by:					
Highest 10% of households	NA	NA	NA	NA	NA
Highest 20%	NA	NA	NA	NA	NA
Lowest 20%	NA	NA	NA	NA	NA
Lowest 40%	NA	NA	NA	NA	NA
Estimated absolute poverty income level (US$ per capita):					
Urban	NA	NA	NA	NA	NA
Rural	NA	NA	NA	NA	NA
Estimated population below absolute poverty income level (%):					
Urban	NA	NA	NA	NA	NA
Rural	NA	NA	NA	NA	NA
Passenger cars/thousand population	12.0	9.8	NA	NA	323.7
Newspaper circulation (per thousand population)	11.5	9.2	NA	27.4	308.0

Notes: NA = Not Available. Most recent estimates of population and GNP per capita are for 1986 unless otherwise noted. Group averages are population weighted. Country coverage depends on data availability and is not uniform. Unless otherwise noted. 1965 refers to any year between 1962 and 1968; 1973 between 1970 and 1976; and most recent estimate between 1980 and 1986.

Definitions of Social Indicators

The definition of a particular social indicator may vary among countries or within one country over time. For instance, different countries define "urban area" or "safe water" in different ways. For more detailed definitions, see the technical notes to the World Development Indicators.

Area *(thousand square kilometers).*

- Total—Total surface area comprising land area and inland waters.
- Agricultural (percentage of total)—Estimate of agricultural area used for crops, pastures, market and kitchen gardens or lying fallow, as a percentage of total.

GNP per Capita. *(US$)*—1986 GNP per capita estimates at current market prices, calculated by the conversion method used for the World Bank Atlas.

Population and Vital Statistics.

- Total population—Midyear (millions), 1986 data.
- Urban population (percentage of total)—Different countries follow different definitions of urban population, which may affect comparability of data among countries.
- Population growth rate (percent)—Total and urban—annual growth rates of total and of urban populations.
- Life expectancy at birth (years)—Number of years a newborn infant would live if prevailing patterns of mortality at the time of its birth were to stay the same throughout its life.

Population projections

- Population in 2000—Projections of population given total population by age and sex, fertility and the demographic parameters of mortality rates, and migration in the base year 1980.
- Stationary population—Projected population level when zero population growth is achieved: that is, the birth rate is constant and is equal to the death rate, the age structure is stable, and the growth rate is zero.
- Population density and agricultural land—Population per square kilometer (100 hectares) of agricultural area.
- Population age structure (percent)—Children 0-14 years, working age group 15-64 years, and people of 65 years and over as percentages of population.

- Crude birth rate—Annual live births per thousand population.
- Crude death rate—Annual deaths per thousand population.
- Total fertility rate—Average number of children that would be born alive to a woman during her lifetime, if during her child-bearing years she were to bear children at each age in accordance with prevailing age-specific fertility rates.
- Infant (aged 0-1) mortality rate—Number of infants per thousand live births, in a given year, who die before reaching 1 year of age.
- Child (aged 1-4) mortality rate—Number of deaths of children, aged 1-4, per thousand children in the same age group, in a given year.
- Family planning—acceptors (thousands)—Annual number of acceptors of birth-control measures received under the auspices of a national family planning program.
- Family planning—uses (percentage of married women)—Percentage of married women of child-bearing age who are practicing, or whose husbands are practicing any form of contraception. Child-bearing age is generally 15-44, although for some countries contraceptive usage is measured for other age groups.

Food, Health, and Nutrition.

- Index of food production per capita (1979-1981 = 100)—Index of per capita annual production of all food commodities. Production excludes animal feed and seed for agriculture. Food commodities include primary commodities (for example, sugarcane, instead of sugar), which are edible and that contain nutrients (for example, tea and coffee are excluded). They include nuts, fruits, pulses, cereals, vegetables, oil seeds, sugarcane and sugar beets, livestock, and livestock products. Aggregate production of each country is based on national average producer price weights.
- Per capita supply of calories—computed from energy equivalent of net food supplies available in a country, per capita, per day. Available supplies comprise domestic production, imports less exports, and changes in stock. Net supplies exclude animal feed, seeds for use in agriculture, quantities used in food processing, and losses in distribution.
- Per capita supply of protein (grams per day)—protein content of per capita net supply of food per day. Net supply of food is defined as above. Requirements for all countries, established by United States Department of Agriculgure, provide for minimum allowances of 60 grams of total protein per day, and 20 grams of animal or pulse protein.

- Population per physician—Population divided by the number of practicing physicians qualified from a medical school at university level.
- Population per nursing person—Population divided by the number of practicing graduate nurses, assistant nurses, practical nurses, and nursing auxiliaries.
- Population per hospital bed—Population divided by the number of hospital beds available in public and private, general and specialized hospitals, and rehabilitation centers. Hospitals are establishments permanently staffed by at least one physician.
- Access to safe water (percentage of population)—Total, urban, and rural—People (total, urban and rural) with reasonable access to safe water supply (includes treated surface waters or untreated but contaminated waters such as that from springs, sanitary wells, and protected boreholes). In an urban area, this may not be more than 200 meters away. In rural areas, this implies that members of the household do not have to spend a disproportionate part of the day fetching water.

Labor Force.

- Total labor force (millions)—Economically active, including armed forces and unemployed, but excluding housewives and students.
- Female (percent)—Female labor force as a percentage of total labor force.
- Agriculture (percent)—Labor force in farming, forestry, hunting, and fishing, as a percentage of the total labor force.
- Industry (percent)—Labor force in mining, construction, manufacturing and electricity, and water and gas, as a percentage of the total labor force.
- Participation rate (percent)—total, male and female—Participation rates are the percentage of population of all ages in the labor force. These are based on ILO data on the age-sex structure of the population.
- Age dependency ratio—Ratio of population under 15, and 65 and over, to the working age population (age 15-64).

Housing.

- Average size of household (persons per household)—total, urban, and rural—A household consists of a group of individuals who share living quarters and main meals.
- Percentage of dwellings with electricity—total, urban, and rural—Conventional dwellings with electricity in living quarters, as a percentage of all dwellings.

Education.

- Enrollment rates:

  Primary school enrollment—total, male and female—Gross enrollment of all ages at primary level as a percentage of school-age children as defined by each country, and reported to UNESCO. While many countries consider primary school age to be 6-11 years, others use different age groups. For some countries with universal education, gross enrollment may exceed 100 percent since some pupils are younger or older than the country's own standard primary school age.

  Secondary school enrollment—total, male and female—Computed in a similar manner, but including pupils enrolled in vocational, or teacher training secondary schools. The age group is usually 12-17.

  Pupil-teacher ratio—primary and secondary—Total students enrolled in school divided by the total number of teachers.

  Percentage of pupils reaching grade six—The percentage of children starting primary school who continue until grade six.

Income, Consumption, and Poverty.

- Energy consumption per capita (kilograms of oil equivalent)—Annual consumption of commercial primary energy (coal, lignite, petroleum, natural gas, and hydro, nuclear and geothermal electricity).
- Income distribution—Income (both in cash and kind) accruing to percentile groups of households ranked by total household income.
- Passenger cars (per thousand population)—Includes motor cars seating fewer than eight persons.
- Newspaper circulation (per thousand population)—Average circulation of a "daily, general interest newspaper," defined as a news periodical published at least four times a week.
- Estimated absolute proverty income level (US$ per capita)—urban and rural—Absolute poverty income level is that below which a minimal nutritionally adequate diet plus essential nonfood requirements are not affordable.
- Estimated population below absolute poverty income level (percent)—Percentage of urban and rural populations who live in "absolute poverty."

Table AV.4a. Economic Indicator Data Sheet, Saudi Arabia, 1966-1976

	1966	*1967*	*1968*	*1969*	*1970*	*1971*	*1972*	*1973*	*1974*	*1975*	*1976*
Current $GNP Per Capita	440	490	500	530	570	680	820	980	1,710	2,880	5,520
Population (thousands)	4,970	5,153	5,848	5,541	5,745	6,019	6,306	6,606	6,921	7,251	7,633
	(Billions of Current Saudi Arabian Riyals)										
Origin and Use of Resources											
Gross National Product (GNP)	9.68	11.21	11.70	12.77	13.91	19.10	24.02	30.09	82.35	125.40	165.39
Net Factor Income (+) or Payments	-2.24	-1.94	-2.96	-3.20	-3.49	-3.82	-4.23	-10.46	-16.97	-14.20	0.87
Gross Domestic Product (GDP)	11.92	13.14	14.66	15.98	17.40	22.92	28.26	40.55	99.32	139.60	164.53
Indirect Taxes Net of Subsidies	0.16	0.14	0.14	0.18	0.16	0.35	0.36	0.53	0.51	-0.52	-0.90
GDP at factor cost	11.76	13.00	14.51	15.80	17.24	22.57	27.90	40.02	98.81	140.12	165.43
Agriculture	0.82	0.85	0.88	0.96	0.98	1.02	1.06	1.14	1.24	1.39	1.59
Industry	7.43	8.16	9.27	9.91	11.03	15.89	20.45	30.93	86.62	120.24	134.27
(o/w Manufacturing)	1.00	1.07	1.25	1.37	1.67	1.96	1.98	2.43	5.08	7.37	8.17
Services, etc.	3.67	4.13	4.50	5.10	5.38	6.01	6.75	8.48	11.46	17.97	28.67
Resource Balance	4.05	4.11	4.20	4.24	5.31	9.98	13.56	21.74	70.39	87.20	77.42
Exports of Goods & NF Services	7.19	7.65	8.59	9.09	10.30	15.19	19.86	30.01	85.68	114.46	120.28
Imports of Goods & NF Services	3.13	3.54	4.39	4.85	4.99	5.20	6.30	8.27	15.29	27.26	42.86
Domestic Absorption	7.86	9.03	10.46	11.74	12.09	12.94	14.70	18.81	28.93	52.40	87.11
Private Consumption, etc.	3.83	4.00	4.58	5.36	5.86	6.41	6.91	7.89	9.83	18.04	23.90
General Gov't Consumption	2.10	2.67	2.75	3.03	3.42	3.80	4.28	5.33	9.86	15.91	28.88
Gross Domestic Investment	1.94	2.36	3.13	3.35	2.81	2.73	3.50	5.58	9.23	18.45	34.32
(o/w Fixed Investment)	2.27	2.16	2.39	2.63	2.60	2.93	3.40	5.69	8.40	17.70	33.54
Memo Items:											
Gross Domestic Saving	5.99	6.47	7.32	7.59	8.12	12.71	17.06	27.32	79.62	105.65	111.74
Gross National Saving	—	3.99	3.39	3.36	3.44	7.30	10.99	13.33	57.20	78.45	97.40

	(Billions of 1980 Saudi Arabian Riyals)										
Gross National Product	77.77	88.73	90.83	97.64	108.41	131.69	158.40	169.60	217.83	233.84	279.57
GDP at factor cost	94.88	103.17	113.03	121.21	134.43	155.29	183.01	222.22	258.81	259.98	279.63
Agriculture	2.55	2.51	2.62	2.71	2.79	2.88	2.98	3.09	3.20	3.33	3.46
Industry	74.78	81.15	89.27	95.33	107.20	126.95	152.67	188.39	218.55	215.96	227.98
(o/w Manufacturing)	5.04	6.52	7.56	8.38	10.00	11.00	11.05	11.83	12.45	12.09	13.08
Services, etc.	18.84	20.68	22.27	24.54	25.71	27.82	29.63	33.53	38.33	39.76	46.71
Resource Balance	79.61	83.35	89.38	94.80	111.39	133.71	163.15	198.52	214.49	189.67	161.23
Exports of Goods & NF Services	86.27	90.80	98.65	104.77	121.05	143.24	174.43	212.56	238.34	227.49	222.64
Imports of Goods & NF Services	6.66	7.45	9.27	9.96	9.67	9.53	11.27	14.04	23.85	37.82	61.41
Domestic Absorption	16.56	20.98	24.78	27.78	24.32	23.95	22.12	26.49	45.58	69.39	116.92
Private Consumption, etc.	—	—	—	—	—	—	—	—	—	—	—
General Gov't Consumption	—	—	—	—	—	—	—	—	—	—	—
Gross Domestic Investment	4.16	5.01	6.61	6.95	5.55	5.06	6.19	9.52	14.59	29.58	51.30
(o/w Fixed Investment)	—	—	—	—	—	—	—	—	—	—	—
Memo Items:											
Capacity to Import	15.28	16.11	18.12	18.66	19.96	27.81	35.52	50.95	133.63	158.82	172.33
Terms of Trade Adjustment	-70.99	-74.69	-80.53	-86.10	-101.10	-115.43	-138.90	-161.61	-104.71	-68.67	-50.31
Gross Domestic Income	25.18	29.64	33.63	36.48	34.61	42.23	46.37	63.40	155.36	190.38	227.84
Gross National Income	6.78	14.03	10.31	11.54	7.32	16.26	19.50	7.99	113.12	165.17	229.26
	(Index 1980 = 100)										
Domestic Prices (Deflators)											
Overall (GDP)	12.4	12.6	12.8	13.0	12.8	14.5	15.3	18.0	38.2	53.9	59.1
Domestic Absorption	47.5	43.0	42.2	42.3	49.7	54.0	66.5	71.0	63.5	75.5	74.5
Agricultural	32.3	33.8	33.6	35.3	35.3	35.2	35.6	36.9	38.8	41.8	45.8
Industrial	9.9	10.1	10.4	10.4	10.3	12.5	13.4	16.4	39.6	55.7	58.9
(o/w Manufacturing)	16.6	16.4	16.5	16.4	16.7	17.8	18.0	20.5	40.8	60.9	62.5

(continued)

Table AV.4a. *(continued)*

	1966	1967	1968	1969	1970	1971	1972	1973	1974	1975	1976
				Index 1980 = 100)							
Manufacturing Activity											
Employment (1980 = 100)	—	—	—	—	—	—	—	—	—	—	—
Real Earnings per Empl. (1980 = 100)	—	—	—	—	—	—	—	—	—	—	—
Real Output per Empl. (1980 = 100)	—	—	—	—	—	—	—	—	—	—	—
Earnings as % of Value Added	—	—	—	—	—	—	—	—	—	—	23.8
				(Billions of Current Saudi Arabian Riyals)							
Monetary Holdings											
Money Supply, Broadly Defined	2.12	2.42	2.80	2.97	3.14	3.59	5.04	6.81	9.78	17.78	29.61
Money as Means of Payment	1.72	1.92	2.20	2.32	2.40	2.65	3.78	5.29	7.33	14.18	24.27
Currency Outside Banks	1.06	1.20	1.45	1.56	1.63	1.67	2.42	3.05	4.14	6.68	10.59
Demand Deposits	0.66	0.72	0.75	0.77	0.77	0.98	1.36	2.23	3.19	7.50	13.68
Quasi-Monetary Liabilities	0.40	0.50	0.60	0.64	0.74	0.94	1.26	1.52	2.44	3.60	5.34
				(Millions of Current Saudi Arabian Riyals)							
Government Deficit (-) or Surplus	—	—	—	—	—	—	—	—	—	—	—
Current Revenue	—	—	—	—	—	—	—	—	—	—	—
Current Expenditure	—	—	—	—	—	—	—	—	—	—	—
Current Budget Balance	—	—	—	—	—	—	—	—	—	—	—
Capital Receipts	—	—	—	—	—	—	—	—	—	—	—
Capital Payments	—	—	—	—	—	—	—	—	—	—	—
				(Millions of Current US Dollars)							
Foreign Trade (Customs Basis)											
Value of Exports, fob	1,520	1.692	2,026	1,992	2,424	3,845	5,491	9,089	35,562	29,669	38,282
Nonfuel Primary Products	1	1	4	4	4	4	9	14	49	31	30
Fuels	1,518	1,691	2,021	1,987	2,417	3,792	5,391	8,993	35,482	29,466	38,164
Manufactures	1	1	2	2	2	49	91	82	31	172	89

Value of Imports, cif	457	502	562	734	692	806	1,125	1,977	2,848	4,141	8,409
Nonfuel Primary Products	148	168	191	224	241	256	308	480	639	743	1,233
Fuels	5	6	6	10	8	10	11	13	29	28	62
Manufactures	304	328	365	500	443	539	806	1,484	2,180	3,370	7,113
(Index 1980 = 100)											
Terms of Trade	14.0	14.2	14.2	14.0	13.1	16.4	16.5	18.0	61.3	57.1	61.1
Export Prices, fob	4.3	4.3	4.3	4.3	4.3	5.6	6.3	8.9	36.8	35.9	38.4
Nonfuel Primary Products	36.0	34.3	36.6	38.3	40.9	37.2	42.2	50.8	60.4	70.0	65.4
Fuels	4.3	4.3	4.3	4.3	4.3	5.6	6.2	8.9	36.7	35.7	38.4
Manufactures	32.6	35.4	34.0	35.4	41.7	42.4	45.8	50.0	86.1	69.4	74.3
Import Prices, cif	30.4	30.1	30.2	30.6	32.7	34.4	38.3	49.5	60.0	62.8	62.9
(Millions of 1980 US Dollars)											
Trade at Constant 1980 Prices											
Exports, fob	35,307	39,322	47,019	46,217	56,236	67,846	87,168	101,240	96,798	82,830	99,550
Imports, cif	1,503	1,666	1,862	2,402	2,115	2,344	2,943	3,992	4,749	6,593	13,365
(Millions of Current US Dollars)											
Balance of Payments											
Exports of Goods & Services	—	1,700	1,937	2,020	2,372	2,926	4,381	8,264	32,735	30,569	40,272
Merchandise (FOB)	—	1,522	1,725	1,785	2,089	2,581	3,911	7,489	30,132	27,294	35,632
Nonfactor Services	—	131	161	184	222	279	364	569	1,383	1,436	1,756
Factor Service Receipts	—	47	51	51	61	67	106	205	1,220	1,839	2,884
Imports of Goods & Services	—	1,482	1,812	1,879	2,037	1,600	1,867	4,856	8,177	12,503	21,600
Merchandise (FOB)	—	616	786	825	829	805	1,197	1,853	3,569	6,004	10,385
Nonfactor Services	—	259	330	330	313	374	509	955	2,163	4,375	7,935
Factor Service Payments	—	607	696	724	895	421	162	2,048	2,445	2,124	3,280
(o/w Long-Term Interest)	—	—	—	—	—	—	—	—	—	—	—
Net Current Transfers	—	-120	-217	-227	-264	-354	-425	-888	-1,532	-3,682	-4,312
(o/w Workers' Remit. Rec'd)	—	—	—	—	—	—	—	—	—	—	—

(continued)

Table AV.4a. (continued)

	1966	*1967*	*1968*	*1969*	*1970*	*1971*	*1972*	*1973*	*1974*	*1975*	*1976*
	(Millions of Current US Dollars)										
Current Account Balance	—	98	-92	-86	71	972	2,089	2,520	23,025	14,385	14,360
Long-Term Capital Inflow (+)	—	98	93	8	93	-127	26	-912	-8,873	-9,137	-11,156
Direct Investment	—	96	-31	-37	20	-111	34	-626	-3,732	1,865	-397
Official Capital Grants	—	—	—	—	—	—	—	—	—	—	—
Long-Term Loans, Net	—	—	—	—	—	—	—	—	—	—	—
Disbursements	—	—	—	—	—	—	—	—	—	—	—
Repayments	—	—	—	—	—	—	—	—	—	—	—
Other LT Inflows (Net)	—	2	124	45	73	-16	-7	-286	-5,141	-11,002	-10,759
Other Net Capital Inflows (+)	—	-136	-57	-49	-77	-172	-1,059	-691	-3,761	3,819	513
Increase (-) in Reserves	-26	-60	56	127	-87	-673	-1,057	-917	-10,391	-9,067	-3,717
	(Saudi Arabian Riyals per US Dollar)										
Memo Item:											
Exchange Rate (Annual Average)	4.50	4.50	4.50	4.50	4.50	4.49	4.32	3.98	3.56	3.53	3.53
	(Millions of US Dollars, Outstanding at End of Year)										
External Debt, etc.											
Public/Publicly Guar. Long-Term	—	—	—	—	—	—	—	—	—	—	—
Official Creditors	—	—	—	—	—	—	—	—	—	—	—
(o/w IBRD & IDA)	—	—	—	—	—	—	—	—	—	—	—
Private Creditors	—	—	—	—	—	—	—	—	—	—	—
Private Nonguaranteed Long-Term	—	—	—	—	—	—	—	—	—	—	—
Use of Fund Credit	—	—	—	—	—	—	—	—	—	—	—
Identified Short-Term Debt	—	—	—	—	—	—	—	—	—	—	—

(Millions of US Dollars)

Memo Items:											
Int'l Reserves Excluding Gold	679	692	543	488	543	1,327	2,383	3,747	14,153	23,193	26,900
Gold Holdings (at market price)	69	69	142	120	127	135	200	346	575	432	415
Social Indicators											
Total Fertility Rate	7.3	7.3	7.3	7.3	7.3	7.3	7.3	7.3	7.3	7.3	7.3
Crude Birth Rate	48.3	48.1	48.0	47.9	47.8	47.7	47.6	47.3	46.9	46.6	46.2
Infant Mortality Rate	—	—	—	—	—	—	—	—	—	—	—
Life Expectancy at Birth	48.7	49.5	50.3	51.1	51.9	52.7	53.5	54.3	55.1	55.9	56.7
Food Production (1979-1981 = 100)	62.0	66.0	59.0	70.0	76.0	103.0	66.0	77.0	108.0	112.0	104.0
Labor Force, Agriculture (%)	67.1	66.4	65.6	64.9	64.2	62.6	61.0	59.5	57.9	56.3	54.7
Labor Force, Female (%)	4.5	4.6	4.8	4.9	5.0	5.2	5.4	5.5	5.7	5.9	6.0
School Enroll. Ratio, primary	—	—	—	—	45.0	—	—	—	—	58.0	59.0
School Enroll. Ratio, secondary	—	—	—	— 12.0	—	—	—	—	22.0	24.0	

Table AV.4b. Economic Indicator Data Sheet, Saudi Arabia, 1977-1986

	1977	*1978*	*1979*	*1980*	*1981*	*1982*	*1983*	*1984*	*1985*	*1986*
Current $GNP Per Capita	7,200	7,780	8,690	10,510	14,400	15,620	13,040	10,510	8,620	6,940
Population (thousands)	8,035	8,458	8,903	9,372	9,804	10,231	10,658	11,093	11,542	12,007
	(Billions of Current Saudi Arabian Riyals)									
Origin and Use of Resources										
Gross National Product (GNP)	207.72	227.18	256.18	392.45	568.05	536.88	417.05	348.78	315.24	275.18
Net Factor Income (+) or Payments	2.67	1.78	6.64	6.64	47.46	12.16	1.82	-23.24	-15.64	-11.51
Gross Domestic Product (GDP)	205.06	225.40	249.54	385.81	520.59	524.72	415.23	372.02	330.88	286.69
Indirect Taxes Net of Subsidies	-0.67	-0.90	-0.93	—	—	—	—	—	—	—
GDP at factor cost	205.73	226.30	250.47	—	—	—	—	—	—	—
Agriculture	1.87	3.91	4.20	4.65	5.57	6.74	8.73	9.61	11.14	12.59
Industry	164.26	169.32	179.85	301.25	419.19	405.43	272.68	221.80	180.64	142.81
(o/w Manufacturing)	9.28	9.97	12.62	19.29	25.75	22.38	23.97	26.94	27.07	26.20
Services, etc.	38.93	52.17	65.50	79.91	95.83	112.55	133.82	140.61	139.09	131.28
Resource Balance	77.62	49.26	39.76	126.14	210.97	167.16	38.18	-19.24	-24.76	-26.11
Exports of Goods & NF Services	140.32	140.76	147.24	258.49	368.43	354.92	219.45	167.17	134.65	102.61
Imports of Goods & NF Services	62.70	91.50	107.48	132.35	157.46	187.76	181.27	186.41	159.41	128.72
Domestic Absorption	127.43	176.14	209.78	259.67	309.62	357.55	377.06	391.26	355.64	312.80
Private Consumption, etc.	34.37	54.61	68.61	102.45	114.90	126.51	137.30	157.37	145.99	122.07
General Gov't Consumption	41.03	47.03	71.90	77.50	81.92	128.53	126.85	121.33	115.65	113.47
Gross Domestic Investment	52.03	74.50	69.27	79.72	112.80	102.52	112.90	112.56	94.00	77.26
(o/w Fixed Investment)	51.19	66.89	76.65	97.07	106.38	122.32	115.45	103.23	91.21	74.93
Memo Items:										
Gross Domestic Saving	129.65	123.76	109.03	205.86	323.77	269.68	151.08	93.32	69.24	51.15
Gross National Saving	113.23	102.02	92.63	179.04	334.39	248.55	121.14	39.09	23.45	11.15

	(Billions of 1980 Saudi Arabian Riyals)									
Gross National Product	324.54	336.93	361.91	392.45	451.45	421.88	346.22	313.97	291.97	264.70
GDP at factor cost	321.53	335.65	353.89	—	—	—	—	—	—	—
Agriculture	3.63	4.20	4.39	4.65	4.92	5.21	5.73	6.48	7.32	8.27
Industry	262.60	268.38	278.15	301.25	319.30	308.65	231.26	218.97	192.36	169.43
(o/w Manufacturing)	14.82	16.12	17.72	19.29	20.67	22.12	24.21	27.38	26.90	26.24
Services, etc.	54.27	61.75	70.05	79.91	89.27	98.21	107.57	112.10	108.98	99.95
Resource Balance	157.39	134.42	131.48	126.14	113.18	46.37	-45.50	—	—	—
Exports of Goods & NF Services	242.86	246.60	249.03	258.49	273.62	241.17	156.42	—	—	—
Imports of Goods & NF Services	85.47	112.18	117.55	132.35	160.44	194.79	201.81	—	—	—
Domestic Absorption	163.12	199.91	221.11	259.67	300.30	365.70	389.96	—	—	—
Private Consumption, etc.	—	—	—	—	—	—	—	—	—	—
General Gov't Consumption	—	—	—	—	—	—	—	—	—	—
Gross Domestic Investment	71.26	91.35	75.78	79.72	114.95	106.38	139.49	140.79	—	—
(o/w Fixed Investment)	—	—	—	—	—	—	—	—	—	—
Memo Items:										
Capacity to Import	191.27	172.57	161.03	258.49	375.40	368.23	244.32	—	—	—
Terms of Trade Adjustment	-51.58	-74.03	-88.00	—	101.78	127.06	87.90	—	—	—
Gross Domestic Income	268.93	260.30	264.59	385.81	515.27	539.13	432.47	—	—	—
Gross National Income	272.96	262.89	273.91	392.45	553.23	548.94	434.12	—	—	—
	(Index 1980 = 100)									
Domestic Prices (Deflators)										
Overall (GDP)	64.0	67.4	70.8	100.0	125.9	127.3	120.5	110.2	107.2	103.3
Domestic Absorption	78.1	88.1	94.9	100.0	103.1	97.8	96.7	—	—	—
Agricultural	51.3	93.0	95.5	100.0	113.3	129.3	152.2	148.3	152.2	152.2
Industrial	52.6	63.1	64.7	100.0	131.3	131.4	117.9	101.3	93.9	84.3
(o/w Manufacturing)	52.6	61.9	71.2	100.0	124.6	101.2	99.0	98.4	100.7	99.9

(continued)

Table AV.4b. (continued)

	1977	*1978*	*1979*	*1980*	*1981*	*1982*	*1983*	*1984*	*1985*	*1986*
	Index 1980 = 100)									
Manufacturing Activity										
Employment (1980 = 100)	—	—	—	—	—	—	—	—	—	—
Real Earnings per Empl. (1980 = 100)	—	—	—	—	—	—	—	—	—	—
Real Output per Empl. (1980 = 100)	—	—	—	—	—	—	—	—	—	—
Earnings as % of Value Added	—	—	—	—	—	—	—	—	—	—
	(Billions of Current Saudi Arabian Riyals)									
Monetary Holdings										
Money Supply, Broadly Defined	45.56	58.03	65.98	77.44	102.99	123.79	137.08	145.34	147.01	—
Money as Means of Payment	38.41	49.21	54.70	58.96	72.98	83.78	84.93	82.97	81.83	—
Currency Outside Banks	16.25	19.18	23.71	25.68	29.49	34.44	35.42	35.11	35.77	—
Demand Deposits	22.16	30.03	31.00	33.28	43.49	49.34	49.51	47.86	46.06	—
Quasi-Monetary Liabilities	7.14	8.82	11.28	18.48	30.01	40.01	52.15	62.37	65.18	—
	(Millions of Current Saudi Arabian Riyals)									
Government Deficit (-) or Surplus	—	—	—	—	—	—	—	—	—	—
Current Revenue	—	—	—	—	—	—	—	—	—	—
Current Expenditure	—	—	—	—	—	—	—	—	—	—
Current Budget Balance	—	—	—	—	—	—	—	—	—	—
Capital Receipts	—	—	—	—	—	—	—	—	—	—
Capital Payments	—	—	—	—	—	—	—	—	—	—
	(Millions of Current US Dollars)									
Foreign Trade (Customs Basis)										
Value of Exports, fob	43,458	40,715	63,419	109,113	119,913	79,125	45,861	37,530	27,403	24,064
Nonfuel Primary Products	27	95	107	181	153	136	153	126	88	—
Fuels	43,311	40,383	62,847	108,226	119,039	78,165	44,928	35,959	26,600	—
Manufactures	120	237	465	705	721	824	780	747	715	—

Value of Imports, cif	14,289	20,177	24,384	29,957	35,042	40,473	39,206	33,696	23,697	20,909
Nonfuel Primary Products	1,830	2,639	3,583	4,965	5,770	5,967	5,732	5,955	3,949	—
Fuels	81	136	156	191	254	192	247	237	157	—
Manufactures	12,378	17,403	20,646	24,801	29,018	34,314	33,227	27,504	19,592	—
				(Index 1980 = 100)						
Terms of Trade	61.6	52.8	66.1	100.0	121.1	113.8	105.9	108.0	106.7	—
Export Prices, fob	42.0	42.5	61.2	100.0	112.5	101.9	92.8	90.6	88.1	—
Nonfuel Primary Products	69.2	67.8	89.7	100.0	94.5	86.4	85.3	83.1	81.1	—
Fuels	42.0	42.3	61.0	100.0	112.5	101.6	92.5	90.2	87.5	44.3
Manufactures	79.9	111.8	95.8	100.0	116.7	143.8	123.6	117.9	117.9	130.8
Import Prices, cif	68.2	80.5	92.6	100.0	92.9	89.5	87.6	83.9	82.6	—
				(Millions of 1980 US Dollars)						
Trade at Constant 1980 Prices										
Exports, fob	103 311	95,821	103,633	109,113	106,592	77,664	49,381	40,651	31,115	24,064
Imports, cif	20,954	25,054	26,332	29,957	37,729	45,207	44,743	40,169	28,689	20,909
				(Millions of Current US Dollars)						
Balance of Payments										
Exports of Goods & Services	46,447	43,461	65,817	111,983	127,855	92,828	65,782	55,017	43,887	34,400
Merchandise (FOB)	40,351	36,993	58,099	100,717	111,831	73,876	45,662	37,425	27,400	20,000
Nonfactor Services	2,108	2,168	2,803	3,824	5,067	4,892	4,252	4,228	4,067	3,200
Factor Service Receipts	3,989	4,300	4,915	7,443	10,956	14,060	15,868	13,363	12,420	11,200
Imports of Goods & Services	29,049	38,929	47,783	59,235	75,678	75,507	73,499	64,530	48,694	39,600
Merchandise (FOB)	14,698	20,020	23,530	25,563	29,889	34,444	33,218	28,557	20,367	16,600
Nonfactor Services	10,272	14,396	22,188	26,756	36,189	34,852	37,259	32,856	25,992	21,400
Factor Service Payments	4,079	4,512	2,065	6,917	9,599	6,210	3,022	3,116	2,336	1,600
(o/w Long-Term Interest)	—	—	—	—	—	—	—	—	—	—
Net Current Transfers	-5,407	-6,745	-6,867	-9,995	-11,048	-9,746	-9,237	-8,882	-8,449	-7,800
(o/w Workers' Remit. Rec'd)	—	—	—	—	—	—	—	—	—	—

(continued)

Table AV.4b. (continued)

	1977	*1978*	*1979*	*1980*	*1981*	*1982*	*1983*	*1984*	*1985*	*1986*
	(Millions of Current US Dollars)									
Current Account Balance	11,991	-2,212	11,167	42,754	41,129	7,575	-16,953	-18,395	-13,257	-13,000
Long-Term Capital Inflow (+)	-7,503	-2,733	-3,148	-27,381	-27,725	-2,975	-880	-9,739	-7,254	-2,700
Direct Investment	783	556	-1,351	-3,192	6,498	11,128	4,944	4,839	1,419	2,100
Official Capital Grants	—	—	—	—	—	—	—	—	—	—
Long-Term Loans, Net	—	—	—	—	—	—	—	—	—	—
Disbursements	—	—	—	—	—	—	—	—	—	—
Repayments	—	—	—	—	—	—	—	—	—	—
Other LT Inflows (Net)	-8,286	-3,289	-1,797	-24,189	-34,223	-14,104	-5,824	-14,578	-8,673	-4,800
Other Net Capital Inflows (+)	-1,790	-1,744	-7,785	-11,425	-3,808	-6,910	16,294	26,633	19,809	6,300
Increase (-) in Reserves	-2,697	6,689	-233	-3,947	-9,596	2,310	1,539	1,501	701	9,400
	(Saudi Arabian Riyals per US Dollar)									
Memo Item:										
Exchange Rate (Annual Average)	3.53	3.49	3.35	3.35	3.33	3.42	3.44	3.49	3.57	3.65
	(Millions of US Dollars, Outstanding at End of Year)									
External Debt, etc.										
Public/Publicly Guar. Long-Term	—	—	—	—	—	—	—	—	—	—
Official Creditors	—	—	—	—	—	—	—	—	—	—
(o/w IBRD & IDA)	—	—	—	—	—	—	—	—	—	—
Private Creditors	—	—	—	—	—	—	—	—	—	—
Private Nonguaranteed Long-Term	—	—	—	—	—	—	—	—	—	—
Use of Fund Credit	—	—	—	—	—	—	—	—	—	—
Identified Short-Term Debt	—	—	—	—	—	—	—	—	—	—

(Millions of US Dollars)

Memo Items:										
Int'l Reserves Excluding Gold	29,903	19,200	19,273	23,437	32,236	29,549	27,287	24,748	25,004	18,324
Gold Holdings (at market price)	508	1,026	2,338	2,692	1,815	2,100	1,753	1,417	1,503	1,797
Social Indicators										
Total Fertility Rate	7.3	7.2	7.2	7.2	7.1	7.1	7.1	7.1	7.1	—
Crude Birth Rate	45.9	45.1	44.4	43.6	42.9	42.1	42.2	42.3	42.4	—
Infant Mortality Rate	—	—	—	10.2	20.3	30.5	40.7	50.8	61.0	—
Life Expectancy at Birth	57.5	58.2	58.8	59.4	60.0	60.9	60.6	61.7	62.0	—
Food Production (1979-1981 = 100)	112.0	113.0	112.0	101.0	87.0	124.0	157.0	157.0	239.0	—
Labor Force, Agriculture (%)	53.1	51.6	50.0	48.4	—	—	—	—	—	—
Labor Force, Female (%)	6.0	6.1	6.2	6.3	6.3	6.4	6.5	6.6	6.7	6.8
School Enroll. Ratio, primary	58.0	60.0	62.0	64.0	66.0	68.0	68.0	—	—	—
School Enroll. Ratio, secondary	26.0	28.0	30.0	30.0	31.0	33.0	38.0	—	—	—

References

Books/Reports

Abdeen, M. and Shook, D.N. (1984) *The Saudi Financial System.* New York: John Wiley and Sons.

Amuzegar, J. (1983) *Oil Exporters' Economic Development in an Interdependent World.* Occasional Paper No. 18. Washington, DC: International Monetary Fund (April).

Askari, H. and Dastmaltschi, B. (1987) "Evolution of a GCC Oil Policy." In J.A. Sandwick (ed.), *The Gulf Cooperation Council: Moderation and Stability in an Interdependent World.* Boulder, CO: Westview Press.

Bowen-Jones, H. (1984) "The Philosophy of Infrastructural Development." Pp. 81-90 in M.S. Elazhary (ed.), *The Impact of Oil Revenues on Arab Gulf Development.* Boulder, CO: Westview Press.

Corbo, V. and deMelo, J. (1986) "Lessons from the Southern Cone Policy Reforms." Unpublished report. Washington, DC: World Bank (October).

El-Kuwaiz, A. (1986) "OPEC and the International Oil Market: Age of Realism." *OPEC Review* (Winter): 393-408.

Fesharaki, F. and Issac, D.T. (1983) *OPEC, the Gulf and the World Petroleum Market: A Study in Government Policy and Downstream Operations.* Boulder, CO: Westview Press.

Fesharaki, F. and Yamaguchi, N. (1984) *The New Saudi Export Refineries: The Role of Shipping Costs in Determination of Product Prices and Competitiveness.* OPEC Downstream Project. Hawaii: East-West Center.

Fisher, S. (1987) "Economic Growth and Economic Policy." Pp. 31-32 in *Symposium on Growth-Oriented Adjustment.* Washington, DC: World Bank and the International Monetary Fund.

General Saline Water Conversion Corporation, The (1979-1986) *Annual Report.*

Harberger, A.C. (1984) "Economic Policy and Economic Growth." In A.C. Harberger (ed.), *World Economic Growth.* San Francisco: Institute for Contemporary Studies.

Ibbotson, R. and Sinquefeld, R.A. (1986) *Stocks, Bonds, Bills, and Inflation: The Past and the Future.* Charlottesville, VA: The Financial Analysis Research Foundation.

International Energy Agency (1983) *World Energy Outlook.* Paris: IEA.

International Monetary Fund (IMF), (various issues, 1975-1986) *International Financial Statistics.* Washington, DC: IMF.

International Monetary Fund (IMF), (1982) *World Economic Outlook.* Occasional Paper No. 9. Washington, DC: IMF (April).

Johany, A.D., Berne, M. and Mixon, Wilson J., Jr. (1986) *The Saudi Arabian Economy.* Baltimore, MD: The Johns Hopkins University Press.

Kingdom of Saudi Arabia, Central Department of Statistics (1986) *Foreign Trade Statistics.*

Kingdom of Saudi Arabia, Central Department of Statistics (1986) *Statistical Yearbook.*

Mattione, R.P. (1985) *OPEC's Investments and the International Financial System.* Washington, DC: The Brookings Institution.

Meir, S. (1986) *Strategic Implications of the New Oil Reality.* Boulder, CO: Westview Press.

Ministry of Agriculture and Water, Saudi Arabia (1980-1985) *Annual Report.*

Ministry of Industry and Electricity, Division of Electricity Affairs, Saudi Arabia (1986) Unpublished document.

Ministry of Information, Saudi Arabia (1404 [1984]) *A Decade of Progress.*

Ministry of Municipal and Rural Affairs, Saudi Arabia (1400-1405 [1980-1985]) *Some Achievements of the Third Development Plan.* Unpublished document, Riyadh.

Ministry of Planning, Saudi Arabia (1984) *Achievements of the Development Plans, 1390-1403 (1970-1983).*

Ministry of Planning, Saudi Arabia (1985) *Fourth Development Plan, 1405-1410 (1985-1990).* Riyadh: Ministry of Planning Press.

Neary, P.J. and van Winjnbergen, S. (eds.), (1985) *National Resources and the Macroeconomy.* London: Basil Blackwell.

Public Investment Fund (PIF), (1980-1986) *Annual Reports.*

Quandt, W.B. (1982) "Saudi Arabia's Oil Policy." Staff Paper. Washington, DC: The Brookings Institution.

Real Estate Development Fund (REDF), (1980-1986) *Annual Reports.*

Ryan, M. (1984) *Health Services in the Middle East.* Economist Intelligence Unit, Special Report No. 184, Ch. 2.

Sampson, A. (1975) *The Seven Sisters: The Great Oil Companies and the World They Made.* New York: Viking Press.

Saudi Arabian Agricultural Bank (SAAB), (1980-1986) *Annual Reports.*

Saudi Arabian Airlines (Saudi), (1980-1986) *Annual Reports.*

Saudi Arabian Basic Industries Corporation (SABIC), (1981-1986) *Annual Reports.*
Saudi Arabian Monetary Agency (SAMA), (1973-1988) *Annual Reports.*
Saudi Consolidated Electricity Companies (SCECOs), (1980-1985) *Annual Reviews of Achievements.* Unpublished document.
Saudi Fund for Development (SFD), (1980-1986) *Annual Reports.*
Saudi Industrial Development Fund (SIDF), (1980-1986) *Annual Reports.*
Saudi Ports Authority (SPA), (1980-1986) *Annual Reports.*
Saudi Public Transport Company (SAPTCO), (1980-1986) *Annual Reports.*
Stauffer, T.R. (1981) "Measuring Oil Addiction." *Middle East Economic Survey* (September).
Stoga, A. and Bennett, P. (1981) "How Fast is OPEC's Surplus Disappearing?" *The Banker* (September): 115-121.
Turner, L. (1979) *Middle East Industrialization: A Study of Saudi and Iranian Downstream Investments.* New York: Praeger.
Turner, L. and Yorke, V. (1986) *European Interests and Gulf Oil.* Brookfield, VT: Gower Publishing.
World Bank, The (1983, 1984, 1985, 1986) *World Development Report.* New York: Oxford University Press.

Periodicals/Pamphlets

Al-Jarbou, A. (1985) "Basic Industries Development by SABIC: Eight Years' Experience," *Forum* 56: 193-200.
Allen, R. (1985a) "Saudi Industry," *MEED Special Report* (November):1-28.
Allen, R. (1985b) "Saudi Construction," *MEED Special Report* (October):1-40.
Allen, R. and Ritchie, M. (1986) "Saudi Arabia," *MEED Special Report* (May): 1-52.
BP Statistical Review of World Energy (1979-1988).
Exxon Corporation (1984) *Middle East Oil and Gas* (December): 24.
"GCC Survey" (1986) *The Economist* (February 8): 18.
Grost, I. (1984) "Entering the Downstream Markets" *Petroleum Economist* (November): 407-409.
Petroleum Intelligence Weekly (1979-1986).
Platt's Oilgram Price Report (1979-1986).
Ritchie, M. (1985d) "Saudi Petrochemicals Come Out Fighting," *MEED* (November) 47: 6-11.
Salomon Brothers Inc. (1986) *International Oils* (April 1).
Salomon Brothers Inc. (1986) *International Oils* (April 10).
"Saudi Arabia" (1985c) *MEED* (April): 23-24.
"Saudi Arabia" (1987) *MEED* (June 20): 27.
"Saudi Arabian Petrochemical Exports: The EEC Protectionist Measures and SABIC's Prospects." (1985) *Arab Gulf Journal* 1: 9-20.

Subject Index